AFTER THE PUBLIC TURN

AFTER THE PUBLIC TURN

*Composition, Counterpublics, and
the Citizen Bricoleur*

FRANK FARMER

UTAH STATE UNIVERSITY PRESS
Logan

© 2013 by University Press of Colorado
Published by Utah State University Press
An imprint of University Press of Colorado
5589 Arapahoe Avenue, Suite 206C
Boulder, Colorado 80303

 The University Press of Colorado is a proud member of
The Association of American University Presses.

The University Press of Colorado is a cooperative publishing enterprise supported, in part, by
Adams State University, Colorado State University, Fort Lewis College, Metropolitan State University
of Denver, Regis University, University of Colorado, University of Northern Colorado, Utah State
University, and Western State Colorado University.

~The paper used in this publication meets the minimum requirements of the American National
Standard for Information Sciences—Permanence of Paper for Printed Library Materials. ANSI
Z39.48-1992

ISBN: 0-978-0-87421-913-5 (paper)
ISBN: 0-978-0-87421-914-2 (e-book)

Complete cataloging information for this title is available from the Library of Congress.

Portions of the introduction originally appeared in an article published by *JAC* 23 (3), "Wayward
Inventions: He(u)retical Experiments in Theorizing Service-Learning" (see Harper, Donnelli, and
Farmer 2003). An earlier version of chapter 4 appeared in *JAC* 28 (3–4) (see Farmer 2008).

To the memory of
DON CLIFFORD,
FRIEND

CONTENTS

ACKNOWLEDGMENTS

As I write these words, the country is in the midst of another presidential campaign, and the media scorecard of brilliant moves and clumsy mistakes, of zingers and gaffes (if you prefer), is already in full force. While the Republican candidate has already managed to accumulate an impressive record of strategic errors, verbal blunders, and assorted infelicities, the Democratic incumbent has made some notable missteps as well. Perhaps the most famous (and controversial) of President Barack Obama's recent campaign statements was his remark, endlessly repeated in stories and clips, and removed from any contextual frame: "You didn't make that!" Obama's statement was roundly criticized (at least in some quarters) as a kind of heresy—a wholesale rejection of such enduring American values as private initiative, entrepreneurship, self-reliance, true grit, and the celebrated theme of the self-made individual.

I heard President Obama's statement in a different way, though, as I believe he intended it—as a reminder that, in our democracy, private achievements, however admirable, are always, in some degree, made possible by public resources, whether these resources occur at the material level (i.e., roads, schools, public spaces, etc.) or at more abstract levels as well (i.e., laws, trade agreements, subsidies, tax policies, etc.). What I thought was an obvious affirmation of public life and its fundamental importance to our democracy was interpreted very differently by the many pundits, commentators, and experts who occupy our political landscape today. A remark that I did not hear as particularly controversial nonetheless sparked the flames of outrage, especially among those whose political viewpoints, not surprisingly, I do not share.

I was reminded of this campaign episode as I began to compose my expressions of gratitude to the many friends, students, and colleagues who made this book possible. In the crowded solitude of authoring a book, I was continually reminded of just how much this effort is a collaborative project, enabled by the generosity, advice, support, and thoughtful exchange of ideas I have had with many others along the way. Yes, I wrote this book, but I did not write it alone. I am therefore abundantly grateful for the inspiration, encouragement, and assistance I received from the following persons, without whose contributions this work simply would not be.

First, I wish to thank the University of Kansas Department of English for the material support I received as a 2011 recipient of the department's Haines Faculty Research Fellowship. I wish also to thank the university for granting me a Keeler Intra-University Professorship, an award that provided me with the time needed to make significant progress on my manuscript. In addition, the same award allowed me to design, along with my colleague, Dave Tell, an advanced seminar on the rhetoric of counterpublic discourses, which we co-taught in the spring of 2012. Many of the ideas elaborated in these pages were first tested in that seminar, and I would be remiss if I did not acknowledge the remarkable student members of that class and the often amazing discussions they provoked. Thank you Jeff Arterburn, Rachel Bloom, Brett Bricker, Chelsea Graham, Justin Kirk, Vince Meserko, Erin Murray, Meaghan Varieur, Justin Wilson, and Mark Wonnacott. I also wish to thank Cedric Burrows, Daryl Lynn Dance, Kendra Fullwood, and Lisa Stockton, who, in completing their own projects, taught me a great deal about my own.

Among my departmental colleagues, I owe a special note of gratitude to members of the Literature, Rhetoric, and Social Justice Group, most of whose members read and responded to an early draft of my first chapter. My sincere appreciation to Marta Caminero-Santangelo, Katie Conrad, Amy Devitt, Maryemma Graham, Laura Mielke, and Mary Jo Reiff for their excellent insights and many helpful comments. Several colleagues outside of my department also read portions of this manuscript, and to these friends and colleagues I must also extend my thanks: Jeff Williams, Emily Donnelli-Sallee, Paul Butler, Jason Barrett-Fox, and, of course, my three anonymous peer reviewers, all of whom offered enormously helpful comments and criticisms.

In my wanderings underground, so to speak, I was extremely fortunate to have a number of guides who led me through some unfamiliar territory and who provided me with a new appreciation for alternative communities, alternative perspectives, and, ultimately, an alternative view of what a public is. I wish, then, to thank members of my Cultural Advisory Board (CAB): Iain Ellis, Jim Gardner, Sarah Madden, Richard Noggle, Ailecia Ruscin, Rachel Vaughn, and Erin Williams. (I like to believe that none of these friends would be especially happy about serving on anyone's advisory board, even my fictitious one.) I also wish to extend my gratitude to the Solidarity! Revolutionary Center & Radical

Library in Lawrence, Kansas, for allowing me to access their amazing zine collection.

Preparing a manuscript for publication comes with its own travails, as any author knows, but this task was made significantly easier by the help I received from Brittany Brannon and Paula Courtney. And to Michael Spooner, my enduring gratitude for your expert advice and your unfaltering encouragement, not to mention the opportunity to publish with Utah State University Press one more time.

Finally, I must give a special word of thanks to my colleague, Dave Tell, of our Communication Studies Department at the University of Kansas, whose enthusiasm for this project was unabated, even when its author had his doubts. His influence on the final shape of this text, its featured themes, its strengths and virtues (whatever readers may judge them to be)—such influences can neither be minimized nor overlooked. Thank you, Dave Tell, for helping make this a better book than it would have been without your involvement.

And Linda, I'm home!

RIOT LOVE POEM

For Maria Alyokhina and Nadezhda Tolokonnikova

A riot   an order   a call in the night to say I love
you and you and you and most especially
the street and open space and our bodies
unbound by restraint and moneyed constriction
and in dreams last night you spoke of fire
of labor and building and soft nests   no armor-clad
SUVs on urban boulevards not oil money not Stoleshnikov Lane

This morning I exhale across continents breath joined
with yours and ours and wanting more than boundaries
street lamps awakened   petals unfurling   hands opening
burn treasury burn prison burn credit burn churches
burn drones burn austerity burn banks burn office buildings
sing certainty and mass gatherings   totalities
I opened to I into we

Now we are in Moscow now Perm now Mordovia
Now we are in Paris now Wall Street now Guantanamo
Now Atchison now Waco now Oakland
Now the avenue the bakery the café
Text springing from fingers
Language from mouths

Megan Kaminski

Introduction
TURNING AND TURNING

One of the commonplace devices in writing disciplinary histories is to construct momentous shifts in scholarly attention as "turns," a reflexive trope that has come to take the place of "paradigms," or "disciplinary matrices," or perhaps the less formal "governing gazes" that shape any field's dominant research interests.[1] The obvious advantage of labeling such shifts as "turns" probably ensues from the fact that this descriptor, more than others, lends a certain dynamism to how scholarly knowledge advances and thus how disciplines progress. In any case, one does not have to look far to notice how much currency this term has had. In mid-twentieth century philosophy, for example, the *linguistic turn* is widely acknowledged to have informed both analytic and continental traditions in philosophy departments, even though there remain (and will remain) stark differences between the two. In critical theory, the late twentieth century has been characterized as a moment when a *spatial turn* occurred, perhaps owing to the influence of thinkers like Henri Lefebvre, Pierre Bourdieu, and David Harvey, each of whom thematized spatiality in exceptionally productive ways. In recent economic theory, the *geographic turn* has been used to describe the work of Paul Krugman, Michael Porter, and several other leading thinkers in the field.

Composition studies, too, has had its turns, the most heralded of which is the *social turn* of the mid- to late 1980s. While this turn was primarily concerned with what theory (or theories) of knowledge should inform our understanding of the writing process, it also had implications for pedagogy (e.g., collaborative learning and writing) as well as for a new political awareness emerging among scholars and practitioners in our discipline. In fact, one of the figures most associated with the social turn, James Berlin, advocated an explicitly materialist approach to understanding our work and, toward the end of his life, was a major influence in the increasing prominence of cultural studies approaches to composition. As our discipline moved into the 1990s, "social" concerns broadened to include inquiries into cultural identities and practices not previously addressed with sustained attention in the disciplinary literature. It could legitimately be argued that the 1990s saw a *cultural turn* in composition studies, but in retrospect, if such a turn did occur, it tended to go largely unannounced and was probably subsumed (incorrectly, I think) as a part of the social turn that occurred a decade earlier. And moreover, this cultural turn persisted well beyond the decade of the 1990s and continues into our current moment.

More recently, however, Paula Mathieu has observed that composition studies has made a *public turn*. Our interest in community literacies, service-learning programs, public writing pedagogies, etc., taken as a whole, would seem to confirm this turn, but perhaps our naming of such a turn ought to come with a necessary proviso: our public turn is not a substitute for our cultural turn just as our cultural turn was not a substitute for our social turn and just as none of our earlier turns relieve us of the responsibility to attend to what is likely the most pressing challenge facing our discipline at the moment, our *digital turn*. My point is that while our discipline advances as a result of the many turns it makes, composition studies remains too varied and too complex for any one turn to supplant or govern all others. Rather, in the busy intersection that is composition, a number of turns are being made, executed in a more or less orderly fashion but not always with the knowledge of where exactly our turns may be taking us.[2]

Still, despite the rich multiplicity of our turns, some may wonder why a distinctly public turn was needed in the first place. After all, when our discipline first emerged in the 1960s, did we not situate ourselves within the traditions of Western rhetoric, so much so that "rhetoric and composition" became the preferred name for our collective inquiries and remains so for many of us?[3] And if these traditions, from their origins in ancient Greece until our present moment, are so thoroughly implicated in the history of public discourse in the West, ought we not wonder why a public turn is needed at all? To reiterate a familiar locution, isn't rhetoric always already public? Has not rhetoric—along with its traveling companion, instruction *in* rhetoric—always had a public orientation and purpose?

One way to answer this question, of course, is to affirm the public character of rhetorical practices but to point out that rhetoric is not limited to strictly public uses. Nonpublic rhetorics may, of course, be found in interpersonal conversations, literary texts, and distinct cultural practices as well as the discursive customs of such entities as private clubs and associations. But the more typical way to answer this question is to point out the obvious—namely, that not all publics are the same, and therefore, whether rhetoric has a democratic space within which to operate remains, historically speaking, a matter of considerable importance because this question speaks to where rhetoric locates itself at any given time. One classic illustration of this point is to compare the Rome of Cicero, where opportunities for the practice of oratorical skills were plentiful, with the Rome of Quintilian, a century later, where such occasions had diminished greatly and rhetoric was increasingly consigned to the schools, a trend that continued throughout the following three centuries, the period known as the Second Sophistic.[1]

Still, as a general truism, it can hardly be denied that "[w]hen democracy flourishes, so does rhetoric and its study. When democracy declines, rhetoric also declines as its role as the method of free public discourse is diminished" (Herrick 2005, 115). Yet, by conflating "rhetoric and its study," Herrick overlooks what many others are often quick to point out—namely, that when "democracy declines," rhetoric beats a hasty retreat to the schools where, figuratively speaking, it seeks refuge until more fortuitous conditions prevail. In other words, the relationship between rhetoric and the schools is far more complicated than that posited by the Ciceronian ideal, a situation where schools devoted their entire curriculum to the education of future citizen-orators who would then use their acquired knowledge to influence public affairs. What, then, does this historical illustration—this stark contrast between the Romes of Cicero and Quintilian—say to us about our present circumstances; and more pointedly, what does it say to us (if anything) about why composition studies felt it necessary to make a public turn at all?

In recalling her days as a graduate student, Nancy Welch reflects upon her first encounter with S. Michael Halloran's (1983) essay, "Rhetoric in the American College Curriculum: The Decline of Public Discourse," an essay, I would confirm, that was assigned reading for many of us who received our disciplinary training in the mid-1980s. In any case, Welch uses Halloran's article as a springboard into ruminations on experiencing no identification whatsoever with the Ciceronian tradition that Halloran celebrates in his essay. In contrast to the (by then) well-established yoking of rhetoric *and* composition, Welch tells us that the brief history of rhetoric offered by Halloran "spoke to [her] not at all" (Welch 2008, 41). Instead, Welch was drawn to the composition side of the tandem—the part that did, indeed, speak to her teaching, her scholarly interests, and her social commitments. Writing some two decades after Halloran's essay, Welch allows that much recent scholarship has deepened her appreciation of what a more informed conception of rhetoric might entail:

Investigations not only into the practices of individual women rhetors, but also into schools, associations, unions, clubs, broad social movements, and countercultural affinity groups as crucial sites for rhetorical training have dramatically expanded our understanding of rhetorical history. If we look at history as the story of widening layers of people contesting their exclusion from public participation and visibility . . . our potential understanding of the available means to make arguments broadens and deepens. Moreover, the history of our field becomes a history of contestation over what is and what is not within rhetoric's realm and who will or will not have speaking rights on those debates concerning what is and is not the public good. (41–42)

It would seem that Welch's understanding of rhetoric represents something of a challenge to the version offered by Halloran (and others) inclined to invoke a (particular) rhetorical tradition for the purpose of restoring some aspects of that tradition's past glory. For Halloran, while some part of this tradition had, in fact, been recovered by the new pedagogies emerging at that time, what got ignored was the classical imperative to "address students as political beings, as members of a body politic in which they have a responsibility to form judgments and influence the judgments of others on public issues." By reinstating a "focus on public discourse," Halloran seems to say that we might yet restore a still vital tradition and, at the same time, participate in the making of a better public than we have now (Halloran 1996, 194). In contrast, Welch seems to say that our historical rhetorics fail us if they do not compel us to attend to the struggles of those who have been excluded from participation in public life and, by implication, rhetorical action. If we are to have a rhetoric for our own time, and not for another, we must also have an informed understanding of the ways that rhetorics and publics mutually construct one another—that is to say, how each is able to form and rewrite the other. Such a task requires an understanding of the continuously shifting relationship between rhetorics and publics, an understanding that is perhaps more historicist than historical in its orientation, a little more Welch than Halloran.

Does this, then, partially explain why composition studies found it necessary to make a recent public turn? Was our disciplinary turn not so much one that suddenly discovered publics but rather one that suddenly discovered the extent to which we had merely taken for granted our relationship to the publics that shaped the formation of our specialty? Had we laid bare our prior conception of public life (and the rhetorics suitable for it) because we finally came to realize that something about public life in America had been profoundly altered, and that as a discipline we felt obligated to respond to new urgencies that, as Welch points out, bear upon the work we do not only inside our classrooms but outside of them as well?

Well, yes, at least partially. Our disquieting sense that the publics we now inhabit—and that inhabit us—are something less than desirable seems to be a widely felt misgiving. In this respect, Halloran's lament about the decline of public discourse might be more generously interpreted not merely as a comment about discourse or rhetorical traditions or the best methods for teaching writing. It might also be understood as an observation about the kind of public, or publics, now embarked upon a trajectory of decline. Seen this way, I think Halloran's argument may be better situated within a broader literature that aspires to chronicle the inexorable fading away of "the public" from American consciousness. About ten years prior to Halloran's article, for example, Richard Sennett (1974) published *The Fall of Public Man*, a work that traces the historical demise of a genuine public realm for late twentieth-century America. A decade after Halloran's essay, Bruce Robbins (1993), in a collection entitled *The Phantom Public Sphere*, questions whether a public sphere is even possible in our postmodern moment. And in this century, two recent (and more popular) works—Richard Posner's (2001) *Public Intellectuals: A Study of Decline* and Robert Putnam's (2000) *Bowling Alone: The Collapse and Revival of American Community*—together, but in their distinct ways, contend that our national sense of meaningful public participation is an increasingly diminished one. Clearly, these works (and others) seek to address what seems to be nothing less than a crisis in our public life, a curtailment of genuine opportunities for democratic action in the public realm.[5]

Composition studies, as well, responded to these changes, both in our scholarship and our teaching. The 1990s saw an abrupt increase of commentary devoted to making sense of our discipline's relationship to a public that seemed to be, if not exactly a phantom, then certainly a slowly vanishing arena of discursive opportunity—unless, that is, we as a discipline pressed the issue, unless we took it upon ourselves literally to "re-model" the existing public sphere through our intellectual work as well as our teaching practices. Such a large goal, in fact, seems to underwrite much of our scholarship during that decade. In *A Teaching Subject: Composition since 1966*, Joseph Harris urges us "to imagine new public spheres which they'd [our students] like to have a hand in making" (Harris 1996, 124). To make room for this new emphasis on publics, Harris interrogates two of our most cherished metaphors, communities and contact zones, and, for different reasons, finds each to be lacking when compared to how turning our collective attention to publics might better guide our inquiries and our teaching. A like emphasis on making publics is found in Susan Wells's much-cited article "Rogue Cops and Health Care: What Do We Want from Public Writing?" Wells observes, "[W]e have been sheltered from a vibrant public sphere. Our public sphere is attenuated, fragmented, and colonized; so is everyone else's." That exigency duly noted, Wells argues that "all speakers and writers who aspire to intervene in society . . . face the task of constructing a responsive public" (Wells 1996, 328–29). To this end, she sketches four pedagogical strategies that may help us construct, along with our students, those responsive publics we desire for them as well as for ourselves.

One of Wells's strategies is that we imagine our classrooms as models, or "concentrated version[s] of the public [at large]" (Wells 1996, 338). This notion gets further attention in the last chapter to Rosa A. Eberly's *Citizen Critics: Literary Public Spheres*, when she asks teachers to regard our classes as "protopublics," staging grounds for the publics our students will someday enter. For Eberly, this means that "texts are inventional prompts for discussion about various publics and their possible reaction to the texts in question" (Eberly 2000, 170). And while we ought never to confuse our classrooms with publics, Eberly argues that we may still "help students imagine themselves as—and then act as—citizen critics" (169). Patricia Roberts-Miller reiterates this view but more pointedly in the context of democratic processes. As she argues, "If public argument is bad, then perhaps there is something wrong with the teaching of public argument. Instead of replicating exactly the practice that leads to the consequences we dislike, we can reflect on it, and try to enact a practice that might get us the kind of public discourse we would like to see" (Roberts-Miller 2004, 228).

Christian R. Weisser also charts a variety of ways by which our writing classrooms can be made more answerable to public concerns, but, according to Weisser, all such approaches need to embrace his suggestion that we bring a sociohistorical awareness to bear upon public issues and public texts. Doing so will best allow students to see "the political, social, economic, cultural, and ideological forces that have influenced any public issue" (Weisser 2002, 99). Given this starting point, it is not difficult to understand why Weisser considers our newfound interest in publics to be continuous with the social turn discussed at the outset of this chapter. But it should be noted, as well, that Weisser considers the likelihood that our interest in publics and publics' theory might be something more than a continuation of what already was, and in fact might "well become the next dominant focal point around which the teaching of college writing is theorized and imagined" (Weisser 2002, 42). Weisser, in other words, anticipates what will be formally announced three years later by Paula Mathieu: the public turn in composition.

In the subtitle to *Tactics of Hope*, Mathieu (2005) proclaims what had for some time become apparent in our disciplinary conversations—namely, that composition had indeed made a public turn, and that this turn was still in the process of being executed. While Mathieu finds ample warrant for her claim in much of the same literature I discuss here, it is important to observe that she has a very specific idea in mind as to what constitutes the public turn as it relates to her work.[6] For Mathieu, the public turn in composition signifies the discovery of an absent but much needed "street" dimension to our inquiries. With that sensibility in mind, she articulates a rallying cry to encourage composition studies to "go public" in our myriad efforts to understand writing and the teaching of writing. As Mathieu explains:

> At the heart of this call to the streets is a desire for writing to enter civic debates; for street life to enter classrooms through a focus on local, social issues; for students to hit the streets by performing service, and for teachers and scholars to conduct activist or community-grounded research. While much has been written about these initiatives . . . when taken together, they could be considered a significant turn in composition studies toward the public and the streets. (Mathieu 2005, 1)

Given her rather broad and inclusive description of what she means by "street," as well as her conflation of "the public and the streets" in this passage, we could reasonably conclude that *street* functions here as a kind of synecdoche, a term that encompasses many of the ways that composition studies imagines its relationship to the larger public. And in fact, Mathieu herself acknowledges street as a metaphor—a "problematic" metaphor, no doubt, but one whose problems are "generative" of the kinds of inquiries we ought to be pursuing. Thus, we hear her ask, "Aren't the *streets* largely where we and our students are heading to read, to write, and to serve?" (Mathieu 2005, xiii). Certainly, for those of us engaged in local literacy and service-learning projects, community writing groups, activist scholarship, and so on, the answer to Mathieu's question could only be an unqualified yes.

However, by yoking the street to the public, Mathieu by no means suggests a facile equivalence between these terms. In an important sense, she is making a comment about what our public realm has become: an evacuated, abandoned space inhabited, for the most part, by those who "live the streets," who do not have the resources necessary to (comfortably) partition their daily lives. As she notes, "wealthy people tend not to spend much time in the streets, and when they do it's often within regulated and semiprivatized spaces, such as gated communities or sidewalks in gentrified neighborhoods" (Mathieu 2005, xiii). Therefore, from a street perspective, our public has been converted into something of a residual phenomenon, a leftover (and left behind) space for the subordinated, the marginalized, and the poor. Small wonder, then, that "the lives of lower-income people tend to be more public . . . than the lives of the wealthy" (xiii). And yet, for those academics like Mathieu, who insist that their scholarly work have meaning beyond the campus proper, her "call to the streets" represents nothing less than a call to respond to the situation of disadvantaged citizens and, by implication, the publics they increasingly define. Mathieu's story of her activist work with the homeless in Chicago and Boston illustrates how answering this call to the streets might productively join our disciplinary commitments with our social commitments.

About the same time that Mathieu's work appeared, Barbara Couture and Thomas Kent (2004) published *The Private, the Public, and the Published: Reconciling Private Lives and Public Rhetoric*, a collection of essays that further examined a key theme in public scholarship: to wit, the public-private distinction addressed by Mathieu and others. Couture and Kent approach this distinction in four ways: through expression and experience, through written language, through mediated identities, and through the discipline of composition studies. Just a few years later, Nancy Welch (2008) critically reexamines this distinction (and the politics it entails) in *Living Room: Teaching Public Writing in a Privatized World*, a work briefly mentioned above. Like Mathieu, Welch brings an activist commitment to her understanding of how we ought to engage the public in our teaching and our scholarship. This same activist desire is obvious, as well, in Linda Flower's *Community Literacy and the Rhetoric of Public Engagement*, a work that, among other things, chronicles her longstanding efforts at the Community Literacy Center (CLC) in Pittsburgh. In this most recent volume, Flower develops a theory of "local publics" that emerges from, and is appropriate for, the practices of "intercultural inquiry" noted here but introduced in her much earlier work (Flower

2008, 24–43). Likewise drawing upon her experiences with the CLC, Elenore Long's (2008) *Community Literacy and the Rhetoric of Local Publics* further elaborates Flower's theory and offers guidelines for teachers who want to develop pedagogies that foster an awareness of community literacies and their relationship to local publics.

As might be expected among those who profess "a teaching subject" such as ours, most of the works mentioned here, no matter how critically or theoretically oriented, reveal a concern with how our public turn gets manifested in our pedagogies. And as we should also expect, our literature alludes to a wide range of teaching approaches. Emily Donnelli (2008) suggests one very useful way of organizing our classroom efforts in those works where pedagogy is front and center. In her bibliographic review, Donnelli (2008) recontextualizes three familiar terms that we may use to categorize our efforts to teach with a public emphasis.[7]

Much of our literature, Donnelli points out, sees the writing classroom as a *micropublic*, wherein students are asked to think of their writing course as part of a larger, external public, one that is both defined and circumscribed by its tetherings to the composition classroom. More commonly, the writing course is figured as a *protopublic*, a term she uses to cast the classroom as a rehearsal site where preparatory work is taken up in anticipation of that moment when, fully fledged, our students will take center stage in their roles as committed, informed, and rhetorically effective citizens. A third term constructs the writing classroom as a *counterpublic*, a term Donnelli borrows to designate those classrooms that aspire to introduce students to the notion of multiple, contending publics. "The classroom as *counter*-public," Donnelli argues, "privileges openly critical and oppositional discourses about the relationship of schooling to society" (Donnelli 2008, 37). Not too surprisingly, Donnelli aligns counterpublic pedagogies with critical pedagogies, especially through the work of Henry Giroux, Ira Shor, and Peter McLaren.

One striking feature of her map, for both micropublics and protopublics, is that Donnelli provides examples gleaned directly from the literature of composition studies. However, when she discusses counterpublic pedagogies, she moves outside of composition proper in order to find examples (and exemplars) to discuss. As noted above, the locus for her examination of counterpublic writing instruction is critical pedagogy. And, doubtless, the literature of critical pedagogy has been enormously influential to the work of writing teachers, particularly over the last three decades. But as a discourse in its own right, critical pedagogy encompasses much more than an interest in writing instruction. Its own premises, it would seem, require critical pedagogy to regard itself as transdisciplinary, even while it embraces a distinct literature of its own, along with conferences, journals, associations, and other assorted markings of disciplinarity. However such a paradox may be understood, and notwithstanding our close, productive relationship with critical pedagogy, it is obvious that composition studies and critical pedagogy are not the same discipline. Why, then, did Donnelli explore the literature of critical pedagogy to make a case for the writing classroom as counterpublic? Why did she choose critical pedagogy as the sole entry point for the idea that our writing classrooms can be figured as counterpublics?

The best answer to that question is the obvious one: because she had no choice. Prior to Donnelli's analysis, very little published work in composition studies sought to address counterpublics, and even less tried to understand counterpublics and their potential implications for the teaching of composition. While it is no doubt true that some of the scholars discussed here gave passing mention to counterpublics—Wells, Michelle Comstock, and Weisser, for example—very few in our discipline gave any sustained attention to the problems posed by counterpublic discourses, especially as such discourses might bear relevance to the practices of those who study and teach writing. I should note that since the time of Donnelli's analysis, scholarship devoted to counterpublics has markedly increased; but that said, and despite our field's "public turn," there remains a relative scarcity of composition scholarship on counterpublics.[8] How, then, to explain our seeming lack of interest in counterpublics? I doubt that any answer to that question could avoid speculation and uncertainty. But allow me to offer three possible explanations as to why this may be so.

First, we may not know for certain exactly what a counterpublic is. This definitional ambiguity should hardly be surprising because, as I intend to show, the term itself has an impressive track record of mutability and redefinition. And while such conceptual instability might speak well of its intellectual liveliness, this same volatility could be off-putting to writing scholars who require more consistency in their efforts to discover how counterpublics might be relevant to our purposes. Second, despite its inconsistencies, one abiding feature of counterpublic discourse is its overwhelming attention to oppositional identities. In this respect, inquiries into counterpublics often tend to overlap with, and frequently resemble, already established inquiries into cultures and subcultures, and thus they may possibly (though unwittingly) cultivate a kind of vying for our disciplinary attention. Indeed, where exactly does our work with (sub)cultures end, and our work with (counter)publics begin? Or vice versa? Must these seemingly distinct objects of inquiry be kept absolutely compartmentalized, separate at all costs? Or might hybrid forms exist, social arrangements that function simultaneously as publics and cultures? These are difficult questions, and I will attempt to broach such concerns in later chapters. For now, though, I wish only to suggest that if writing scholars do, in fact, choose between investigating publics or cultures, the latter overwhelmingly triumph as the preferred object of our research and teaching.

Finally, our apparent lack of interest in counterpublics might have something to do with the intellectual heritage of the concept itself. Even though composition studies has made good (if not extensive) use of public sphere theory—a line of inquiry prompted by critical theorist Jürgen Habermas—we have yet to explore what is no doubt the most formidable critique of Habermas's idea of the public sphere: namely, the genuine vitality of "actually existing" counterpublics.[9] To understand counterpublics better than we presently do, however, will require us to make forays into other discourses, other literatures, other conversations, the larger share of which will seem at a considerable remove from our disciplinary purposes. And yet, as I hope to demonstrate in the pages to follow, a more discerning examination of publics and counterpublics may prove to be rewarding to composition studies in ways that we did not foresee. To commence that task, the first question to be asked is this: Where does the idea of counterpublics come from?

* * *

In *Structural Transformation of the Public Sphere: An Inquiry into a Category of Bourgeois Society,* Habermas (1991) details the historical conditions accompanying what he calls the bourgeois public sphere in its course of development. In tracing the emergence and demise of the public sphere, Habermas attempts to delineate "the material conditions . . . for a rational-critical debate about public issues conducted by private persons willing to let arguments and not statuses determine decisions" (Calhoun 1992, 1). In addressing this problem, Habermas discovers the bourgeois public sphere arising out of ideas of civil society and "representative publicness" to be found in the European High Middle Ages, but later evolving along with the emergence of the modern, depersonalized state and early trade capitalism of the seventeenth and eighteenth centuries.

For Habermas, the bourgeois public sphere is traceable, in part, to two important and related developments. First, Habermas points to the reconstitution of the family as a private, intimate sphere—a cloistered domain of human relations ostensibly immune from market forces, free to develop its own separate rules, unencumbered, in large measure, to external purposes or needs. Habermas claims the reconstituted family actually offered a new subjectivity founded upon the idea of something essentially human that eluded the overdeterminations of economic, official (or any other vested) status that might otherwise limit or consummate the human subject. The intimate sphere thus provided a locus from which a critique of state or other official authorities, of rank and status difference, might originate. It suggested the possibility of such a realm serving as a necessary forerunner for the emergence of the bourgeois public sphere.

Habermas points to another model, the world of letters in the late seventeenth and eighteenth centuries. According to Habermas, the appearance of opinion and literary journals, of print news, of salons in Paris and coffeehouses in London all contributed to the emergence of a discursive space set aside for purposes of rational-critical debate. In this way, the literary public sphere is, for Habermas, a prototype for the broader, more politically interested bourgeois public sphere of the late eighteenth century, the summit of its historical ascendancy.

What, then, are the hallmarks of the public sphere? First, notes Habermas, while the bourgeois public sphere never assumed an equality of status among participants, it did assume that such differences in rank, wealth, and social status could be temporarily set aside—or, to use the more familiar term *bracketed*—for purposes of rational discussion. The presumed value of doing so lay in the notion that ideas, debates, propositions, etc. could be judged best on their purely argumentative merits, uncompromised by the external identity of the disputants involved. A second feature resides in the expansion of possible topics for discussion, and thus of interpretive freedom, the result of a gradual loosening of ecclesiastical and state monopolies on the received ways in which discourses were distributed and regulated. A third feature could be discovered in its principle of inclusiveness. Habermas allows that any given instance of the public sphere might very well be exclusive in its membership. Nevertheless, he observes, "it could never close itself off entirely and become consolidated as a clique; for it always understood and found itself immersed within a more inclusive public" and thus came to represent a new, bourgeois version of representative publicness (Habermas 1991, 36–37).

In the nineteenth century, the blurring of strict demarcations between state and society—between the previously distinct realms of public and private—made the old concept of a public sphere largely untenable, obsolete. Models of "fairly negotiated compromise among [competing] interests" supplanted received notions of a general, common interest (Calhoun 1992, 22). In the last half century, Habermas points to a culture of passive consumerism as the most likely substitute for a locus of rational-critical debate, an actuality that effectively renders the public sphere "an arena for advertising" promulgated by a mass media primarily designed for orchestrating consent (Calhoun 1992, 26). One hope, however limited, for a functioning public sphere might yet be discovered in "special interest associations" and what Habermas refers to as the "intraorgazinational public sphere" and "intra-associational democracy" (Habermas 1991, 209). Needless to say, these are a far cry from the bourgeois public sphere of the eighteenth century.

Some critics point to a certain methodological inconsistency to be found in Habermas, pointing out how apparently normative intentions compromise Habermas's exemplary historicist scholarship. Such critics observe that Habermas is not merely examining the conditions that allowed for the historical emergence of the bourgeois public sphere; he is also making an argument for its restoration in our moment—and perhaps worse, for *all* moments. Thus, for many critics, behind Habermas's detailed historical scholarship is an idealized public sphere, a public sphere that somehow manages to transcend historical determination altogether. Needless to say, this sort of idealism is more than a little hard to square with Habermas's Frankfurt School Marxism, out of which much of his work emerges. And even non-Marxist critics, such as Richard Rorty, part ways with Habermas when, as Rorty claims, Habermas "goes transcendental" (Rorty 1982, 173). Clearly, many readers of Habermas reject the seemingly tagged-on idealism of what remains otherwise a remarkable work of historicist scholarship.

A second criticism of Habermas centers upon his apparent indifference to praxis, to action. Harry C. Boyte, echoing such feminist critics such as Mary P. Ryan, Geoff Eley, and Nancy Fraser, claims that Habermas's notion of the public sphere turns its back on the subaltern, popular, decentered publics "created through a turbulent, provisional, and open-ended process of struggle, change, and challenge" (Boyte 1992, 344).[10] But, as Boyte points out, even many of Habermas's severest critics share his tendency to divorce public discourse from public action. What kind of rational-critical argument is even possible,

Boyte asks, if "common action is separated from public debate?" (345). What is the quality of our public discourse if it is wholly sundered from civic involvement?

For Boyte, a public sphere that eschews praxis, that isolates action from rational-critical debate, is, among other things, one that merely reproduces the traditional knowledge endorsed by formal schooling—distanced, analytical, and socially uncommitted knowledge. Worse yet, by assuming that public action is irrelevant to public debate, by ignoring the rich problem-solving traditions of American democracy, the Habermasian public sphere has the potential, at least, to render citizens into something akin to garrulous spectators and to construct the public intellectual as a figure more properly looked upon as a celebrity than an agent of social change.

And yet the most enduring (not to mention the most prolific) challenge to Habermas emanates from those critics who dispute the normative ubiquity of a single public sphere. In its wish to bracket all such differences in rank that might warp, or otherwise distort, rational-critical debate, this idealized Habermasian public sphere ends up being exclusionary as well—not just of privileged groups but of marginal and subaltern groups too, including such social formations that might call into question the very desirability of a universal public sphere in the first place. Such critics argue that there exists no uniform, general public but rather, multiple, contending publics that often have an oppositional relationship with the larger public, and with each other. These "other" publics are most often referred to as *counterpublics*, and in the wake of the original publication of Habermas's *Structural Transformation*, the idea of counterpublics has represented the foremost challenge to his conception of the public sphere.

The first mention of counterpublics comes a decade after the original publication of Habermas's *Structural Transformation* in 1962. Oskar Negt and Alexander Kluge's (1993) *Public Sphere and Experience: Toward an Analysis of the Bourgeois and Proletarian Public Sphere* appeared in its original German version in 1972 and is generally considered to be the first sustained critique of Habermas's ideas.[11] As the title of Negt and Kluge's work suggests, they introduce the idea of a "proletarian public sphere," a dialectical negation of the (by then) familiar "bourgeois public sphere" that Habermas reconstitutes as a normative model. As the counter-term itself implies, the *proletarian public sphere* is clearly (and thoroughly) concerned with labor and, as Miriam Hansen points out in her foreword to the English translation, *Public Sphere and Experience*, "gives little attention to non-labor issues or constituencies that might project an alternative organization of the public sphere." Yet by positing a more encompassing and historically restored proletariat, and then by describing the proletarian public sphere as a *counterpublic*, Negt and Kluge not only offered an important new term to our critical lexicon, but they also "provided a rallying point for a whole spectrum of groups and movements . . . because [they] allowed the groups to think of themselves as oppositional and public" (Hansen 1993, xvi).

This last point is of crucial importance. In the Habermasian bourgeois public sphere, to be radically oppositional is to be at odds with the very idea of publicness itself—and be located outside of the public sphere, outside of public discourse. Stated a bit differently, to be radically oppositional is to be *illegitimate*, at least in the received sense of what demarcates a public. Yet by allowing groups and movements to consider themselves as, simultaneously, oppositional *and* public, Negt and Kluge's work announces a watershed moment in our thinking about the public sphere. Not only do they challenge what they see as the "singular, foundational, and ahistorical" model of the Habermasian public sphere, they also provide their own definition (Hansen 1993, xi). According to Negt and Kluge, "We . . . understand the public sphere as an aggregate of phenomena that have completely diverse characteristics and origins. The public sphere has no homogenous substance whatsoever" (13). While the Habermasian model is based "on the formal conditions of communication (free association, equal participation, deliberation, polite argument)," Negt and Kluge's understanding revises this formulation considerably. Although they neither identify nor examine specific counterpublics, they nonetheless make a profound shift away from Habermas by directing attention to "questions of constituency, concrete needs, interests, conflicts, protest, and power" (xxx).[12] In sum, Negt and Kluge create an opening for future inquiries into counterpublics as a feature of what actually constitutes an existing public.

The first mention of counterpublics in English appears in Rita Felski's *Beyond Feminist Aesthetics: Feminist Literature and Social Change*.[13] Drawing upon Habermas, as well as Negt and Kluge, Felski introduces the idea of a "feminist counter-public sphere." Although she uses "feminist public sphere" and "feminist counter-public sphere" interchangeably, she contends with the debilitating notion that feminism must be "understood as a unified interpretative community governed by a single set of norms and values" (Felski 1989, 10). To the contrary, a feminist counter-public sphere, Felski argues, establishes a site and a framework for the critical pluralism necessary for a new solidarity, one that surmounts a misguided desire for unanimity of interest or opinion.

While Felski's work is groundbreaking, Nancy Fraser is more widely known for promoting the idea of counterpublics, or more exactly, what she calls "subaltern counterpublics." In her much-cited and highly influential essay, "Rethinking the Public Sphere: A Contribution to the Critique of Actually Existing Democracy," Fraser offers a critical summary of Habermas's *Structural Transformation*, and then proceeds to challenge his argument by interrogating four key assumptions that inform his work. First, she observes, Habermas posits "that societal equality is not a necessary condition for political democracy"—in other words, that it is necessary merely to "bracket" social inequalities rather than address them. Second, she points out that Habermas assumes uniformity always to be preferable to diversity and that from a Habermasian point of view, "a multiplicity of competing publics is necessarily a step away from, rather than toward, greater democracy." Third, Fraser disputes Habermas's premise that deliberations about the "common good" must, by definition, exclude any concern with "private interests" or "private issues." And finally, she critiques "the assumption that a functioning democratic public sphere requires a sharp separation between civil society and the state" (Fraser 1990, 62–63). After identifying these assumptions, she provides a compelling refutation of each, concluding that the idealized public sphere offered by Habermas does not take into account historically or actually existing publics, "discursive arenas" whose purpose is to contest forms of domination. Such arenas, Fraser points out, may be accurately designated as subaltern counterpublics.

Fraser offers what is likely the clearest, most succinct definition of counterpublics to be found in the entire literature. Counterpublics, she argues, are not merely alternative publics but "parallel discursive arenas where members of subordinated social groups invent and circulate counterdiscourses, which in turn permit them to formulate oppositional interpretations of their identities, interests, and needs" (Fraser 1990, 67). She further directs our attention to the fact of their "dual character," observing, "On the one hand, they [counterpublics] function as spaces of withdrawal and regroupment; on the other hand, they also function as bases and training grounds for agitational activities directed toward wider publics. It is precisely in the dialectic between these two functions that their emancipatory potential resides" (68). As with Felski (whom she cites), her exemplary case is the "feminist subaltern counterpublic, with its variegated array of journals, bookstores, publishing companies, film and video distribution networks, lecture series, research centers, academic programs, conferences, conventions, festivals, and local meeting places. In this public sphere, feminist women have invented new terms for describing social reality" (67).

But in giving too much attention to formal definition and distinguishing features, we risk losing sight of other, often less discussed, contributions that Fraser makes to our understanding of counterpublics. Especially noteworthy among her many insights: her awareness that counterpublics are saturated in discursivity and that their existence in large part depends upon the texts they both create and circulate; her recognition that not all counterpublics are necessarily committed to social justice, equality, and greater democratic participation (i.e., that it is possible for reactionary counterpublics to exist); and her suggestion, not elaborated here, that counterpublics frequently align with specific identities, and that these identities may be either chosen (as in feminist subaltern counterpublics) or given (as in "peoples of color," "gays and lesbians," etc.). As I indicated, Fraser does not expand upon these secondary insights in her essay but later theorists of counterpublics do.

Foremost among these is Michael Warner. In *Publics and Counterpublics*, Warner elaborates and critiques Fraser's understanding of counterpublics, yet surpasses its limitations. Early on, for example, Warner proclaims a "need for both concrete and theoretical understandings of the conditions that currently mediate the transformative and creative work of counterpublics," especially what "counterpublics of sex and gender" might teach us about "new worlds . . . new privacies, new individuals, new bodies, new intimacies, and new citizenships" (Warner 2005, 62). While Warner is primarily interested in queer counterpublics, he obviously intends his discussion to apply to all counterpublics. While he does not provide a formally concise definition of counterpublics, as does Fraser, he does offer a full discussion of their defining qualities, most of which I discuss in chapter 2.

Even though Warner affirms much of what Fraser has to say, especially her suggestion of the importance of texts to counterpublics, he also parts ways with and goes beyond her understanding.[11] Among other things, he challenges her assertion that counterpublics must, by definition, be *subaltern*, by which he means that not "all counterpublics are composed of people *otherwise* dominated as subalterns" (Warner 2005, 57). One's day job, in other words, might not have anything to do with one's "after hours" membership in this or that counterpublic. Warner also contributes an awareness of the specifically aesthetic features of counterpublic membership. This is evident in a chapter devoted to style and its importance to counterpublic identity. But this aesthetic sense is perhaps nowhere more obvious than in his claim that counterpublics enact a function of "poetic world making," or what he calls "the performative dimension of public discourse" (114). Through the reflexive circulation of texts, and thus through the stylized expressions embodied in those texts, counterpublics make and maintain alternate worlds for their members.[15] Furthermore, because those worlds exist as a result of whatever attention they are able to invoke and sustain through texts, counterpublics tend to be a great deal more evanescent and volatile than what earlier commentators, including Fraser, might have us believe.

But the most profound revision Warner makes is his opposition to a key premise that both Fraser and Habermas share—namely, that the ultimate purpose of publics (and counterpublics) is "to deliberate and decide." In other words, he contests the widely held assumption that what publics are about is "rational discussion writ large" and that, therefore, public discourse must be "propositionally summarizable." Of course, Warner is not arguing that rational-critical debate is irrelevant to understanding publics and counterpublics. He is saying, however, that this emphasis has been "ideologized" to such an extent that it obscures "the poetic or textual qualities of any utterance." Propositions, arguments, resolutions, position statements, opinions—each is thought to be reducible to its content, and therefore, each is endlessly repeatable, conveniently "fungible" in ways that "other aspects of discourse, including affect and expressivity, are not" (Warner 2005, 115). Warner believes that counterpublic discourse is much more than its ability to debate a point. Although he does not put it exactly this way, he implicitly asks us to think about how these "other aspects of discourse" have a bearing on the rhetoric of publics and counterpublics.

Warner, Fraser, Felski, Negt and Kluge—these are the major theoretical statements on counterpublic discourse. Tucked away in the interstices between and beyond these statements there exists a substantial commentary that emerges within the literatures of various disciplines. Scholars in fields as diverse as literary studies, sociology, history, women's studies, education, public relations, and urban theory have all contributed to the conversation about counterpublics. Our institutional "next door neighbor," communication studies, has in fact developed an ample record of published inquiry devoted to counterpublics. Scholars such as Robert Asen, Erik Doxtader, and Daniel C. Brouwer have all made important contributions to a specific understanding of the rhetoric of counterpublics for those working in this field. But as I indicated earlier, with a few notable exceptions, composition studies has not done likewise.

* * *

After the Public Turn: Composition, Counterpublics, and the Citizen Bricoleur responds to what I see as our discipline's general inattentiveness to counterpublics. As I note above, our general neglect of counterpublics, while by no means absolute, may be explained in a variety of ways. But the urgency that motivates this work is that by devoting relatively little attention to counterpublics, we limit our students' understanding of what qualifies as democratic participation, of what counts as authentic public engagement, of what a *citizen* is. To whatever degree might be possible, then, it is my hope that *After the Public Turn* alters and broadens our present understanding of publics and public discourse to include, more fully than we do now, those oppositional social formations known as counterpublics. I also hope that this work prompts future inquiry into both counterpublics and those who *make* counterpublics—those mostly unsung figures I call "citizen bricoleurs," such figures who, as my title suggests, embody a theme woven throughout the entirety of this work. If I am able to persuade other composition scholars and teachers that counterpublics (and those who make them) are worthy of far more scrutiny than we have yet to extend to them, I will have met one of the main purposes of this book. For by encouraging my colleagues to consider this direction, it may yet be that counterpublic inquiry will assume a more prominent role in our classrooms, and our students will leave those classrooms with a deeper understanding of what democratic citizenship means in our time.

This work is structured upon two main sections; each section is composed of two chapters that investigate a particular kind of public and, by implication, a particular kind of counterpublic. In the first section I look at what I call *cultural publics*, certain social formations that can be seen, at once, as publics and cultures, so long as we are willing to examine the public aspects of cultural inquiry and, correspondingly, the cultural aspects of public inquiry.[16] I argue that some publics and cultures are made through texts and that textual circulation is, therefore, essential to this making enterprise, one that I see as emblematic of the arts of bricolage. I use as my central example zines and zine making, and I pose the question: What else gets made when zines get made?

Chapter 1, then, attempts to provide a concrete illustration of my basic idea. Drawing upon three major commentators on bricolage—Claude

Lévi-Strauss, Dick Hebdige, and Michel de Certeau, I review how these three thinkers have used this concept and are especially alert to its wider implications. Following their lead, I attempt to show how bricolage can help us understand how certain social formations get made, and to illustrate this, I trace the history of zines—with a particular emphasis on anarchist zines—which, for my purposes, exemplify how certain forms of resistance can be surreptitiously crafted, jerry-rigged, assembled from the discards of others. Here I introduce the figure of the citizen bricoleur and suggest that zine makers embody precisely what I have in mind. Chapter 2 further details my exploration of zines but shifts from cultural theory to public sphere theory as a way to frame my discussion. In particular, I acknowledge that zines can, of course, be looked upon in the usual way—that is, as a subculture of only marginal significance to the culture at large. But they can also, and at the same time, be understood as a certain kind of public—a counterpublic—and from this vantage, they may prove to be more significant than some have previously thought. To make my case, this chapter examines the contemporary situation of zines—the challenges they face, the promises they hold.

In my second section, I turn my attention to what I call *disciplinary publics* and pose a very different set of questions: Is it possible to construe academic disciplines as counterpublics? And if so, whom or what are they counter to? What exactly is it that they oppose, and why should we regard their oppositional stances to be, in any meaningful sense, *public*? Might it not be the case that their institutional placement does not even permit us to entertain the idea that disciplines can be thought of as counterpublics? What is to be gained by looking upon certain disciplines this way? And what is to be lost? One purpose of this section is to offer an alternative model of public participation for scholars and teachers, one that surpasses our received models that tend to limit us to our fascination with public intellectuals, policy experts, and, to some extent, the varieties of activist scholarship available to us.

In chapter 3, I elaborate the rather counterintuitive (if not outrageous) idea that *some* academic disciplines in *some* contexts may be regarded as counterpublics. In support of this claim, I provide three abbreviated cases wherein I examine texts by scholars who discuss whether their disciplines—architecture, teacher education, and science and technology studies (STS)—might be legitimately defined as counterpublics. Based on what they tell us, I attempt to craft a provisional description of a disciplinary counterpublic. With this description in hand, I argue in chapter 4 that composition studies sometimes finds itself performing the role of a counterpublic, one whose oppositional stances largely arise because of the historical (and current) representations it faces both in and out of the academy. I argue, further, that composition studies is a liminal counterpublic because it has yet to achieve a full awareness about the public significance of the work it performs—whether in the classroom, the streets, or the venues of publicity available to it. I end this chapter by returning to bricolage as a way to assist composition in locating a needed space for itself within and among public discourses.

In sum, two major sections form the body of this work—one that inquires into cultural publics, using zines as its preeminent example, and the other that inquires into disciplinary publics, using composition studies as its most fully elaborated illustration. If the contrast between the two seems dramatic, I intended it to be so. My hope is to put into relief, to make conspicuous, the stark differences in the manner by which texts circulate in two discursive yet contrastive worlds—a realm of the street and a realm of the institution; a realm of officially authorized legitimacy and a realm of no (apparent) legitimacy at all; a realm of amateurish, self-published texts and a realm of immaculately professional ones.

I offer these contrasts, however, to make a point. Counterpublics do not exist prior to or outside of the varied contexts within which they emerge. As counterpublics, their peculiar forms are thus shaped by those contexts. Such is why there can be anarchist counterpublics, subaltern feminist counterpublics, queer counterpublics, black counterpublics, green counterpublics, street art counterpublics, Internet counterpublics, "grassroots documentary" counterpublics, biker counterpublics, and so on. To qualify as a counterpublic, the minimal requirements are generally acknowledged to be the following: an oppositional relationship to other, more dominant publics; a marginal, subaltern, or excluded status within the larger public; and an identity wrought by, and refined through, the reflexive circulation of texts. Drawing especially upon the work of Nancy Fraser and Michael Warner, I will elaborate this description at length in the pages to follow. But I hope it obvious that counterpublics can be discovered in some surprising places and can express a range of very different social, cultural, and political viewpoints.

In an epilogue to this work, I return to those who make counterpublics, those I refer to as citizen bricoleurs. In a brief essay that attempts to offer a composite sketch of the citizen bricoleur, I show who qualifies as a citizen bricoleur, where the citizen bricoleur is likely to be found, what projects he or she undertakes, and why the citizen bricoleur is so crucial to the making and maintenance of counterpublics. Most important, I illuminate why the citizen bricoleur is so important to any understanding of contemporary and future rhetorics on our horizon and, hence, to any informed teaching of writing.

* * *

The title of my introduction is taken from the opening line of William Butler Yeats's iconic poem "The Second Coming." As most readers know, the entirety of that famous first line is "Turning and turning in the widening gyre," and it is to that closing phrase, "the widening gyre," that I now turn to elaborate the closing phrase to my own first line, so to speak.

Earlier I used the metaphor of an intersection to describe how composition is a discipline that has made, and continues to make, several turns, and that it executes these turns in a mostly organized way. The intersection metaphor is evocative of many laudable qualities, not the least of which are orderliness, social cooperation, turn taking, courtesy, respect for laws, and the conventions of movement. What's more, the turns made at these figurative crossroads are decidedly angular matters, typically hard left or hard right, as fitting, perhaps, the right-angle imaginary of traffic engineering.

But Yeats's image of a widening gyre evokes a different kind of turning, a turning that describes a spiral or vortex, a whirling outward, circular and expansive in its motions. It is the majestic image of a galaxy in deep space or, less gloriously, the swirling funnel in your bathtub drain. This gyre has its own symmetries, its own inexorable movements, its own order. And it is sometimes two motions at once, circling as it expands. *Pace* Yeats, if its center should indeed hold, it will continue to balance these two motions for ages, or for moments.

I think of counterpublics this way—circling the larger public sphere to which they are bound while at the same time expanding in number and influence, coming into and fading from view, disappearing and being born. As they turn and turn in the widening gyre, they seek always to be more public than they are because they cannot help but to do so. As Nancy Fraser reminds us, "the proliferation of . . . counterpublics means a widening of discursive contestation, and that is a good thing." To be a member of a public or counterpublic, in other words, is to be aware of oneself "as part of a potentially wider public" (Fraser 1990, 67). To be a member of any public is in fact to want more publicity, more publicness, more of what one already has.

If this is true of publics and counterpublics, might it not be true of our *inquiries into* publics and counterpublics as well? Should not our scholarship about publics seek to cultivate and increase its own horizons, its own broadening expanse, its own widening gyre? I believe so, and it is my hope that one way to widen the gyre of our public turn is to direct more sustained attention to counterpublics and what they mean for the study of rhetoric and writing.

This is one contribution to that end.

NOTES

1. The terms *paradigms* and *disciplinary matrices* come to us from Thomas Kuhn's (1996) *The Structure of Scientific Revolutions*. In the second and third editions of this work—and most likely in response to a good deal of criticism—Kuhn revised his original formulation of "paradigm" and offered a substitute term he referred to as a "disciplinary matrix." Kuhn's work was enormously influential while the emerging discipline of composition studies was consolidating in the 1970s and 1980s. Janet Emig, for example, in "Inquiry Paradigms and Writing," extended Kuhn's idea and introduced us to yet another term to describe how scholarly work in our field proceeds: the *governing gaze*, which she elaborates in this article. See Emig (1982, 65–69).

2. Busy intersection indeed. At the time of this writing, two additional turns have been announced. Drawing especially on the work of Bruno Latour, Paul Lynch (2012) notes that an "apocalyptic turn" has informed much of our recent composition scholarship, if not always explicitly, then certainly by sensibility. In addition, Jenn Fishman (2012) has guest edited a recent special issue of *CCC Online* devoted to "The Turn to Performance" in composition studies.

3. I do not wish to rehearse the fascinating debates about what we ought to call ourselves except to say that throughout this work, I will, at various junctures, use most all of the available terms. I regard our many self-descriptors—composition, composition studies, writing studies, rhetoric and composition, etc.—as a valuable resource, lexical *topoi* that may help me illuminate specific points in the rhetorical way I intend.

4. Patricia Bizzell and Bruce Herzberg point out that this contrast may be somewhat overstated, noting that while in Quintilian's time "it could be fatal to express views inimical to the Emperor . . . good forensic oratory and epideictic oratory were still needed" (Bizzell and Herzberg 2001, 359). Moreover, precisely dating the period of the Second Sophistic is likely impossible, judging by the fact that many scholarly sources differ widely on this question. While all sources rightly attribute the term to Philostratus's (230 CE) *Lives of the Sophists*, the years used to demarcate this period vary a great deal, ranging anywhere from 50 CE to 400 CE. Most observers, however, mark its origins to about the time of the reign of Nero, 54 CE–68 CE, and its prominence is generally considered to have occurred during the second and third centuries CE.

5. Critiques of American public life were, of course, available long before the last quarter of the twentieth century. Most notable among them are Walter Lippmann's (1925) *The Phantom Public* and John Dewey's (1954 [1927]) *The Public and Its Problems*, both of which are considered important, though the latter is generally interpreted as a rather pointed answer to the former. But on the matter of "the public," Lippmann's rather antipopulist work has proven itself to be more enduring, if for no other reason than that its memorable locutions have inspired the titular frames for both Bruce Robbins's (1993) recent collection *The Phantom Public Sphere*, as well as Edward S. Herman and Noam Chomsky's (2002 [1988]) collaborative work *Manufacturing Consent: The*

Political Economy of the Mass Media. Two more works deserve note here. The acknowledged "father of public relations," Edward Bernays (2004 [1928]), is often lauded for
Propaganda, his compelling how-to manual for shaping public consent in a modern
democracy. And Hannah Arendt's (1958) *The Human Condition* explores the private-
public binary in the context of Ancient Greece; Arendt sees the modern polis in
inexorable decline. The works mentioned here articulate much the same lament. As
Robbins notes, "The list of writings that announce the decline, degradation, crisis, or
extinction of the public is long and steadily expanding. Publicness, we are told again
and again and again, is a quality we once had but have now lost, and that we must
somehow retrieve" (Robbins 1993, viii).

6. For other evidence that a public turn was well underway, see also Mortensen (1998),
Trimbur (1989), George (2010), Comstock (2001), Isaacs and Jackson (2001),
Goodburn (2001), Cushman (1999), among others, not to mention the ample literatures on service-learning and community literacies that were establishing themselves
during this time as well. My purpose is not to offer an exhaustive account of composition scholarship focused on publics and public sphere theory. Rather, by acknowl-
edging a number of select works, I want to confirm what others had noticed too—
namely, that a discernible shift occurred in our literature in the 1990s, a shift that
marked a new line of inquiry into the significance of *publicness* for our discipline. I
do this not only to lend support to Mathieu's claim that we have made a public turn
but to illustrate (by virtue of my selections) that our turn is wide-ranging, one that
subsumes a multiplicity of emphases—whether the critical analysis of public texts,
service-learning pedagogies, activist learning that moves us outside our classroom
walls, or the notion that compositionists might themselves need to perform the role
of "public intellectuals"—and, at the same time, broadens our understanding of
what that might mean. In other words, our public turn is not a seamless, narrow one;
it encompasses a variety of concerns—pedagogical, institutional, disciplinary, and
cultural. For a more comprehensive survey of this early public-oriented scholarship,
see Weisser and Mathieu.

7. For Donnelli, the term *micropublic* is suggested by Weisser's use of the term *microcosm*
to describe how service-learning pedagogies enable our classrooms to have a "point
of contact" with the "real world" and yet still remain sites devoted to writing instruction (Donnelli 2008, 31). From Eberly, she borrows the term *protopublic* to describe
the many genres of public writing that we ask our students to read and, more important, the public genres we ask them to write. And from Nancy Fraser, Donnelli recontextualizes the term *counterpublics* to describe our application of critical pedagogy
to writing instruction. In this pedagogy, students are challenged to understand how
"diverse and often competing interests are negotiated to construct public spheres,
with a focus on studying the histories and material practices of publics" (47).

8. See, for example, Linda Flower's (2008) excellent discussion of counterpublics
in *Community Literacy* and, in a similar vein, Elenore Long's work emerging out
of the same project. See also Susan Jarratt's (2009) "Classics and Counterpublics
in Nineteenth-Century Historically Black Colleges"; Christian Weisser's (2008)
"Subaltern Counterpublics and the Discourse of Protest"; and Paul Butler's
(2008) "Style and the Public Intellectual"; as well as my response essay to Butler,
"Composition Studies as Liminal Counterpublic" (Farmer 2008), an essay that is an
earlier version of chapter 4 of this book. Three recent works also incorporate discussions of counterpublics: Shane Borrowman and Theresa Enos's (2009) *Renewing
Rhetoric's Relation to Composition*, David Wallace's (2011) *Compelled to Write*, and a
recent collection by John M. Ackerman and David J. Coogan (2010), *The Public
Work of Rhetoric*, in which counterpublics receive some treatment in several chapters,
though not especially sustained attention.

9. My phrasing is both borrowed and purposeful. I intend to echo Nancy Fraser's (1990) locution from her important article "Rethinking the Public Sphere: A Contribution to the Critique of Actually Existing Democracy."

10. Each of the scholars mentioned here is anthologized in Calhoun's (1992) seminal collection.

11. It is somewhat remarkable that given the wide influence of both works, especially *Structural Transformation*, neither work was translated into English until several years after its original publication in German. The English translations of *Structural Transformation* and *Public Sphere and Experience* appeared in 1989 and 1993, respectively.

12. One possible exception to this claim is that in the appendix to their volume, Negt and Kluge briefly discuss "the public sphere of children" (Negt and Kluge 1993, 283). Such a sphere could readily be interpreted as a counterpublic because it represents opposition to "adults' interests" in the bourgeois public sphere with which it must contend (284). Related to such a sphere, in chapter 1, I offer a highly condensed history of self-publication in America and note Paula Petrik's (1992) work on the toy printing presses known among adolescents in the mid- to late nineteenth century. Although Negt and Kluge do not say how a children's public sphere might be able to self-organize, it would seem that access to the mechanisms of publicity, such as what Petrik describes, would be a basic requirement.

13. I reprise here a claim made by Daniel C. Brouwer (2005), but I feel compelled to point out that Henry Giroux and Peter McLaren (1987a) mention counterpublics in a chapter published two years earlier. Giroux and McLaren argue for seeing teacher education as a counterpublic, but they seemingly do not rely strictly on Habermasian-inspired scholarship to make this claim. I discuss their article at length in chapter 3 of this volume.

14. Sandra Gustafson (2008) has challenged Warner on his exclusive interest in *texts*, if by that term we mean to refer to print publications only. She notes that Warner gives short shrift to the crucial role played by oratory in the making of counterpublics and implicitly suggests that, in doing so, he has overlooked the rhetorical importance of embodied voices, embodied performances, and the historical role oratory played in the construction of the kind of publics he extols. From her point of view, Warner's interest in rhetoric, then, would necessarily be an abridged one, at least to the extent that it did not take into account oratory and the spoken word.

15. It is both tempting and, I would argue, mistaken to see Warner's emphasis on style, as well as "poetic world making," to be emblematic of some larger shift away from rhetoric (i.e., "rational-critical debate") toward literary or aesthetic texts. As noted, perhaps the best critique of Warner's limited understanding of rhetoric comes from Gustafson (see previous note). That said, it seems that Warner is clearly interested in the implications of his argument for rhetorical study. In 2002 Warner contributed to a symposium of articles in the *Quarterly Journal of Speech*, each of which responded to a short version of his "Publics and Counterpublics" chapter that later appeared in his book by the same title. Those who participated in this forum sought to understand the specific implications of his work for rhetorical studies.

16. I will continue to refine what I mean by cultural publics in the first section of this book. But perhaps one preliminary way to understand what I am after is simply to reverse the title words of a major journal in public scholarship. The journal I refer to is *Public Culture*, and implicit in its ordering of terms is the notion that a public exists, and that this public may be interpreted as a culture in its own right. Even though *public* modifies *culture* in this phrase, the two terms are clearly meant to be considered as a piece, a uniform singularity—notwithstanding the fact that *culture* is the privileged term in the pair. And yet to echo a question once posed by Ann Berthoff (i.e., "How does it change the meaning if I put it this way?" [Berthoff 1981, 72]), I ask readers to

consider instead the possibility of *cultural publics*. By rendering the latter term plural, I hope to draw attention away from uniformity toward multiplicity, and by reversing the terms, I hope to suggest that *some* publics (though certainly not all) have distinct cultural qualities, and that by functioning as both publics and cultures, they occupy a special category, one that bears a special relevance to counterpublic inquiry.

PART ONE

Cultural Publics

1

ZINES AND THOSE WHO MAKE THEM
Introducing the Citizen Bricoleur

> La perruque *is the worker's own work disguised as work*
> *for his employer. It differs from pilfering in that nothing*
> *of material value is stolen. It differs from absenteeism in*
> *that the worker is officially on the job.* La perruque *may*
> *be writing a . . . love letter on "company time" or . . . "bor-*
> *rowing" a lathe to make a piece of furniture for [the] living*
> *room . . . [T]he worker who indulges in* la perruque *actu-*
> *ally diverts time (not goods, since he uses only scraps) from*
> *the factory for work that is free, creative, and precisely not*
> *directed toward profit.*
> —Michel de Certeau, *The Practice of Everyday Life*

In an amusing illustration of how acts of resistance get mustered into serving that which they resist, Walker Percy tells of how sightseers at the Grand Canyon must exercise considerable savvy if they wish to reclaim a sovereign view of the canyon from those who intend that it be seen in the officially approved ways. Percy offers a number of tactics by which ordinary tourists can seize or "recover" the canyon for themselves. One of the most obvious is simply choosing to get off the beaten track—in other words, refusing the organized, planned tours in favor of venturing forth through the canyon on one's own. Problems arise, however, when a park official notices that maybe a few too many tourists are electing to get off the beaten track, thereby calling into question the very necessity (and profitability) of organized tours in the first place. When this happens, only one solution recommends itself: tourists are advised to "*consult ranger for information on getting off the beaten track.*" Perhaps for a slightly higher fee, tourists can now buy tickets for the official *Off the Beaten Track Tour* and thereby maneuver around the standard tours designed for those who, sadly, cannot afford a more authentic view of the Grand Canyon (Percy 2008, 483).

Percy's essay is a complex, somewhat desultory examination of the difficulty in exercising some measure of autonomy—or, to use his term, *sovereignty*—over one's experiences. While Percy would not put it in these terms, he shows how the marshaling forces of power can so easily deputize resistant others on behalf of the complete hegemony such power seeks to enforce. In making this point, Percy raises the unsettling question of whether resistance is even possible. Is there any way to get beyond the reach of appropriating power (what Percy calls the "symbolic complex") (Percy 2008, 482)? Are there any loopholes or escape routes through which one might pass in order to establish a site of resistance outside of that power? Is it, in other words, even possible to get off the beaten track? If we were to draw reasonable inferences from this and his other examples, Percy's answer to these questions would be a qualified yes—qualified because, for Percy, resistance occurs not in the forum, the streets, or the public square but rather in the ad hoc, ingenuous, and quotidian strategies that individuals deploy in everyday contexts. For Percy, acts of resistance would likely seem to be rather innocuous and happenstance affairs, designed primarily to allow individuals to live lives that are genuinely their own.

Might not the same be said of the office or factory employee who "borrows" workplace time and resources for private purposes? Are these not acts of resistance as well? Certainly, in his illustration of *la perruque*, Michel de Certeau wishes us to believe as much. The ethically questionable practices described in the above epigraph are legitimized by the fact that "nothing of material value is stolen" and that tools are merely borrowed, not taken. Most significant of all are the virtuous ends that the activity of la perruque serves, ends that are "free, creative, and precisely not directed toward profit" (de Certeau 1984, 25). Even though it is easy to imagine other, less noble purposes that such borrowings might serve, de Certeau is not as much interested in a formal, ethical analysis of this situation as he is in identifying everyday, tactical forms of resistance. In his illustration, de Certeau wishes to draw our attention to the ordinary resourcefulness, the very *unheroic* cunning of those who "make do" with, or make the best of, the situations in which they find themselves.

On the surface, then, Percy's tourists and de Certeau's workers would seem to share at least this much in common: a repertoire of imaginative, calculated tactics for resisting the various perceived oppressions that accompany the experience of lived life. But, unfortunately, it seems that they also share a profoundly limited vision of resistance. Judging by the illustrations mentioned here, we could only conclude that everyday resistances must be solitary, unseen, and mostly inconsequential events—here and there acts of isolated subterfuge that seemingly do not require *anyone else* for their enactment. After all, it would be hard to conceive of Percy's sightseers as participants in a "resistant tourists collective" or de Certeau's workers as members of Perruque Workers International, Marseille Local 17. What is needed, in other words, is a way to pay tribute to ordinary acts of resistance and yet not relegate those acts to innocuous, privatized domains of irrelevance. Is it even possible, then, to understand everyday resistances as having a distinctly *public* significance, and if so, how is that public character revealed?

De Certeau provides us with one answer by asking us to consider *la perruque* not as disconnected, solitary events but rather as an ensemble of practices already writ large in the culture, as something that far surpasses the confines of the workplace. When *la perruque* is discovered outside the office or factory, according to de Certeau, it becomes what is more familiarly known as *bricolage*, the artful "making do" of the "handyman" who, using only those materials and tools readily available to him, constructs new objects out of worn ones, who imagines new uses for what has been cast aside, discarded (de Certeau 1984, 29). Of course, it is possible to consider bricolage in its most restricted, literal sense, as simply the cobbling together of new things out of old materials, but de Certeau sees bricolage as having much larger significances than that.

In the pages to follow, I will examine the role of bricolage in the making of publics, counterpublics, and alternative publics. Drawing on three major commentators on bricolage—Claude Lévi-Strauss, Dick Hebdige, and Michel de Certeau—I will first review how these three thinkers, alert to its wider implications, have used this concept. Following their lead, I will show how to apply bricolage to the task of public making through a discussion of zine culture—particularly anarchist zines—which, for my purposes, exemplify how resistance can be, at once, both everyday and public, as long as we understand publics in certain ways. I argue for a way of seeing publics as not merely formations that sometimes intersect with already established cultures but instead as formations that can be said to be cultures in their own right. Put differently, I want to posit the importance of *cultural publics* to the work of composition, an idea I wish to introduce in this chapter and elaborate in the next.

THE RAG AND BONE SHOP OF CULTURAL PRODUCTION

Several years ago, I came to appreciate the larger significances of punk and the cultural meanings that punk, rasta, hipster, reggae, and

glitter subcultures conveyed. Like many, I came to this larger awareness through a reading of that compact, incisive, and remarkable work,
Subculture: The Meaning of Style, by Dick Hebdige. Writing in 1979,
Hebdige provides a retrospective account of postwar, British working-
class youth and their embrace of identities affiliated with a variety of
musical subcultures—subcultures not only in conflict with the dominant culture but also, and frequently, with each other. And because
these conflicts, whether internal or external, could shift or transform
suddenly—that is, because alliances and oppositions emerged and
receded with some volatility—the meaning of subculture could never
be said to be stable. Definitions of subcultural styles were always in dispute and, according to Hebdige, "style [was] the area where . . . oppos-
ing definitions clash[ed] with dramatic force" (Hebdige 1979, 3). Style,
from this perspective, signified a Refusal with a capital *R*, and the ges-
tures that embodied this refusal had a public meaning, a subversive
value that could be, and was intended to be, read by others.

Punk and other subcultures, Hebdige points out, *refuse* to be part
of a willingly dominated majority, *refuse* to grant consent (tacit or otherwise) to be normalized within a system of pervasive control. Not surprisingly, therefore, subcultural styles are seen to go "against nature,"
interrupting the "myth of consensus" and challenging the principles
of unity and cohesion upon which that myth depends (Hebdige 1979,
18). Subcultural style, then, is an insult, an affront, a sneer, an outrage,
an ironic smile, a slur, a provocation. It is a T-shirt that reads "Fuck Off
and Die." But it is also a task to be accomplished: subcultural style does
not merely happen on its own—though, to be sure, there are spontaneous elements to it. Rather, subcultures must be made—constructed
out of cultural materials or, more accurately and from a punk perspective, cultural debris. For this reason, in his elaboration of subcultural
style, Hebdige refers approvingly to a term first used by anthropologist
Claude Lévi-Strauss—*bricolage*—to describe how a subcultural style such
as punk finds expression (103).

In *The Savage Mind*, Lévi-Strauss observes that there is no accurate
English equivalent for the term *bricolage*. Noting that in its older senses
bricolage referred to human movement, especially motions accompanying sports and pastimes—ball and billiards, "hunting, shooting, riding,"
and the like—Lévi-Strauss tells us that in our times, bricolage refers
to a kind of radically flexible handiwork, an eclectic method by which
the practitioner of bricolage, the *bricoleur*, employs all the available
tools and materials "at hand" to accomplish some purpose, typically in

innovative, unpredictable, and cunning ways. Yes, the bricoleur is truly someone who, to quote Lévi-Strauss, "undertakes odd jobs and is a Jack of all trades, a kind of professional do-it-[yourself-er]" (Lévi-Strauss 1962, 16–17n). But she is much more than just a resourceful fixer of things. And to understand why these Jacks and Jills of all trades interest Lévi-Strauss, I want to revisit his argument briefly.

Lévi-Strauss desires to rescue what others refer to as "primitive magic" from its thoroughly discredited status in the wake of Enlightenment reason. He does not endorse the usual opposition between magic and science, the common opinion that sees them as incommensurable world-views. Nor does he see magic as an evolutionary stage, a harbinger of a yet fully realized science. "Magical thought," he tells us, "is not to be regarded as a beginning, a rudiment, a sketch, a part of a whole . . ." Rather, magic constitutes a viable system in its own right, and for this reason, it invites comparisons to "that other system which constitutes science," so that we may see them as "two parallel modes of acquiring knowledge." Indeed, Lévi-Strauss devotes much of his argument to the task of illuminating how magic and science "require the same sort of mental operations and [how] they differ not so much in kind as in the different types of phenomena to which they are applied" (Lévi-Strauss 1962, 13). He concludes that it would be more accurate to say that we are actually examining two kinds of science, with primitive magic now renamed by Lévi-Strauss as "prior science" (15–16). To glimpse how these two "sciences" differ, Lévi-Strauss asks us to compare the situation of our mythical handyman bricoleur (underscore *mythical*) and his counterpart, the trained engineer.

Lévi-Strauss observes that the bricoleur "is adept at performing a large number of diverse tasks," but those tasks, given their number and variety, as well as their ad hoc and unplanned nature, are not necessarily to be called "projects"—at least not in the way that an engineer might refer to her work. In other words, the bricoleur "does not subordinate each of [his or her tasks] to the availability of raw materials and tools conceived and procured for the purpose of the project." His materials and tools are finite and heterogeneous, and "they bear no [necessary] relation to the current project, or indeed to any particular project" (Lévi-Strauss 1962, 17). They are, rather, the accumulations—the remains—of earlier constructions and destructions, and they thus represent always and only potential uses that are not yet foreseen: "Elements are collected or retained on the principle that 'they may come in handy.'" Unlike the engineer, the bricoleur does not possess nor want the specialized tools required of every particular project. Instead, she wants tools that are specialized enough *not* to require "the equipment and knowledge of all trades and professions," but not so specialized that each tool is limited to "one definite and determinate use" (18). This is all very interesting, especially when each of us recalls how we once jerry-rigged a temporary fix to that broken showerhead or improvised a gate lock out of an old bike chain and a rusty C-clamp.

While Lévi-Strauss acknowledges the importance of bricolage at the purely mechanical level, his larger purpose is to show how mythologies, as well as things, are made, sustained, and transformed by "the new arrangement of [existing] elements" and the "continual reconstruction of the same forms" even, or perhaps especially, when those same forms are in disrepair, relegated to the junk heap—when, in other words, those forms don't work anymore (Lévi-Strauss 1962, 21). The mythmaker bricoleur, at this point, improvises new structures out of old ones, and in doing so, improvises useful analogies between the natural and the social realms that can, in the words of one observer, "satisfactorily explain the world and make it able to be lived in" (Hawkes 1977, 51).

Now it should be apparent that both Hebdige and Lévi-Strauss understand bricolage primarily in terms of culture and myth, respectively, even though Hebdige seems more intent to align bricolage with critique, to show how it may be used to expose and resist the hegemonic "myth of consensus" that I mentioned earlier. Or, to put things differently, one might argue that Hebdige regards bricolage as myth*breaking* rather than myth*making*. Yet that distinction would still be too simplistic and too misleading, I think, for Hebdige, too, sees in subcultural style the promise of alternative ways of being that point to the need for social arrangements not based upon the domination of one group by another. In any case, both Hebdige and Lévi-Strauss see in bricolage a practice that is simultaneously resistant and constructive.[1]

Similarly, another way to understand bricolage is to observe how it overcomes the usual dichotomy between consumption and production. Bricolage, according to de Certeau, is able to surmount this opposition by rendering consumption itself into an alternative kind of production, a special and clever form of "making" that, as a consequence of its furtive deployment, goes mostly unnoticed. In fact, de Certeau suggests that the best way to observe this appropriative form of making is not through its own products but its "*ways of using* the products imposed by a dominant social order" (de Certeau 1984, xiii). He explains:

The "making" in question is a production, a *poiēsis*—but a hidden one, because it is scattered over areas defined and occupied by systems of "production" (television, urban development, commerce, etc.), and because the steadily increasing expansion of these systems no longer leaves "consumers" any *place* in which they can indicate what they *make* or *do* with the products of these systems. To a rationalized, expansionist, and at the same time centralized, clamorous, and spectacular production corresponds *another* production called "consumption." The latter is devious, it is dispersed, but it insinuates itself everywhere, silently and almost invisibly, because it does not manifest itself through its own products. (xii–xiii)

Because "people have to make do with what they have" and because "what they have" is largely determined for them, individuals and groups resort to various tactics through which they might enact a productive agency while, at the same time, consuming the imposed, ready-made products of a dominant social order (de Certeau 1984, 18). According to de Certeau, they do this through any number of ruses, tricks, moves, insinuations, ploys, tropes, poachings, and mutations—any of which might be creatively exercised when the right opportunity presents itself.

It is not difficult to see how what de Certeau describes here is emblematic of the arts of bricolage, and thus we should not be surprised at de Certeau's frequent and favorable allusions to bricolage even though he typically is more inclined to speak of "uses" and "tactics" to describe these arts.[2] And while de Certeau acknowledges his debt to Lévi-Strauss and the mythmaking potential of bricolage, he clearly sees bricolage as having neither the unity nor the coherence that Lévi-Strauss posits in his description of "mythological universes." Rather, in de Certeau's broader understanding, bricolage represents " 'another kind of 'mythology' dispersed in time, a sequence of temporal fragments not joined together but disseminated through repetitions and different modes of enjoyment, in memories and successive knowledges" (de Certeau 1984, 174–75). If, in fact, bricolage is implicated in mythmaking at all, it is a very different kind of myth than the one that informs Lévi-Strauss's conception—a piecemeal, forever incomplete mythology of seemingly discrete, unrelated temporal acts.

But is this not an extremely limited understanding of bricolage, one that precludes our exploring the larger meanings of its importance? If what de Certeau says is true—namely, that what he intends to elaborate is a "*science of singularity* . . . a science of the relationship that links everyday pursuits to particular circumstances," (de Certeau 1984, ix), then are we not severely hamstrung in our efforts to entertain the possibility

that bricolage might mean something more than its random and particular instantiations? Even de Certeau seems uneasy with this conclusion, for elsewhere he suggests that we do indeed need a larger frame by
which to understand bricolage. Thus, in commenting upon the repertoire of tactics available to the bricoleur, de Certeau observes that "a politics of such ploys should be developed." While he does not offer such a
politics, he does provide the contours for what this project would likely
entail. De Certeau thus maintains that "such a politics should . . . inquire
into the public ('democratic') image of the microscopic, multiform, and
innumerable connections between *manipulating* and *enjoying*, the fleeting and massive reality of a social activity at play with the order that contains it" (xxiv).

Taking my lead from de Certeau's suggestion, and drawing upon the
earlier work of Hebdige and Lévi-Strauss, I wish to propose a different
approach to bricolage. I offer that we might find something of value in
linking our received understandings of bricolage conceived in terms of
myths, subcultures, and everyday practices to publics, counterpublics,
and alternative publics, and rather more generally toward what I call
cultural publics. If we should make this move, the bricoleur would then
become a figure we might properly entitle the "citizen-handyman" or
citizen bricoleur, an intellectual activist of the unsung sort, thoroughly
committed to, and implicated in, the task of understanding how publics
are made, unmade, remade, and made better, often from little more
than the discarded scraps of earlier attempts—constructions that, for
whatever reason, are no longer legitimate or serviceable. Of necessity, it
seems to me, the citizen handyman and handywoman must, therefore,
take up residence at the crossroads of publics and cultures—counterpublics and subcultures—and from this border location, try to understand the relationships between these terms, making use of such inquiries for the purpose of enacting a more just and democratic society. But
do we, at present, have available to us an elaboration of this notion of
the citizen bricoleur, as I have suggested here? Do we have any illustrations of where publics and cultures intersect and where both might be
regarded as products made from imaginative and appropriative consumption, that is to say, from the arts of another kind of bricoleur, the
citizen handyman?

A BRIEF PREHISTORY OF ANARCHIST ZINES

Arrayed before me I have about a dozen publications with titles like
Dropping Out; Slingshot; Fighting for Our Lives; Stolen Sharpie Revolution;

Infiltration; *Loitering is Good*; *Off the Map (The Vagrancy Manifestos)*; *No Gods, No Masters Degrees*; *Nights of Rage*; and others. Within these assorted pages, readers will find travel stories, rants on a variety of topics, alternative history lessons, cartoons, letters, music reviews, political essays, interviews, survival strategies, and lots of advice on how to dumpster dive, organize pranks, loiter, squat churches, drop out, make paper, start a distro (distribution source), and scam free photocopies. The publications I refer to, of course, are *zines*, those homemade, amateurish pamphlets and newsletters circulated among readers whose primary bond is the experience of shared alienation, and who, as members of a loose but collective identity, reject the trappings of consumerist capitalism and its accompanying vision of a putative "good life." One thoughtful interpreter on zines, Stephen Duncombe, defines them as "noncommercial, nonprofessional, small-circulation magazines that their creators produce, publish, and distribute by themselves" (Duncombe 1997, 10–11). This definition, while formally useful, is, as Duncombe knows better than most, profoundly incomplete, for zines are much more than just amateur self-publications. In fact, Duncombe (and other informed observers) have attempted to elaborate what precisely characterizes the world of zines. In the following paragraphs, I will review those qualities that make zine publishing distinct—and ultimately, I argue, illustrative of bricolage writ large.

Zines, it would seem, possess something of an eternally contemporaneous quality, largely devoted to promoting and understanding the current "scene" and its music, events, politics, and shifting concerns. Of course, zines have a history too—though, to be sure, it is one that has gone largely unwritten. It is true, for example, that there exist longstanding American traditions of self-publishing, a lineage that extends back to eighteenth-century pamphlets (Duncombe 1997, 32–33) and, later, women's conduct books of the early nineteenth century (Downing 2000, 153–54). But in addition to conduct books, the first decades of the nineteenth century also saw the emergence of "amateur papers," sometimes called "juvenile newspapers," originally and often published by children but increasingly popular among adults as well, especially in the years leading up to and immediately following the Civil War. As a testament to the vitality and popularity of amateur papers, the National Amateur Press Association was fully constituted in 1876 (Petrik 1992), giving rise to satellite amateur press associations (APAs) such as the Ladies Amateur Press Association and a Negro APA as well. While the publications distributed by these organizations could hardly be called "zines," at least in our present understanding of that term, they did anticipate the contemporary zine in a number of important respects. In some instances, for example, they were produced "using toy presses and printing equipment scavenged from the professional press" (Duncombe 1997, 54)—or more exactly, "their youthful editors scavenged used type, cast off composing sticks, and put their mothers' abandoned cheese presses back into service" (Petrik 1992, 127). And as with many of today's zines, "they printed pretty much anything their publishers felt like expressing." Associative networks of readers and like-minded authors and editors often distributed these publications, which, especially in their late nineteenth-century forms, are sometimes regarded as the immediate forerunners to the earliest science fiction *fanzines* that emerged in the late 1920s and early 1930s (Duncombe 1997, 54–55).

According to Duncombe, "zines as a distinct medium" were born with the appearance (and subsequent popularity) of science fiction fanzines from the 1930s onward (Duncombe 1997, 11). They offered a venue for enthusiasts of a nascent, marginalized genre—science fiction—to circulate within their communities new fiction, announcements, reviews, opinion, and so forth. The remarkably enduring publication *Amazing Stories* first appeared in the late 1920s, and *The Comet*, arguably the first science fiction fanzine, was published in 1930. In decades to follow, science fiction fanzines became increasingly popular, but so did fanzines devoted to other genres and subcultures. Avant-garde movements, for example, developed publications very much akin to fanzines, as did enthusiasts of various literary genres such as poetry and detective fiction, and significantly, of musical genres as well. Jazz fanzines, rhythm and blues fanzines, and rock 'n' roll fanzines all thrived in the 1960s and 1970s and were typically obscured by what might be called the mainstream underground presses of the day—that is, such famous newspapers and magazines as *The Village Voice*, *Rat*, *Oz*, and even *Rolling Stone*. Unlike these publications, specialized fanzines evolved and flourished somewhere beneath even the so-called underground publications of their times (Rau 1994; Atton 2002, 56).

Out of this milieu came *the* watershed moment in the emergence of the modern zine—namely, the arrival of punk music of the early 1970s.[3] It is difficult to overstate the importance of punk music to an understanding of contemporary zines. According to the anonymous editor of *Hippycore*, "zines *are* punk," a proclamation that could be read, at least in part, as an answer to the question "What happened to punk music?" (quoted in Atton 2002, 57). A good case can be (and has been) made that while other musical styles have overshadowed punk music, punk, as a distinct cultural expression, lives on in the form of the present-day zine. If this is so, what exactly is being sustained? What aspects of punk culture are affirmed and reasserted in zine publications?

As noted earlier, punk music (and the identity it spawned) was, according to Hebdige, centrally devoted to "the destruction of existing codes and the formulation of new ones" (Hebdige 1979, 112), although, it should be noted, the latter purpose usually gets overlooked by the attention given to the former. In any event, and to reprise Hebdige, punk is negation, resistance, opposition—a refusal to stand in line for the ready-made existence offered by straight society. In its strategic opposition to the hand-me-down norms of mainstream culture, punk's obvious first line of attack was its music. Characteristically rough and roughhewn, loud, fast, anarchic in impulse and relentlessly confrontational in style, punk music gave expression to those who felt that the culture at large offered nothing of value other than something to turn away from. Punk music, I think it safe to say, would eschew the very notion of an anthem, but if one recommended itself, a likely candidate might be *The Ramones*' (1978) "I'm Against It." Here listeners find not merely the wholesale rejection of all things mainstream but the seeming rejection of all things *period*:

> I don't like Jesus freaks; I don't like circus geeks
> I don't like summer and spring; I don't like anything
> I don't like sex and drugs; I don't like water bugs
> I don't care about poverty. All I care about is me
> And I'm against . . .

In retrospect, lyrics such as these help us understand the predictable, dismissive criticisms of punk as nihilistic—as standing for, or affirming, essentially nothing. The singer of these words tells us that he doesn't like certain cultural identities (Jesus freaks), certain occupations (circus geeks), certain seasons (summer and spring), certain creatures (water bugs), and, surprisingly, certain recreational pleasures (sex and drugs). And what's more, he doesn't really care about poverty. In fact, he doesn't care about or much "like anything"—not people, not nature, not even the sorts of diversions he might be presumed to like. As he tells us, "All I care about is me." Such a credo will most likely (and correctly, I think) be heard in the way it is intended: as effrontery of the first order. But is it anything more than that?

To take punk seriously, to understand its larger cultural importance, lyrics like these must be read not merely for what they say but rather for what they do. What's being crafted here is not simply lyrical expression but a particular identity, and thus the ensuing basis for an affiliation recognizable to others who share this identity: a community. What, then, are the shared qualities of punk identity?

To state the obvious, punk places a high premium on personal freedom, originality in expression, honesty, authenticity, and what might be called a radical individualism. As noted above, punk also embraces an unshakable contrarianism, forever defining itself against straight society, without which one has to wonder if punk has an identity at all. As Duncombe observes,

> For a self-consciously rebellious subculture, such identity formation makes a certain sense, but it also contains a serious contradiction. A negative identity only has meaning if you remain tied to what you are negating. Reveling in the fact that you are a loser only makes sense if there is a society that rewards winners you despise. (Duncombe 1997, 48)

Such a criticism, of course, can be directed to most oppositional movements and cultures, not just punk. But being in a dependent relationship to that which you revile cannot help but invite a measure of self-loathing and, for that reason, make punk identity a rather precarious but highly charged matter. The question of what counts as true punk— authentic punk—provokes a great deal of heated discourse, which, in the end, has not resulted in a settled definition or consensus. On this matter, Duncombe reports, "punks have been slugging it out" for nearly three decades, "setting up and tearing down the rules of being punk" (Duncombe 1997, 67). Such a pastime, needless to say, will likely be a self-refuting endeavor if one is antagonistic to any and all normative prescriptions—in a word, *rules*—to begin with.

Further complicating punk identity is the anarchistic ethos that it adopts for itself, an ethos that, unwittingly perhaps, raises the question of whether a punk community is even possible. How does one square a radical individualism with the concerted, affiliative spirit that communities both presuppose and require? How is solidarity to be wrought out of disparate individuals whose shared characteristic appears to be, as the Ramones tell us, a complete negation of everything except the individual? "What sort of community do you have," Duncombe asks, "if everybody has to have his or her own idea of that community? Answer: an unstable one" (Duncombe 1997, 68). For Duncombe, one revealing sign of this instability can be found in the frequent and nostalgic invocation of a Golden Age of Punk, a magical time when such tensions did not predominate and punk life was always, indisputably *better*. Duncombe thinks it likely that such an invocation functions as a salve for the painful contradictions that inhere in what a punk ethos tries to advance.

Despite the many challenges that accompany the making of a distinct punk identity, as well as the many challenges involved in forging a punk community, it would be a mistake to suggest that neither exist. Many still identify as punk, and the majority of these regard themselves as belonging to something resembling a loose-knit community, even if that community is a vexed and tenuous one. Again, the key to understanding both identity and community is to see these as aspects of a larger, more encompassing formation—namely, culture (or any of its several glossed variants—subculture, microculture, alternative culture, etc.). And while punk itself was overwhelmingly identified with its distinct musical expressions, it was never solely about music. In characteristic punk fashion, Johnny Rotten told an interviewer, "We want to be amateurs . . . We're into chaos, not music." And the putative first punk fanzine, *Sniffin' Glue*, according to Hebdige, published three fingering diagrams for guitar and told its readers, "Here's one chord, here's two more, now form your own band" (Hebdige 1979, 109, 112). Punk was (and is) much more than its music. Punk was also more than its fashions, its attitudes, its outrages, its scenes, its adornments, its ethos, and even its self-understanding.

In light of its cultural influence, then, it seems odd how little impact punk had on the emergent field of composition studies. Geoffrey Sirc offers the most insightful and detailed account of composition's apparent indifference to punk culture. Sirc reminds us that before the arrival of punk's heyday in the mid- to late 1970s, composition instructors (at least some of them) had freely and enthusiastically borrowed music from the prior decade, often discovering lively and innovative ways to incorporate '60s music into their writing pedagogies. By 1975, however, that earlier enthusiasm had all but disappeared, replaced with an ethos that saw its mission as "righting writing," a disciplinary quest for objectivity, expertise, and strategies to manage what Sirc refers to as the "ordering of texts and selves and worlds" (Sirc 1977, 11). Needless to say, punk represented a direct negation of those values. Punk could not be made to fit comfortably (or, as I think Sirc demonstrates, retrofitted comfortably) within the official story of composition studies as it went about the business of legitimizing its disciplinary status. And thus an important cultural moment was not noticed at all, and with it went an unrealized perspective, however aberrant and fleeting, on writing and writing pedagogy. But what would a punk-inspired pedagogy entail? What could that possibly mean?

For Sirc, any punk pedagogy worthy of its name would have allowed "students to write against the inhibitory," and would have been founded on the principle that "anything could be negated," a principle that directs its hopes and aspirations not, as commonly thought, toward annihilation but rather toward transformation. Thus, while comp had discovered the authorizing enchantments of process, punk, according to Sirc, was far more interested in *passages*, of the unknown destinations where writing might be headed, those places it might be *en route to*. It is in this sense that Sirc observes, "we never taught writing as a way of hating writing" (Sirc 1977, 22). And it's a good bet that most teachers of writing consider the very thought of doing so repellent. But for punks, hating writing essentially meant hating something that had already been named by others, owned by others, packaged and delivered by others. Hating writing was a necessary passage to reclaiming writing for one's own purposes, of taking it back, of having the freedom to write writing in one's own way. And while many writing teachers enact practices that affirm our widely held belief that students own their own texts (or ought to), punks challenge this commonplace in a more fundamental way, pointing out that whatever writing may be, it is presently something that belongs to other people—teachers, published writers, official media, certifying institutions, etc.

Perhaps it is both understandable and fortuitous that Sirc makes no attempt to specify what constitutes a punk writing pedagogy. To make explicit such a pedagogy would be an inescapably reductive, if not self-refuting, exercise in futility. After all, how is it possible to institutionalize negation? What's more, the durability of any punk pedagogy would rightly, I think, be suspect. As Sirc reminds us, punk is evanescent, volatile, located in temporary spaces and occurring in the fleeting transcendence of carnival time. It would be the exceptionally rare artist or writer or teacher or academic discipline that would be able "to marshal enough inner resistance to continuously exploit negation for more than a matter of years" (Sirc 1977, 24). However, if we are required to accept punk negation whole cloth, it its very absoluteness, then it has nothing to offer writing teachers whatsoever. In fact, such a requirement excludes the possibility that we can make tactical, improvisational, appropriative use of punk to suit our classroom purposes—in other words, that teachers, too, can enact their own sort of improvisational handiwork; and that as bricoleurs of a pedagogical stripe, we can therefore make something useful out of the remnants, fragments, and shards of punk. Yet if any basis for a kinship between writing instruction and punk culture exists, it is the centrality of texts to the mission of both.

Indeed, how punk came to know itself, how punk smithied its own realization, no matter how fragile that realization may have been, was a function of its texts, especially the many zines that emerged alongside the music that were crucial to the making of punk culture. But if zines were essential to the formation of punk, their significance endured beyond punk's moment. The rightful heir to punk culture is zine culture, especially anarchist zine culture, since within these publications, punk not only found its continued expression but discovered an articulated politics as well.

"NO GODS, NO MASTERS"

Roughly emergent with (though derived from) punk music was the rise of the punk zine. As I have noted, a number of mainstream and underground publications had already aligned with specific musical genres by the time punk music first appeared. But the acknowledgment that punk was much more than its music shows that the affiliation between punk zines and punk music was an allied, familial, mutually constitutive relationship—one fundamentally different than the relationship between, say, *Rolling Stone*, the rock magazine, and The Rolling Stones, the band. Early punk zines, such as the previously noted *Sniffin' Glue*, along with *Punk*, *Who Put the Bomp*, *Search and Destroy*, *Sideburns*, *Ripped and Torn*, and many others, did not merely report on their favorite bands or list concert schedules or offer musical gossip or review the latest singles—though, to be sure, they did all these things. Punk zines did much more. Up from the streets, from clubs, from hovels, from suburban basements and downtown squats, from hallways and alleyways, punk zines fashioned a cultural identity and a community founded on a shared anarchist point of view toward all things mainstream, official, respectable. As volatile and frayed such a group point of view may have been, it was largely made and sustained through the proliferation of zines—so much so that, paradoxically, the anarchism that enlivened the social space that formed this identity kept the relationship between punk zines and punk music vital (that is, what held the scene together). And if punk zines follow from punk music, as most acknowledge, then it might be useful to briefly examine punk music's anarchistic spirit.

From its very inception, punk embraced and championed an anarchistic politics—though it might be more correct to say that punk anarchism was a politics of sensibility rather than one of enunciated principles and propositions. The peculiar brand of punk anarchism, as incoherent as it may have seemed to many (including punks), might best be understood as an anarchism that extended to the very notion of a coherent politics itself, especially if, from a punk point of view, what counts as legitimate political discourse had already been decided by others and was, therefore, offered *prêt-à-porter*, yet another ready-made commodity. In punk anarchism, even conventional ideas of what counted as proper discourse were negated, so the politics that emerged was, by mainstream standards, flailing, inarticulate, contradictory, and unnamable. But it was also unmistakably real.

Two qualifications, however, might be useful. While it may be true that the ubiquitous descriptor "anarcho-punk" speaks to the degree to which punk and anarchist sensibilities are inextricably coupled, the same phrase also implies the existence of *other* forms of punk (not to mention *other* forms of anarchism). It is important, then, to recognize that anarchism and punk are not identical. In his recent study of how young people construct narratives of entrance into the anarcho-punk scene in Philadelphia, Ed Avery-Natale makes this point by noting,

> In recent years, the anarchist movement in the West has garnered many new "converts," as it were, from the punk rock culture. This is not to imply that all anarchists are punks nor that all punks are anarchists, but only to point out that for at least some there is an integral connection between the two, and that it is not uncommon to find in the contemporary anarchist movement a number of punks and post-punks who have dedicated their lives to anarchism. (Avery-Natale 2009, 2)

Taken in its entirety, punk music, as such, cannot be said to have universally embraced an anarchist politics. And while no one is likely to be surprised at the anarchism that informs and indeed characterizes so much of punk music, neither should anyone be surprised at the sheer number of punk subgenres with a more complicated, if not absent, relationship to an anarchist ethic. While the anarchism of early punk undoubtedly influenced the available varieties of punk—glam punk, crust punk, horror punk, deathrock, Celtic punk, funk punk, art punk, folk punk, to name just a few—all have located themselves in various distances to it. And how could this be otherwise? No punk anarchism worthy of its name would demand allegiance to a uniform point of view—an agenda, a dogma, a program. Yet, even in offering this qualification, I would argue that the sheer variety of punk subgenres is, in some measure, a testament to the very anarchism that is distinctive of punk.

A second qualification emerges from the degree of commitment that various bands expressed toward an anarchist ethos. The refusal of many early bands to sign with major record labels is routinely invoked as an originary emblem of the anarchist, independent spirit of punk groups. But in actuality, as Brian Cogan points out, this may have been "largely because [at first] few alternatives existed." As punk became increasingly visible and popular, many bands signed with independent labels "because they were dropped by or unable to secure a contract from a major label," not because they rejected the commercialism of the latter. And yet the circled letter *A* (for anarchy), as a sign of any particular band's loyalty to anarchism, was frequently inscribed on album covers, posters, handbills, publicity photos, ads, and zines, even when major record labels owned and run by transnational corporations distributed such promotional materials.[1] Moreover, according to Cogan, it remains unclear the degree to which "major bands such as The Clash and Sex Pistols actually believed in the political statements they were making" (Cogan 2008, 78).

Cogan reports on two bands in particular, Crass and Throbbing Gristle, as groups that genuinely lived the anarchism they promoted. In addition to their music, for example, Crass distributed manifestos, organized pranks, initiated graffiti campaigns and street protests, lived communally, and (presciently) addressed feminist issues—an act that was as off-putting to some punk fans as it was to the usual mainstream critics of punk music (Cogan 2008, 81–84). Throbbing Gristle, in contrast, embodied an anarchist aesthetic through testing the boundaries of performance art. Moreover, by controlling the entire distribution and production of their own work, they experimented with not only music but pure sound and unrestrained performance (no matter how harsh or profane), such that, according to Cogan, they "single-handedly created a new genre, industrial noise." Perhaps this genre was not as important as what it signified: an honest attempt to break free of "traditional ideas about pain, disgust, and the body" in order to clear the way for a new conception of personal and aesthetic freedom (Cogan 2008, 86). Crass and Throbbing Gristle undoubtedly viewed punk anarchism differently, but they approached anarchism with an integrity and depth of understanding that, according to Cogan, was frequently missing in many of the more famous bands.

My purpose here is not to revisit the endless (and futile) debates about authenticity in punk music nor even to pursue the question concerning which bands most faithfully embodied the anarchist orientation for which early punk is known. Rather, I wish to acknowledge that not all punk was anarcho-punk, and that the commitment among punks to an anarchist politics was wavering and variable as well as not universally shared. And it follows that the same can be said of punk zines. While most were decidedly anarchist in orientation, not all were interested in promoting an anarchist perspective. That qualification duly noted, it nonetheless remains impossible to deny the intimate kinship between punk zines and the anarchism they espoused. Indeed, as the heyday of punk music waned, many zines that came into existence *because* of punk often found themselves, as it were, carrying the banner of punk anarchism into the years (and decades) after 1977. Again, this is not to say that punk died out completely. In my view, strong evidence exists that it has not. But it is suggestive that the anarchism expressed originally, and most compellingly, in early punk music soon found its continued, and more dominant, expression in anarchist zines. One result of this change was that punk anarchism, however imprecisely defined, eventually became more important than the music from which it derived—that is, more and more removed from its punk origins. It, therefore, became possible to speak of anarchist zine culture as something related to, but distinct from, punk culture per se.

Certainly, the proliferation of anarchist zines and their increasing numbers of readers confirms their emerging prominence. *Punk*, *Sniffin' Glue*, and *Ripped and Torn* were among the first zines but many soon followed. *Factsheet Five*, one of the oldest of zines (or perhaps, in a sense, metazine), served as a useful guide to the world of zines and was replete with music reviews as well as notices and information about the abundance of other zines in circulation at any given time. Similarly, *Maximumrocknroll* started as a punk magazine but eventually began to formulate a politics of "constructive" engagement (Duncombe 1997, 47), thereby becoming increasingly political in its editorial orientation. Neither of these zines jettisoned their affiliation with punk, and they each accommodated changes that marked a revivified interest in punk anarchism. What's important here, though, is that the source of this new interest derived not so much from punk music but rather from the zine culture that had consolidated itself in the wake of punk's zenith moment. One zine writer explains why, in part, anarchist zines surpassed the origins of their collective birth:

Although I think it's possible to be politicized by music, zines give you a sense of the community and the communication and how global it all is. Zines are the place where all the radical thoughts that get condensed down into song lyrix [*sic*] and paragraph explanations get explained in further detail. And they show that punk is so much more than music, or "more than noise," if you will. (Lewis n.d.)

More than anything else, zines were responsible for the emergence and maintenance of an anarchist underground culture in the 1980s and '90s, and indeed, a culture that persists into our present moment. And when we look into how zines made such a culture, we notice a reflexivity that is strikingly consistent with the anarchist ethos that zines trumpeted.

MAKING STUFF AND DOING THINGS[5]

What are the characteristic features, then, of anarchist zines and, more importantly, the brand of anarchism they endorse? Certainly, any-one's checklist would have to include a commitment to what Duncombe calls a vernacular radicalism of unfettered personal freedom and expression; a celebration of all things amateurish, crude, makeshift, and ephemeral—that is to say, of all things insistently *unprofessional*; the restoration of a collage aesthetic (or perhaps more exactly, a cut-and-paste aesthetic, especially in textual presentation); a militant anti-copyright ethos and an oppositional stance toward all the established protocols of life under consumer capitalism as well as the establishment of loose, sometimes evanescent, associative networks (distros) through which zine publications get circulated, bought and sold, loaned, borrowed, given, taken, and so on (Duncombe 1997, 8).

But the most interesting feature—and one common to both punk and anarchist zine cultures—can be found in its passionate allegiance to an ethics of "do it yourself," or DIY. Anarchist zines routinely publish DIY articles that, on first glance, seem mostly devoted to the routine chores of everyday making do, or even the random pleasures of everyday diversions. A brief sampling of article titles from various anarchist zines would include the following: "How to Make a Candle"; "I Made My Own Soymilk"; "11 Places to Dumpster Dive"; "How to Get Rid of Fruit Flies"; "How I Fixed My Harmonica"; "Build Your Own House"; "Homemade Root Beer"; and "How To Make Your Own Paintbrushes." Were it not for the fact that DIY has been so utterly co-opted by commercial culture, we would most likely be struck by how banal these concerns are, and we would rightly be left to wonder what on earth these trivialities have to do with anarchist politics—or any politics for that matter.

But more is being made here than candles and root beer. Kyle Bravo explains that the DIY found in the pages of anarchist zines is qualitatively different from the conventional understanding of that term as it is promulgated in popular media:

> As with most subcultural phenomena co-opted by the mainstream, the term "DIY" has been exploited to the point of mediocrity by advertising agencies and corporate profiteers. Walk into any corporate chain hardware store and you'll be bombarded by a DIY ethos that has become a hollow, menacing mockery of the fervent DIY ethos that fuels much of the subcultural underground . . . We speak of a spirit of action that will never be found in, on, or near Lowes, Home Depot, Wal-Mart, Home and Garden, or DIY Network. (Bravo 2008, 1)

I think it safe to say that for Bravo, as for most zine anarchists, any conception of do it yourself that requires you to purchase additional merchandise at your local, franchised supply store is not DIY at all.

In anarchist circles, the point is to break free of the almost ceremonial dependencies so integral to the ideology of consumer capitalism. This is why, despite the seeming triviality of learning how to make your own soymilk and paintbrushes and candles, such everyday acts, as they are represented in anarchist zines, are understood to be acts of political resistance. Make no mistake: this is not your grandparents' familiar wild-eyed, Molotov cocktail–throwing, street-fighting image of an anarchist. That iconography no longer obtains. Rather, this is an anarchism borne of historical conditions that require ownership of the means of production *and* consumption, even if wresting these operations from others requires that one begin with little more than the ordinary, the humdrum, and the casually dismissed. For anarchist zine writers, however, these isolated acts of homespun resistance are charged with much larger significances. For each act of do it yourself, no matter how outwardly trivial, embodies a critique of consumer capitalism and, at the same time, a making of *something else* in addition to those candles and root beer.

Here again the influence of punk can be instructive. Just as punk music once insisted that the distance between performers and audience must be overcome, anarchist zines insist that the distance between consumers and producers of texts must likewise be surmounted. The DIY spirit in punk culture was aimed at the primary task of reclaiming, of taking back music from corporate ownership and control. Anarchist zine culture redirected that same spirit to the primary task of reclaiming from the officially endorsed venues of communication not music but authorship and publication. Such is why the DIY ethos figures so prominently in the zines themselves. On some basic level, implied or expressed, zinesters rightly apprehend—and challenge—the venerable notion that who owns the power to disseminate ideas owns the ideas themselves. It should hardly come as a surprise, then, that the quintessential paper zine consists of stapled pages of typed, photocopied text arranged in jumbled fonts and columns, usually accompanied by handwritten drawings and notes, typically with a copyright notice that implores readers to steal whatever they find useful, and frequently traded at concerts or through distros. In sum, everything about these publications stands in material and symbolic opposition to corporate media's ownership of ideas, information, and informational resources. This is why one common rhetorical purpose of most zine authors is to encourage readers to "do it yourself," to ask readers to become authors and publishers of their own work. It is telling to consider, if only in passing, how truly exceptional such a request is, owing to the obvious fact that ordinary readers have been so thoroughly conditioned to see publication as a distinction and an achievement rather than a right or an ethical obligation.

Clearly, then, this making of things, this fashioning of items (including zines themselves) to meet the basic needs of everyday (underground) life is intended to represent something more than the sort of helpful hints one might find in the home improvement aisle. No, what's being crafted here is political critique, a stance toward the culture at large—an oppositional stance, no doubt, but a stance that also attempts to imagine an alternate way of being in the world. Duncombe has observed, "Doing it yourself is at once a critique of the dominant mode of passive consumer culture and something far more important: the active creation of an alternative culture. DIY is not just complaining about what is, but actually doing something different" (Duncombe 1997, 124).

In the fragile solidarity that is crafted through this opposition, through the inchoate, topsy-turvy, scattered efforts of zine anarchists, a subculture is made—or to be more exact, and in Gramscian terms, a counter-hegemonic culture is made, one that arises out of unflinching dissent and offers a counternormative vision of another way to live. But how, precisely, does such a culture get made? What do zines do, exactly, to create a common identity, as well as a sense of community, among those who share this view of the world?

As a consolidating ethos, do it yourself is not a difficult concept to understand when applied to the things and the tasks of lived life. Nor is it a hard concept to grasp when applied to the making of zines themselves. But to think of culture as a do-it-yourself project seems, at best, diminishing and, at worst, somewhat audacious. After all, in most conventional understandings, culture is something that is overwhelmingly *received*, whether by culture we mean the rarefied products of Arnoldian genius (of capital *C* culture) or the more familiar idea of culture as an ensemble of traditions, habits, ways, history, and shared perspectives that encompasses what we call identity. In either version, the notion that culture can be made out of whole cloth (or for zinesters, the remnants of someone else's whole cloth) is, for some, heretical. But zines presume to do exactly that—namely, to make a (sub)culture from remnant materials, so to speak, and do so with whatever tools of textual circulation are readily available. While an undeniably utopian emphasis exists in the culture-making enterprise of zines, there is also the very sober, practical realization that this is a world that must be built, and built from the street up. According to Duncombe,

> Zine writers have created vast networks of independent communication in order to share the ideas and thoughts they feel are not being shared elsewhere. These networks make up a distinct material infrastructure of communication that uses the technology of mass commercial society—computers, copy machines, mail system—but steers the use of these technologies toward nonprofit, communitarian ends. The network lends itself to an ideal of social organization. One of the reasons that anarchism is a philosophy so prevalent in the underground world is that it is a close abstraction of the network: voluntary, nonhierarchical, with omnidirectional communication flows, and each citizen a creator/consumer. (Duncombe 1997, 188)

The closing phrase of this passage—"each citizen a creator/consumer"—might well serve as a basic principle of zine anarchism as well as a revealing measure of its utopian aspirations. Notice, for example, that "each citizen" implies universal democratic participation while not, in any way, disavowing the very notion of citizenship, as some might expect certain anarchist theories to do (rather, it is much more likely that anarchists see the term *citizen* in need of critical redefinition).[6] Notice, too, that the typographical yoking of "creator/consumer" suggests a desired conflation of these roles so that "each citizen" performs not one or the other activities but both at once. In other words, the present-day, corporate-enforced division between those who produce (create, make) and those who consume no longer holds sway in an anarchist vision of a just world. And finally, notice yet one more conflation, the one that joins the two emphases of this phrase—namely, the merging of organic democratic participation with organic economic and cultural production. Realizing that the passivity required by consumer capitalism is profoundly anti-democratic, zine anarchism tries to imagine an alternate way of being in the world (which is to say, a culture) that is, at once, both democratic and perpetually self-created, since in anarchist utopias, the old hierarchies obviously will not remain in force.

Idealistic? Quixotic? Utopian? Unrealistic? It would be hard to argue otherwise. But this is precisely why zines tend to stress lived, personal experience (however messy that may be) over immaculately reasoned arguments about propositions or the minutiae of anarchist theory (though neither of these are entirely absent from zines). Given the emphasis in zines on authenticity, on individuality, on a do-it-yourself ethos, anarchism must not merely be thought about, discussed, and championed—*it must be lived*. This suggests why, on the whole, anarchist zines reject the cold comforts of formal debate and dispassionate reason—not because they embrace irrationality (though some do) but because, for most zine writers, to argue about *matters that matter* as if they did not, as if nothing really important was at stake, is simply unconscionable. Better to live your beliefs, your culture, your politics, your identity rather than engage in disputes that require nothing from you and that change nothing in the world. For zine writers, knowing how to make your own toothpaste is not trivial. On the other hand, writing a rational, compelling argument about the "controversy *du jour*" just might be, especially if it is done, as is frequently the case, from a comfortable, privileged, and nonparticipatory distance.

So what kind of politics, then, can be gleaned from zine anarchism? This is a difficult question to answer. Once one assumes a principled opposition to all hierarchies—organizational, institutional, economic, ethical, and political—and once one endorses a do-it-yourself brand of anarchism that seems to valorize individual rather than collective action, what sort of politics remains?

Those observers who comment on zine politics generally offer that such a politics is, of necessity, a micropolitics, one that is simultaneously experiential and anticipatory—or to use their favored term, *prefigurative*, which, according to Duncombe, features a lived "politics by example," a politics that "bears witness to alternative ways of seeing, thinking, and doing" (Duncombe 1997, 198). Echoing this point, but focusing more specifically on DIY itself, Lucy Nicholas argues that anarchist culture, "through the prefiguration of preferable ways of being," is able to suggest those social norms that "[Judith] Butler identified as pre-requisites in any project for change" (Nicholas 2007, 18). And in his examination of radical media, Downing points out,

> For anarchism . . . it has normally been enough to create little islands of prefigurative politics with no empirical attention to how these might ever be expanded into the rest of society. Example has often been considered sufficient. What is needed is a recognition of the many areas of life that are political . . . together with the most painstaking, unremitting search as to how prefigurative politics can expand beyond its islands. (Downing 2000, 72)

Islands may not be the best metaphor to describe the laterally networked communities that presently embody the global anarchist movement.[7] But endorsing that metaphor for the moment, what's most interesting about this passage, then, is its call to leave shore, to set sail in order to find out how a prefigurative politics can be enacted in larger contexts where such a politics might have the opportunity to effect real change. Linked to this call is another—namely, to discover and recognize "the many areas of life that are political." Although Downing does not say as much, apparently this task also requires leaving the island, charting a course for the mainland so that these other "areas of life" that go unacknowledged as political can be correctly identified. But zine anarchists have no need to leave the island at all. These other areas of political life are already known, familiar, and, most important, lived.

At the beginning of this chapter, I noted that Michel de Certeau, realizing the limits of everyday tactics set in opposition to a dominant social order, urged that a politics of such ploys should be investigated. I noted that while de Certeau does not spell out precisely what this politics consists of, he does suggest that "such a politics should . . . inquire into the public ('democratic') image of the microscopic, multiform, and innumerable connections between *manipulating* and *enjoying*, the fleeting and massive reality of a social activity at play with the order that contains it" (de Certeau 1984, xxiv). De Certeau calls for nothing less than a politics of bricolage—a politics of those dispersed, imaginative, and clandestine acts of making do that, when taken together, are able to transform ordinary consumption into an alternate kind of production, a form that "insinuates itself everywhere, silently and almost invisibly, because it does not manifest itself through its own products," but rather though its "*ways of using* the products imposed by a dominant social order" (xii–xiii).

It is in this larger sense that I suggest that zine authors and publishers (almost always one and the same) are bricoleurs, handymen and handywomen fast about the business of making something new from the refuse and rummage of what de Certeau refers to as a "centralized, clamorous, and spectacular production" (de Certeau 1984, xiii). Do it yourself, as I have tried to show, represents, at its most obvious, the concrete, tangible expression of such efforts. But just as bricolage can be (if one so chooses) regarded only at the concrete level of the mechanical and the quotidian, de Certeau, along with Claude Lévi-Strauss and Dick Hebdige, has something larger in mind. For all three thinkers understand bricolage as potentially instrumental in the making of heretofore unrealized social formations.

Peering into the zinester's toolbox, then, we might well notice a pen knife or two, some rusty scissors, a few Sharpies, a utility knife, several cutouts from other zines, three glue sticks, an assortment of rub-on letters, and a ruler. Over in the corner, we might also notice an old Royal typewriter, ensconced by two cardboard boxes full of scraps of homemade or used paper, as well as "drawings and doodles . . . old 70s year books [*sic*], amusing vintage ads, children's books . . . old magazines (like national geographic [*sic*]) and old tabloids, flyers, stickers, travel pamphlets, photographs, photocopier art" and so on (Wrekk n.d., 7). With these tools and materials readily at hand (along with whatever else might be scavenged from friends, yard sales, and the local copy store), the zinester bricoleur crafts the latest installment of her homemade zine, and in so doing, crafts an identity, a politics, an ethic, a culture, and a way of being in the world.

What also gets crafted is a kind of public.

NOTES

1. A very different understanding of bricolage can be seen in recent attempts to refigure it as a qualitative research methodology. Joe Kincheloe has perhaps been most associated with this development, and he most extols the contributions of "research bricoleurs," those investigators who "understand the necessity of new forms of rigor in the research process" (Kincheloe 2001, 681). Kincheloe sees the value of methodological bricolage to reside in its application to what he calls "deep interdiciplinarity," an informed, flexible approach to inquiry as boundary work among the various

disciplines, as multiperspectival inquiry that occurs "in the liminal zones where disciplines collide" (686, 689). From such locations, the research bricoleur looks inside his methodological toolbox to find the instruments best suited for the inquiry at hand as well as those tools that cultivate a larger awareness about the relationship between disciplinary and interdisciplinary knowledge. See also Pinar (2001).

2. The central distinction in de Certeau's argument, and the one most frequently alluded to in our disciplinary literature, is the one between *strategies* and *tactics*. The former is described as a "calculus of force-relationships" imposed upon a place that serves as the basis for certain kinds of official (or to use de Certeau's term, *propre*) relations. Strategies, de Certeau observes, are perhaps best illustrated by "political, economic, and scientific" rationalities, and thus, it must necessarily follow, the various institutions that represent those rationalities. Tactics, on the other hand, are fleeting; they have no identifiable location as such, that is "no base where [they] can . . . secure independence in respect to circumstances." Rather, tactics "constantly manipulate events in order to turn them into 'opportunities.' The weak must continually turn to their own ends forces alien to them," de Certeau argues. Tactics, then are everyday forms of resistance, instances of "knowing how to get away with things," an awareness of how to use an imposed order to serve one's own purposes (de Certeau 1984, xix).

3. Exactly when punk music first appeared is a matter of considerable debate. While widespread agreement points to 1977 as a signal year in punk's musical history, owing largely to the sudden prominence of Johnny Rotten and the Sex Pistols, most observers consider the earlier work of The New York Dolls, The Velvet Underground, and Patti Smith, as well as Detroit's The Stooges and MC5, as clear musical forerunners to punk's zenith moment. Along these lines, a kind of fascinating parlor game often attends discussions of punk history wherein participants try to identify the original, archetypal punk figure. This pastime often leads to amusing possibilities. (For example, "Are you kidding me, Salvador Dali? No, man, John Locke was the first punk.") But missing in these diversions is punk as a distinct phenomenon rooted in cultural history. The most interesting (and informed) look at punk's intellectual and cultural antecedents remains, in my view, Greil Marcus's (1989) *Lipstick Traces*. Marcus carefully teases out punk's twentieth-century lineages, and while there is much speculation in his work, his ideas are neither capricious nor unfounded.

4. As a testament to how easily an anarchist ethos (in general) and zines (in particular) can be co-opted by corporate interests, Duncombe notes that in the early 1990s, Warner Records published its own zine, *Dirt*, "a zine bankrolled entirely by the corporate behemoth, Time-Warner Inc." Duncombe reports that save for its unusual sponsorship, *Dirt* "looked and read like any other zine." Urban Outfitters, according to Duncombe, also published its own zine, *Slant*, and Sirius satellite radio likewise produced a zine advertising its services (Duncombe 1997, 140–41).

5. The title of this section is taken from an anthology of DIY articles edited by Kyle Bravo and printed by Microcosm Publications of Bloomington, Indiana. The articles collected here were culled from various zines across the country and cover a range of topics and projects. Arguably, the most important publisher of underground anarchist writing, especially book-length works devoted to contemporary anarchism, remains CrimethInc. Free Press. See, for example, *Days of War, Nights of Love* (CrimethInc. Workers Collective 2001) or *Expect Resistance: A Field Manual* (CrimethInc. Workers Collective 2008).

6. An early reader of this chapter drew attention to the possible contradictions implicit in the idea of anarchist citizenship (an oxymoron for that reader) because the notion of citizenship seems to require, at the very least, some manner of state apparatus—the very thing that, according to common definition, anarchism is presumed to oppose. However, in our present moment, it is clear that we are now faced with a pressing need

to imagine new forms of citizenship—postnational or transnational—forms that are no longer indentured to traditions of Westphalian sovereignty for definitions of what a citizen is. As Nancy Fraser recently observed, "the equation of citizenship, nationality, and territorial residence is belied by such phenomena as migrations, diasporas, dual and triple citizenship arrangements, indigenous community membership, and patterns of multiple residences" (Fraser 2007, 16). Add to these developments our ever-expanding global technologies and economies and it soon becomes clear that we must now look upon citizenship as something that surpasses, and is perceptibly distinct from, the traditional nation-state. Thus, because citizenship is revealing itself to be a rather fluid concept, and one now in the process of critical revision, I do not think it especially far-fetched to posit an anarchist citizenship. And in fact, among some anarchists, a great deal of attention has been devoted to the question of anarchist citizenship. Indeed, scholars from anarchist (and other) perspectives are now asking us to imagine what seems to be a very counterintuitive idea: the notion of citizens without states. See, for example, Hoffman (2004); Bookchin (2000); Roseneil (2010); Blackstone (2005). For two additional (and important) challenges to received ideas about citizenship, see Rosaldo (1999) and Rodriguez (2001). It is in this larger sense that I refer to punk and zine anarchists as citizen bricoleurs, since the public acts they perform are directed toward an alternate vision of freedom—significantly, a vision that does not require a state apparatus for its realization. Along the same lines, when I describe the activities of citizen bricoleurs as *democratic*, I am referring to actual practices (or habits) executed on behalf of this same vision, and not to a theory of government per se. Indeed, this emphasis on "habits and practices" is one that Amy J. Wan endorses in her recent examination of how the term *citizenship* remains a useful, but nonetheless vexed, descriptor for writing teachers and scholars (Wan 2011, 46). Her overview is more comprehensive than what I provide here and offers further evidence that the concept of citizenship is presently undergoing critical reexamination from a number of intellectual perspectives.

7. Anarchists and anarchism have both received some attention in counterpublic scholarship. For a discussion of one historical counterpublic, see Kathy E. Ferguson's study of Emma Goldman and Alexander Berkman's agitational efforts at the "turn of the last century." According to Ferguson, "viewing anarchism as a counterpublic highlights the significance of its temporalities, social locations, and textual practices" (Ferguson 2010, 193). Much more recently, and a bit more tangentially as well, see Mark Porrovecchio's (2007) "Lost in the WTO Shuffle."

2

OTHER PUBLICS, OTHER CITIZENS, OTHER WRITING CLASSROOMS

Twenty-volume folios will never make a revolution; It's the little pocket pamphlets that are to be feared.
—Voltaire, in a letter to d'Alembert, 1766

Thus far, I have spoken of anarchist zines in terms of culture, and I doubt if any reader would be particularly startled by my frequent use of the phrase "anarchist zine culture" in the previous chapter or this one. In the wake of cultural studies (and its enormous influence in the contemporary academy), we are habituated to thinking of *culture* as a term that encompasses alternative communities, identities, and movements. More problematic, though, is the suggestion I offer here: namely, that the culture of zines (in general) and anarchist zines (in particular) is a public as well—to be sure, a particular kind of public but a public nonetheless. This idea chafes with a commonsense rendering of "the public" as a broad, inclusive social formation concerned with matters of policy that affect all citizens. That matter-of-fact understanding, however, has been found to be incomplete and misleading.

In the pages that follow, I will make the case that zine culture also functions as a public or, more precisely, a counterpublic. Neither wanting to relinquish the many valuable insights gained by understanding zines as a culture nor wanting to limit zines only to that understanding, I argue instead that zines ought to be regarded as exemplary *cultural publics*. I define a cultural public as any social formation, established primarily through texts, whose constructed identity functions, in some measure, to oppose and critique the accepted norms of the society in which it emerges.[1] In Heisenbergian fashion, cultural publics may be seen exclusively as cultures or as publics. The challenge is to see them as both and, ideally, to see them as *both at once.*

As mentioned, I have thus far directed most of my attention to zines as culture. I now turn to the task of understanding zines as publics. To this end, I trace the contours of modern public sphere theory, especially as it relates to my argument.

PUBLICS, COUNTERPUBLICS, AND ZINES

The familiar idea of what constitutes a public (or a public sphere) has been usefully—and brilliantly—critiqued by Jürgen Habermas (1991), who, in *The Structural Transformation of the Public Sphere*, details the historical emergence and subsequent decline of the "bourgeois public sphere." In the process of historicizing our understanding of the public sphere, Habermas demonstrates that the public sphere is identical neither to a governing state apparatus nor to existing market arrangements, even though it is inescapably implicated in both. Rather, a public sphere, in its perfected form, is a rational, discursive arena, a freely accessible space of unfettered, communicative interaction wherein participants debate and deliberate on matters of common concern. While it never attained its idealized form, the bourgeois public sphere, as Habermas describes it, still retains considerable normative value because it offers a model of rational discussion not available to actually existing democracies. In its requirement that differences in social status and privilege be "bracketed"—left at the door, so to speak—it tries to guarantee that rational-critical debate will not be constrained, managed, or distorted by private interests.

Since its original publication a half-century ago, Habermas's *Structural Transformation* has spawned a vigorous line of scholarship, work that has been simultaneously inspired by, and critical of, his notions of what a public sphere is and ought to be. Foremost among recent critics is Nancy Fraser, who forcefully challenges the assumed desirability of a universal, general public, freely accessible to all, even if that notion is meant only to serve as an ideal to which we ought to aspire. In her widely acknowledged critique of Habermas's normative model of the bourgeois public sphere, Fraser points out that "declaring a deliberative arena to be a space where extant status distinctions are bracketed and neutralized is not sufficient to make it so" (Fraser 1990, 60). Indeed, according to Fraser, in order for Habermas to construct an idealized bourgeois public sphere in the first place, he must disregard (or if one prefers an ironic perspective, *bracket*) the long existence of "other" competing publics that go unnoticed or unnamed as publics—publics originating out of cultural, gendered, and communal identities, for example (61). In advocating for their particular self-interests, such publics often find themselves antagonistic toward and disputatious with the public at large and, for that matter, each other.

Because these other publics are multiple, contentious, and largely marginalized, Fraser calls such publics *subaltern counterpublics*—"parallel discursive universes where members of subordinated social groups invent and circulate counterdiscourses to formulate oppositional interpretations of their identities, interests, and needs" (Fraser 1990, 67). Her prime example is the "feminist subaltern counterpublic, with its variegated array of journals, bookstores, publishing companies, film and video distribution networks, lecture series, research centers, academic programs, conferences, festivals, and local meeting places" (67). Moreover, subaltern counterpublics are positioned dialectically in their relationship to larger publics. According to Fraser, subaltern counterpublics thus have a "dual character":

> On the one hand, they function as spaces of withdrawal and regroupment. On the other hand, they also serve as bases and training grounds for agitational activities directed toward wider publics. It is precisely in the dialectic between these two functions that their emancipatory potential resides. This dialectic enables subaltern counterpublics partially to offset, although not wholly to eradicate, the unjust participatory privileges enjoyed by members of dominant social groups in stratified societies. (68)

Despite their tumultuous and often antagonistic relationship to broader publics, subaltern counterpublics (like all publics) nonetheless seek to expand their influence to publics existing outside of their own self-definitions. That is to say, subaltern counterpublics, because they are publics, do what publics do: they "aspire to disseminate [their] discourse to ever widening arenas" whereupon they can potentially effect changes in public opinion en route to effecting changes in public policy (Fraser 1990, 67). As an illustration, Fraser observes that, until quite recently, domestic violence against women was considered "a private matter between what was assumed to be a fairly small number of heterosexual couples." Through the "sustained discursive contestation" of a feminist subaltern counterpublic, such a longstanding (but neglected) form of violence changed into a public issue of common concern (71). Because of the agitational efforts of this counterpublic, domestic violence was *made* into a public issue.

Michael Warner seeks to revise Fraser's understanding of what constitutes a public (or counterpublic) by asking us to consider if there might be alternative rationalities (and, for that matter, irrationalities) that could be accommodated by public discourses. In a major departure from both Habermas and Fraser, Warner asks us to redefine counterpublics as something other than, or more than, "subalterns with a reform program" (Warner 2005, 119). To propose such alternatives is to depart from "the prevailing image [of publicness as] something like parliamentary forensics," and thereby, in turn, to recommend that "rational-critical debate" ought not to be the exclusive or preferred standard by which to proclaim something to be a public or counterpublic (115). Not all publics, Warner argues, subscribe to "the ideology of public discussion" (211), and in this respect, he mentions as examples ACT UP and OutRage!, queer publics that rejected traditional debate styles, believing these to be largely exercises in media management—a view that is, I would note, quite likely shared by anarchist zine publics as well.

Warner maintains that publics (and thus, by definition, counterpublics) are discursive spaces that are ceaselessly under construction—forever unfinished, so to speak—due to the stark and singular fact that they are "organized by nothing other than discourse itself" (Warner 2005, 67). Publics exist, Warner holds, "*by virtue of being addressed*" (67). Publics are thus made, sustained, and altered in the very act of textual address, and only through that act—a fact that leads him to concede what appears to be an inescapable paradox. If, as Warner contends, the mere act of addressing a public is, at the same time, the act of bringing that same public into existence, then for whom, precisely, is the original address intended? What are we to make of our addressee—presumably, the desired public of our imagination—if that public is "conjured into being in order to enable the very discourse that gives it existence"? (67). Rather than seek an easy answer to this paradox, Warner argues instead that this circularity must be appreciated, for it is "essential to the phenomenon" of those discursive spaces we call publics (67).

"To address a public," Warner observes, "is to be a certain kind of person, to inhabit a certain kind of social world, to have at one's disposal certain media and genres, to be motivated by a certain normative horizon, and to speak within a certain language ideology" (Warner 2005, 10). Certainly, it should be obvious, then, that address of this sort has an expressive function, but it might be more exact to say that it performs a *socially expressive* function. The person speaking, in other words, is in search of like-minded others who might also be disposed to inhabit the same discursive space. Public discourse, then, in its very saying, proclaims not merely, " 'Let a public exist,' but [also] 'let it have this character, speak this way, see the world in this way.' It then goes in confirmation that such a public exists." Or as Warner puts it, "Run it up the flagpole and see who salutes. Put on a show to see who shows up" (114). For Warner, publics are typically made this way—in a process of invocation, recognition, and reflexive circulation—a process where texts perform a "world making" function, a task altogether distinct from the summariz-able content of whatever those texts say.

One of the implications of this paradox is that publics must inevi-tably be composed of strangers. This is not to say that publics must be exclusively composed of strangers. No doubt, the public(s) we imagine ourselves belonging to are quite likely to include friends, colleagues, acquaintances, family members, or perhaps any combination of these. But publics must always include strangers too. This can be partially explained by their expansive orientation toward other publics, and thus to larger arenas of influence, which, as both Habermas and Fraser observe, is a distinctive quality of all publics. But for Warner, publics are constituted of strangers primarily because they are self-organized by texts, not by institutions or other "external frameworks" that estab-lish fixed criteria for membership (Warner 2005, 74–75). "Lacking any institutional being," Warner says, publics "commence with the moment of attention, must continually predicate renewed attention, and cease to exist when attention is so longer predicated" (88). Publics, then, are mercurial and, in a sense, virtual too. But ensuing from this curious phe-nomenon of "stranger sociability" is a reversal of our inherited view of the stranger as "marvelously exotic" or a "wandering outsider," a trou-bling, mysterious figure who embodies "a disturbing presence that must be resolved" (75). No, Warner argues, the stranger is no longer someone who must either be banished or received into the common fold because "publics orient us to strangers in a different way." Indeed, insofar as pub-lics are concerned, strangers are "treated as already belonging to our world . . . *They are a normal feature of the social*" (75; emphasis added). And such is why public discourse is "both personal and impersonal," why it is interpreted as, at once, "addressed to us and addressed to strangers" (76, 77). Public speech, in other words, "is not just heard; it is heard (or read) *as* heard not just by oneself but by others" (90). Thus, an aware-ness develops that strangers are "no longer merely people whom one does not know" (75). Rather, "strangerhood" constitutes an essential aspect of a distinctly public understanding of social relations.

Warner's ideas extend our understanding of publics and counter-publics and mark a significant departure from the received ideas of Habermas and Fraser. Most dramatically, Warner sees publics as hav-ing a poetic function, a qualifier that must be understood in its ancient and larger sense of *making*—or more precisely, as Warner says, "poetic world making." To draw our attention to such discursive qualities as "affect and expressivity," or to think seriously about public discourse in

light of its "speech genres, idioms, stylistic markers, address, temporality, *mise-en-scène*, citational field, interlocutory protocols, lexicon, and so
on" is to make a profound shift away from our notion of publics as sites
of "rational discussion writ large" (Warner 2005, 114–15). This conventional understanding of publics as social formations that exist purposefully "to deliberate and then decide" is one that aspires to define a public strictly by its arguments and ideas, its pure contents, which are then
assumed to be "propositionally summarizable" (115). Warner thinks this
to be a severely limited understanding of publics, one founded largely
on the mistaken belief that all publics position themselves in relation to
an imagined "general public" whose participation in state power is simply taken for granted. Publics thus see themselves as important because,
as part of *the* larger public, they bear at least the promise of being able
to change laws, policies, codes, decisions, procedures, etc.—those very
matters about which publics typically deliberate. Even Fraser's subaltern
counterpublics do not attempt to move beyond this ideological legacy,
since, as Warner suggests, they remain faithful to the primacy of rational-critical debate inherited from the Habermasian model. Like Fraser,
Warner regards counterpublics as primarily defined by their oppositional character, but unlike Fraser, Warner questions if such opposition
must be limited to the content of their discourses—namely, the matters
that get talked about or examined. Warner thinks that the oppositional
character of counterpublics, however, is much richer than received
models that limit it exclusively to debate and deliberation, much more
encompassing in its understanding of what discourse actually does and,
therefore, much more significant in its implications.

Much of what Warner says of publics extends to counterpublics, but
there are important differences as well. For example, whereas any public
must inevitably locate itself in relation to other publics and, especially,
"a general or wider public," counterpublics must locate themselves in
relation to publics that are not simply larger or broader but are experienced as *dominant.* The conflicts that ensue from this dominance arise
not only because counterpublics oppose dominant publics on this issue
or that controversy but because the discourse that makes up any counterpublic is itself greeted with hostility and is thus deemed unacceptable
by the dominant publics against which counterpublics define themselves. Warner mentions gay or queer counterpublics wherein a "circulatory space" is produced, a discursive space "freed from heteronormative
speech protocols" that dominant publics merely assume to be in force.
Within the space of a queer counterpublic, however, "the presumptive

heterosexuality that constitutes the closet for individuals is suspended" (Warner 2005, 120). What emerge are discursive protocols that are specific to a particular queer counterpublic.

As with any public, "stranger sociability" remains a characteristic feature of a queer counterpublic, and yet address to strangers is always fraught with risk. Counterpublics, queer or otherwise, still address "indefinite strangers," but those strangers are not thought to be "just anybody." A certain kind of stranger is thus imagined, an anonymous someone who might be (or more likely already is) responsive to "this kind of discourse." Thus, as Warner explains, "ordinary people are presumed not to want to be mistaken for the kind of person who would participate in this kind of talk or be present in this kind of scene" (Warner 2005, 120). Such persons would therefore exclude themselves from membership in this particular counterpublic. Those inclined to membership, though, would be responsive to the manner in which they are addressed by this counterpublic's discourse, and would thus, in turn, be willing to speak this way "to inhabit a certain kind of social world, to have at one's disposal certain media and genres, to be motivated by a certain normative horizon, and to speak within a certain language ideology" (10). This is not to say that counterpublic identities must be either established beforehand or "formed elsewhere." Rather, participation in counterpublic discourses itself "is one of the ways by which its members' identities are formed and transformed" (121). But the question then becomes: To what end? Once debate and deliberation are consigned to secondary status, once rational-critical dialogue is no longer the standard for what constitutes public discourse, then what exactly is the purpose of counterpublic discourses? Is it for identity recognition alone that counterpublics exist?

No, for Warner, counterpublics exist primarily for social *poesis,* for a kind of "world making" that occurs through the reflexive circulation of discourses. The worlds that are made through counterpublic texts (broadly understood) far surpass issues about which we ought to engage in rational-critical debate or, for that matter, the need to establish solidarity among members of a subaltern identity. Both of these functions, while obviously important, are not adequate to the real purpose of counterpublics, which, according to Warner, is to bring into existence "spaces of circulation in which it is hoped that the poesis of scene making will be transformative, nor replicative merely" (Warner 2005, 122). Among other things, this means that we have to imagine a different sense of what agency might mean when it comes to counterpublic discourses and the worlds they make:

A queer public might be one that throws shade, prances, disses, acts up, carries on, longs, fantasizes, throws fits, longs, mourns, "reads." To take such attributions of public agency seriously, however, we would need to inhabit a culture with a different language ideology, a different social imaginary. It is difficult to say what such a world would be like. (Warner 2005, 124)

What can be said, though, is that counterpublics desire such worlds, yearn for the kind of social imaginary that would accommodate more encompassing visions of publicness, however undefined these may presently be. For what motivates counterpublic discourses is "the hope of transforming not just policy but the space of public life itself" (Warner 2005, 124).

I have previously argued that the space within which anarchist zines circulate can rightly be said to demarcate a culture—to be sure, an alternative subculture, but a culture nonetheless. I also suggested earlier that anarchist zine culture might best be thought of as *culture called forth*, culture assembled through the makeshift arts of bricolage, especially bricolage as an expression of a widely endorsed do-it-yourself ethos that is reflexively evident in zines themselves. But in light of my examination of Fraser and Warner, can we not also say that anarchist zines constitute what both refer to as counterpublics? Is there any disputing the fact that the circulatory space of anarchist zines is a counterpublic too, and one made through the arts of bricolage?[2]

Consider, for example, what is for Warner the defining feature of a counterpublic—that publics are "organized by nothing other than discourse itself," that they exist "*by virtue of being addressed*" (Warner 2005, 67). Anarchist zine publics are brought into being, and subsequently maintained, through the act of address in an ongoing process, as I noted earlier, of invocation, recognition, and reflexive circulation. To reiterate Warner's image (and maybe paradoxically so, if one has a hard time imagining anarchists with flags), the anonymous zine author runs his anarchist banner up the flagpole to see who salutes, to discover if there might be likeminded others "out there," kindred strangers (of a certain sort) whom our zine author might never meet but who share a vision of the way things could be, who "inhabit a certain kind of social world," and who, it appears, are similarly "motivated by a certain normative horizon . . . to speak within a certain language ideology" (10). Our unknown zinester, then, having confirmed that, indeed, many such strangers exist, desires to expand this fragile "stranger sociability" to additional others who share his worldview. He thus proceeds to send his zine out to readers through distros; or he drops his zine off at concert venues and coffee shops; or maybe he leaves a few scattered copies on the downtown bus he rode that day. In pursuing such activities—that is, in writing, publishing, and circulating his zine—our nameless zinester is taken up with the assorted chores of what Warner calls poetic world making—though, to be sure, the activities that I just described here seem far more prosaic than poetic.

Warner, of course, uses *poetic* in an almost ironic way, to both counter the tendency to equate publics with an instrumental, exclusively rational politics as well as direct attention to the expressive, aesthetic role of language as something inseparable from what publics truly are. Warner's poetics, I think we can safely say, differs from the sort we usually associate with that term. It is, in fact, the kind of poetics that could easily mock, chide, and caricature poetry itself, especially poetry's status as originary art of arts, its haven in academic curricula and journals, its seeming remove from the lives of ordinary people.[3] From Warner's perspective, then, it is not hard to imagine a public founded upon a (counter)poetics that disputes received views of poetry, or more broadly, any form of imposed, hegemonic discourse. This, in fact, is why Warner offers a description of a queer public as a specific, resistant, discursive space, one that is fundamentally at odds with "heteronormative speech protocols" (Warner 2005, 120). As Warner shows, the poetics of queer publics are typically removed from anything that could be described as elevated, refined, or magisterial nor could such a poetics be properly construed as "timeless overheard self-communion" (82). Such is why that venerated term *poetics* could itself be the target of poetic world making discourses.[4]

Along these lines, anarchist zine publics, while not particularly concerned with poetry, are nonetheless avidly concerned with poetics, with the making of a world that is both intensely expressive and passionately committed to an aesthetic that reflects its DIY values. Like queer publics, anarchist zine publics establish an oppositional discursive space—a space not likely to appeal to any and all strangers but one that will appeal to some strangers who are responsive to its call and who can imagine themselves inhabiting that space, even if only for a while. And while it might seem that an anarchist zine public, precisely because of its anarchist politics, is oriented toward deliberation and rational-critical debate, I hope it remains clear from what I wrote earlier that the kind of anarchism promoted by anarchist zines far surpasses a discourse founded strictly upon propositions. In fact, readers will only sometimes find in anarchist zines, especially older zines, an elaborated articulation of beliefs, principles, arguments, and so on. Rather more likely, these will be simply assumed, as will the shared understanding that merely enunciating propositions about anarchism, paradoxically, diminishes the very anarchism that zine readers desire. For many zinesters, approaching anarchism this way, as something reducible to a position statement or a debate point risks severing anarchism from authentically lived life. And just as worrisome, it implies that the expressive, aesthetic qualities of anarchist zine texts ultimately do not matter, that the poetics of zine publications have nothing to do with the anarchist vision they embody.

In light of Michael Warner's insightful descriptions, then, it is clear that anarchist zines easily qualify as counterpublics. Warner himself does not refer to zine culture as a counterpublic, notwithstanding the fact that queer counterpublics certainly have generated more than their fair share of zines. Other scholars, however, have suggested that the worlds created by and through zines are counterpublics in their own right. As I elaborate below, the originator of *Grrrl Zine Network*, a resource for third-wave feminism, sees zine publishing as crucial to the formation of a transnational counterpublic wherein "people can experiment with ideas, articulate themselves, and describe experiences otherwise suppressed by mainstream society" (Zobl 2009, 10). Mimi Nguyen, former zinester and feminist scholar, likewise interprets grrrl zines to be a "culturally productive, politicized counterpublic" (Nguyen 2000; Zobl 2009, 1). And in composition studies, Michelle Comstock has likewise argued that grrrl zines resemble Fraser's conception of subaltern counterpublics in that they serve "two functions—private enclave and public training ground . . . for cultural and political activities directed toward wider publics" (Fraser 2001, 394). More recently, Daniel C. Brouwer (2010) has demonstrated how two HIV/AIDS zines, *Diseased Pariah News* and *Infected Faggot Perspectives*, invoke counterpublics through their thematization of corporeal expressivity and markers of difference.

But why does this matter? Why attach any special importance to whether or not zines, anarchist or otherwise, qualify as counterpublics? I believe there are three reasons why this move is important.

First, having established the importance of bricolage to the making of cultures—or more exactly, subcultures—I now wish to extend the value of bricolage to the poetic world making function of counterpublics as well. The descriptions offered by Fraser and Warner—especially Warner—leave little doubt that counterpublics get made through the assorted arts of bricolage, even though neither thinker uses that term.

Yet in light of the overwhelming emphasis that each assigns to textuality—for example, Warner's assertion that counterpublics are "organized by nothing other than discourse itself "—we are left to conclude that bricolage, when applied to the making of counterpublics, must refer to the innovative making of texts that, in turn, create the kinds of discursive spaces within which those texts circulate (Warner 2005, 67). And could anyone seriously dispute the fact that of the many texts that most closely resemble practices characteristic of bricolage, zines may very well be the quintessential example?

I remain surprised, then, that so little attention has been given to the role of bricolage in the making of counterpublics. And I remain likewise surprised that, with the exception of the few examples noted above, so little attention has been given to zines and the counterpublics they bring into being through their distinct modes of address. If it is true, as Warner maintains, that a public exists by virtue of being addressed, then such a public will surely be determined, at least in part, by the manner in which one addresses it. For this reason, and to echo Warner, we need to look closely at anarchist zines, not merely for what they say, but also for their assorted registers; their multiple voices; their design, layout, and presentational strategies; their grammars; their arenas of intertextual reference; their common locutions, terministic screens, and all the other discursive resources that might be found in their toolboxes. That anonymous author of your local anarchist zine is someone about the task of making a text as well as a counterpublic. In fact, it is difficult to imagine an actually existing counterpublic without its corresponding zine(s); and it is likewise hard to imagine an actually existing zine without a corresponding counterpublic that it simultaneously invokes and addresses.

Second, the fact that bricolage is common to the making of certain kinds of cultures *and* publics invites us to consider hybridized social formations—what I refer to as cultural publics—that are simultaneously both cultures and publics and that therefore merit a distinct status of their own.[5] With a few notable exceptions, scholarly inquiries directed toward an understanding of culture, or of a particular culture, remain largely severed from those inquiries directed toward to an understanding of publics. Scholars typically investigate one or the other but seldom examine social formations that can be regarded as both at once and that might be understood to possess features common to cultures as well as publics. Make no mistake, I do not wish, in any way, to disparage the separate traditions of intellectual inquiry that orient themselves to either cultures or publics. Rather, I wish only to suggest that some attention be devoted to those social formations that perform double duty—that function, in concert, as both cultures and publics. This idea, I believe, is implied by Fraser's notion of feminist subaltern counterpublics as well as Warner's examination of queer counterpublics—especially queer publics not exclusively devoted to issue advocacy. As I hope is obvious, it is also present in much of the foregoing discussion—namely, in my attempts to explicate anarchist zine culture and show how such a culture easily qualifies as a counterpublic too, particularly in the context of Warner's insightful elaboration of that term.

Now to posit the actuality of something that might be called a cultural public is to posit an expanded understanding of what we conventionally mean by both terms. A cultural public is one where *publicness* assumes a far greater emphasis than it ordinarily does in investigations into cultures and subcultures, where *publicness* becomes not only an interesting aspect or occasional focus but rather a constituent element of specific cultures. In reverse fashion, then, a cultural public also requires a willingness to see that certain publics cannot be understood without an awareness of how they embody the broad concerns of culture—identity, traditions, discourses, values, beliefs, customs, experiences, to name just a few—and yet, at the same time, insist upon the distinctly public significance of all such concerns. A cultural public, in short, is not merely a discursive space where dissenting opinions might be voiced but a space where dissenting ways of being in the world might be articulated as well. Such is why Warner concludes his analysis of counterpublics with the suggestion that what motivates counterpublic discourses is "the hope of transforming . . . the space of public life itself" (Warner 2005, 124). And if counterpublics are best positioned to take on the task of altering "the space of public life itself," of redefining our extant versions of publicness, then it follows that we must likewise redefine what makes a citizen as well. Which brings me to my third and final point.

We need to imagine a new kind of citizen—not only the one who dutifully votes, who takes pleasure in exercising civic pride, who advocates for various causes, who participates in local governance, who devotes time and money to a favored candidate, and so on. Of course, we need such citizens. Any meaningful democracy simply cannot thrive without its received forms of public engagement. But we need another kind of citizen too—the kind of citizen who believes democracy to be something more than law or policy; who understands that democracy remains forever a yet-to-be-completed project; who knows, far better than most, that while any given democracy must be changed from within, it must also be contested from without by those who exist on the margins, who have been excluded from all the usual forms of participation, and who, because of identity, language, style, or preferred ways of being in the world, desire nothing less than an alternative kind of publicness. These, too, are citizens, though they may not often wear the mantle of respectability usually associated with that vaunted honorific.

Such is why I think these citizens may be more correctly referred to as citizen bricoleurs, those improbable handymen and handywomen of alternative world making who, situated at the intersection of (certain) cultures and (certain) publics, are able to craft something new—a range of hybrid social formations assembled from resistant texts that, when considered together, comprise a "fleeting and massive reality of a social activity at play with the order that contains it" (de Certeau 1984, xxiv). Those who make such texts, and the worlds within which they circulate, perform democracy at street level, so to speak, perform democracy at the unmapped sites of its most quotidian expression. Thus, it follows from all I have written here, that those who make, write, draw, assemble, produce, copy, and distribute anarchist zines are exemplary citizen bricoleurs, intellectual activists of the unsung sort, thoroughly committed to and implicated in the task of understanding how democracy, in its largest sense, gets made, unmade, remade, and made better. I will return to the citizen bricoleur in my epilogue, but for now, I wish to pose the question of whether there might be a place for zines and bricoleurs in our classrooms.

As I mentioned in my introduction, composition studies has, for well over a decade now, explored the many ways that our teaching practices can be more directed toward and informed by the diverse publics within which we are situated, and to which we are always, in some unspecified measure, answerable. What we have not explored are the pedagogical implications of taking into account the kinds of cultural publics I have discussed here. To do so, however, I believe it first necessary to establish the ongoing relevance of zines, knowing that the question many readers may be disposed to ask still remains: Whatever happened to zines? If an answer can be provided, then, it is my hope that we teachers of writing might learn something from the zinesters among us, those citizen bricoleurs whom we have to this point mostly ignored but who very well may be sitting in our classrooms.

PUNKS, ANARCHISTS, GRRRLS: IN SEARCH OF A TRAJECTORY

Although my first chapter was not intended as such, I am fairly sure that many readers look upon the foregoing discussion to be a retrospective of sorts—an exercise in nostalgia—since the flourishing of zine publications, especially anarchist zines, clearly occurred from the 1980s to the early 1990s. But once again, another parallel emerges between punk and zine cultures, this time in the form of a question originally (and often) asked of punk. That question—"Whatever happened to punk?"—I now revise as, "Whatever happened to zines?"

For some, the answer to the first question is that punk died at an early age, sometime in the late 1970s, depending on what authority one consults. For others, as punk evolved, as we moved into what is sometimes called the "post-punk" era of the 1980s, it necessarily received much less public scrutiny, as punk's outrages came to be regarded, well, as far less outrageous. Then, in the wake of post-punk, this century saw the emergence of what has been referred to as "post-punk revival." The point here is that for latter-day punks, some measure of the authentic spirit of punk never really died even though it changed profoundly after 1977. Or to put this differently, true punks know that true punk lives.[6] It may be, however, that there are far fewer true punks than there once were—an assertion that, if true, could be the cause for either lament or celebration, depending on one's commitment to purity and authenticity.

But what, then, of zines? What happened to zines? I am not personally aware of any publications called "post-zines" nor have I heard mention of "zine revivals" (though there are any number of zine festivals and exhibitions) located on our present cultural landscape. What I am aware of, though, is an archival impulse to collect zines—to sort them, code them, preserve them, and catalog them—presumably for cultural historians, researchers, and assorted other scholars. This collecting impulse can be discovered not only in underground sites (alternative bookstores and the like) but also in public and academic research libraries, often in special collections devoted to ephemera. Janice Radway mentions important collections at the Cleveland, New York (State), and Salt Lake City Public Libraries. And among academic libraries, Bowling Green, Michigan, Michigan State, Smith, Duke, Barnard, DePaul, and others all have zine collections (Radway 2011, 144). This trend in archiving zine publications is a fairly recent development and probably has much to do with the legitimacy that zines gained, according to Radway, as a direct consequence of Duncombe's *Notes from Underground: Zines and the Politics of Alternative Culture,* cited frequently in my first two chapters (144).

This same legitimacy may, in part, explain the recent academic interest in zines as well. After years of institutional indifference, the fact that zines are finally capturing the attention of librarians and scholars surely would seem to lend force to arguments for their newfound cultural legitimacy. And yet this same attention, because it is overwhelmingly historical in orientation, might also be interpreted as the death knell for zines. In other words, to study zines as artifacts or relics or evidentiary "documents" might itself be construed as proof of their demise. And, in fact, some have made this argument. Many zinesters themselves have already pronounced zines dead, notwithstanding good evidence to the contrary (seemingly forgetful of Johnny Rotten's similarly hasty judgment about punk in 1978).[7] What I hope is obvious, though, is that there is no compelling reason to subscribe to the view that zines must be either vital or studied but not both. These are not mutually exclusive alternatives.

To demonstrate this, one need only consider the emergence of grrrl culture. Dissatisfied with their ongoing second-class status within their chosen community, young women who otherwise identified as punk "broke rank," so to speak, and put forward a distinct, oppositional identity of their own, one based on gender awareness. According to Alison Piepmeier, "the unofficial beginning of the Riot Grrrl movement" can be traced to an event that occurred in August 1991—"Girl Night in Olympia"—the opening of the International Pop Underground Festival, held in Olympia, Washington (Piepmeier 2009, 73).[8] Soon after this event, the first issue of *Action Girl Newsletter* was published, alongside a rapidly proliferating number of other grrrl zines: *Bikini Kill, I'm So Fucking Beautiful, Riot Grrrl,* and, eventually, more recent grrrl zines such as *The East Village Inky* and *Jigsaw,* many of which Piepmeier examines at some length. Even though she offers her readers an "origin story" for the genesis of grrrl zines, Piepmeier sees the narrative of grrrl zines as but one moment, albeit an especially important moment, in the larger story of women's history of self-publishing in America, an account she briefly retells in her study.[9] For Piepmeier, grrrl zines are especially important because not only did they give birth to the grrrl movement, but they performed an accompaniment to the overture of what would become third-wave feminism as well. According to Piepmeier, "the origin stories of the two are inextricably intertwined. Grrrl zines are coterminous with the third wave . . . grrrl zines and third wave feminism respond to the same world . . . grrrl zines are often the mechanism that third wave feminists use to articulate theory and create community" (9–10).

Since their beginnings in the early '90s, grrrl zines have continued to flourish, though this fact is often met with surprise. Confirming the widely held view that zines are typically "seen as a nostalgic medium, harking back to a punk or grunge era that no longer exists" (Piepmeier 2009, 14), Piepmeier is not especially surprised to hear her colleagues ask, "Does anyone even make zines these days"? In the introduction to *Girl Zines*, she offers a direct and unequivocal response to this question:

> The answer is emphatically—and perhaps surprisingly—yes. Zines are still being made, and in great numbers. In the course of writing this book, I've acquired approximately one hundred newly made zines, given to me by the zine creators I've interviewed or my own students, or purchased in my many forays into independent bookstores around the country or online zine distribution sites. (14)

What Piepmeier could have added here is that scholarship *about* zines, especially grrrl zines, is flourishing as well. In addition to Piepmeier, many other scholars have turned their attention to zines. Janice Radway, Mimi Nguyen, Elke Zobl, and Daniel C. Brouwer are only a few of the many recent scholars who have sought to understand the larger cultural significance of zine discourses.

In composition studies, Michelle Comstock and, more recently, Brenda Helmbrecht and Meredith A. Love, have attempted to understand the relevance of zines for writing scholars and teachers. Anticipating a good deal of the argument forwarded in this chapter, Comstock observes that grrrl zines offer "many young women ways to reconceive their participation in the public sphere not just as consumers but also as producers of and writers of culture" (Comstock 2001, 387). Comstock, like Nguyen (2000), even goes so far as to characterize the grrrl zine scene as a counterpublic in its own right, though she draws exclusively on Fraser's conception to do so.[10] Helmbrecht and Love, on the other hand, examine two mainstream zines, *Bitch* and *Bust*, to see how each rhetorically construct specific and multiple *ethe*. They argue for the considerable value in incorporating these two zines into our classrooms because "both zines can teach our students the value of making arguments about personally significant issues" and because each can effectively interrupt "the academy's conception of what 'good writing' looks like" (Helmbrecht and Love 2009, 160).

For writing scholars and teachers, grrrl zines can now be understood to have an important pedagogical value; but this value, I believe, would not have been recognized were it not for the fact that grrrl zines have become the object of an important line of recent feminist inquiry. Their contribution to third-wave feminism, for example, is indisputable, as Piepmeier, Zobl, Radway, and many others have demonstrated. But if grrrl zines are crucial in the development of feminist thinking, it must similarly be noted that they betoken an important step in the evolution of zine discourses as well. While very few scholars would deny that early grrrl zines emerged out of the anarcho-punk culture described in the previous chapter, what's clear is that they went far beyond that culture. Most significantly in this regard, grrrl zines brought an awareness of gendered, as well as racial and ethnic difference, to a discourse that was overwhelmingly white and that (with the not always articulated exception of class) did not usually concern itself with categories of difference. Grrrl zines, after all, first illuminated the "unexamined whiteness" (Piepmeier 2009, 131) of punk zines by way of such early publications as *Evolution of a Race Riot*, a zine that collected in a single issue a variety of scattered harangues, all of which, according to editor Mimi Nguyen (1997), were designed "to subvert the dominant punk rock order & yes whiteboy/girl hegemony" (Nguyen 1997; Piepmeier 2009, 131).[11] Moving beyond a simplistic concern for diversity and multiculturalism— concepts "drained of political power" through their appropriation by consumerist culture—grrrl zines embraced instead "intersectional identities," which, taken together, attempted to account for "identities that don't fit into familiar cultural narratives or stereotypes" but that nevertheless "interlock and affect one another" (Piepmeier 2009, 124–25). If, as Piepmeier claims, intersectionality is now a staple of "mainstream feminist discourse," then we would be wise to return to early grrrl zines to see how this concept was enacted in actual practice (126).

Were it not for grrrl zines, then, it is doubtful that zines would have received the measure of scholarly attention that they have in recent years. Yes, there are scholars whose specific focus is not grrrl zines per se (see Cogan [2008], Duncombe [1997], Avery-Natale [2009], among others). Nonetheless, and as I have indicated above, grrrl zines made a formative contribution to third-wave feminism and they cultivated an awareness of what had been largely absent from zine discourses—a sense of the importance of gendered and cultural difference.[12] These developments, I would offer, made zines a genre more amenable to formal, academic inquiry. I am thus inclined to believe that the attention directed toward grrrl zines resulted in a broader scholarly interest in *all* zines, whatever their particular theme or orientation.

But to return to my earlier point, what should be clear is that scholarship about zines, in itself, does not signify their demise. Nor does a parallel impulse to archive zines necessarily tell us much of anything about their present vitality and currency. And though it may be reasonably asserted that the number of zines has waned since their heyday in the late '80s to mid-'90s, this does not mean that zines are "dead" or that they are trending toward oblivion. Rather, it suggests that the nature of zine publication is changing—and changing profoundly. The obvious source of this transformation is the Internet as the preeminent locus of current self-publishing. For this reason, few writing about zines today can escape the obligation to try to understand them within the context of our ubiquitous new media.

WHAT HATH THE INTERNET WROUGHT?[13]

The relationship of zines to Internet discourse is, in some ways, riddled with certain ironies. Long before the Internet was a staple of everyday life, zines anticipated many of its characteristic features. Duncombe, as noted earlier, argued that "zine writers have created vast networks of independent communication . . . voluntary, non-hierarchical with omnidirectional communication flows" that seek to bring into actuality "an ideal of social organization" (Duncombe 1997, 188). A better description of Internet discourse, especially in its most idealistic conceptions, may be hard to imagine. Anna Leventhal, moreover, notes that zines and Internet discourses both embrace a democratic vision of communication but that, structurally, they also share much in common:

> Zines in a way resemble an early version of the Internet; there is a strong likeness in the way that each medium proclaims itself to be democratic, giving every voice equal weight through access to low-budget production and dissemination. The importance of networking is also analogous, and in the same way that one web page invariably leads to another, contact with one zine or zine-maker inevitably opens up a plethora of access points. (Leventhal 2007, 19)

After noting this kinship, however, Leventhal then asks, "If zines are the predecessors of the Internet, must we now recognize that, having birthed the new generation of minor mediaphiles, they are now dead, or have at least outlived their usefulness?" (19). In other words, could it now be that the very technology able to realize zine ideals will prove to be their undoing? Certainly, this is a question that zinesters and anyone currently writing about zines must address.

In many ways, the familiar Internet genres—blogs, personal websites, online journals and newsletters, discussion boards, Facebook postings, etc.—all would seem to render the vulnerable, precarious zine obsolete, to make it irrelevant (or perhaps worse, *quaint*) owing largely to the typical zine's purposeful lack of sophistication. Claims about the death of zines almost always ensue from the commonplace assumption that the genres of new media have (or very soon will) entirely replace whatever communicative purposes zines once performed. After all, the reasoning goes, Internet discourses have become increasingly accessible to everyone, and hence with few exceptions, they can easily reach transnational audiences. What's more, they offer a seemingly inexhaustible range of visual and verbal resources and readily accommodate existing print genres. Indeed, as is now obvious, most major newspapers and magazines, as well as most academic journals, have online versions of their print editions, and many book titles now appear in digital formats in order to address the burgeoning popularity of e-book readers.

Not too surprisingly, some zines also have online versions, but the more interesting (and predictable) development is the recent emergence of e-zines, specific online publications that seek to approximate something of the look, content—not to mention *attitude*—of their paper counterparts. Like most online newspapers, some e-zines are simply scanned then uploaded versions of already existing print zines. But at the other end of the spectrum can be found those e-zines that originate and flourish on the Internet and nowhere else. While the claim that zines have been dealt a deathblow by the Internet seems overstated, it appears that zines do indeed confront special challenges when attempting to create a vital space for themselves within digital environments. Why? The obvious answer is that the materiality of zines simply cannot be regarded as an incidental or happenstance feature. Put differently, materiality is a constituent feature of what zines are, what they do, and what they say to others. A couple of examples may illustrate why this is so.

In drawing the inevitable comparison between blogs and zines, and in the context of her examination of grrrl zines, Piepmeier refers to a "number of recent studies that have documented the hostility of the Internet for women" (Piepmeier 2009, 15). While she is obviously aware that certain controls exist that can (partially) filter out misogynistic, racist, homophobic, and violent comments, and while she does not want to characterize zine communities as "utopian alternative[s]," she does claim that zines provide a kind of intimacy, and demand a kind of effort, that seems to block some of the more opportunistic aggression that is prevalent online. Writing a hostile anonymous comment on a blog is easy; taking the time to write a letter, on paper, and mail it to someone whose zine you read is a much more labor-intensive endeavor. It's also a more intimate one, since only the person who created the zine will read the letter, as opposed to the ostensibly broader audience for blog comments. (16)

Piepmeier is not denying that genuine online communities can exist. Obviously, many do. But she is suggesting that the communities invoked by zine discourses are qualitatively different, and that for grrrl zinesters in particular, this difference matters in ways that are profoundly important. What's more, this difference originates, she claims, through the very materiality of zines, a fact that "differentiates them from blogs, not only in terms of the artifacts themselves, but in terms of the communities that accrue around them." Zines, Piepmeier maintains, enable "different kinds of community and different modes of activism than digital media" (17). Needless to say, if zine materiality has a shaping effect on the kinds of community that zines make possible, it follows that this same materiality also has a shaping effect on zines understood as what I call a cultural public.

Among librarians and archivists, zines are routinely categorized as *ephemera*, a term that captures, at once, a sense of both their marginality as well as their materiality. As someone who writes from her experience "as a founding member of Montreal's Bibliograph/e Zine Library," Leventhal observes that preserving zines "is a matter of protecting a cultural form whose very materiality is both its strength and potential limitation" (Leventhal 2007, 1–2). The zine preservationist is, however, immediately faced with the paradox of endeavoring to make permanent something that was never intended to be and whose presumed value is discovered neither in its rarity nor in its aesthetics but in its *use*, that is, "from the interwoven histories of the zine's currency":

> Any zine has likely passed through at least a few hands, and the history of one zine is in part the history of zine culture in general . . . While wear-and-tear could devalue a zine in the eyes of a traditional library or artistic collection, for an individual involved in zine-making such decay might be testament to the zine community's continued vitality and presence. Zines store "traces" of their attendant cultural context in their very objecthood; in a sense, their ephemerality and frailty is the source of their strength. (12)

To illuminate this point, Leventhal asks us to contrast zine collecting with the world of comic book collecting. The latter activity prizes most those comics that are in "'mint condition' (that is to say, essentially unread)," and thus the more pristine the artifact, the more market value it is assigned by collectors (12). In contrast, a zine that has passed through many hands is considered to have greater value, at least from the point of view of zinesters, because it will bear visible evidence of its journeys. Among zine readers, "mint condition" more likely refers to a zine that is smudged and tattered from repetitive use, one that shows signs of its lived life in the circulatory channels of zine culture. Distinct, then, from the problem of how zine cultures and counterpublics might be variously understood, it seems likely that the materiality of zines is part and parcel of any definition of zines that might be put forward. But if this is true, how are we to understand zines in the context of digital environments?[14]

Consider, for example, one of the claims I offered earlier—namely, that a distinguishing feature of zines is that they embrace a do-it-yourself ethos, and further, that this DIY ethos is very much related to the arts of bricolage—the inventive, resourceful making do associated with skills that accrue to the handymen and handywomen of the world. But do such arts endure in digital environments? Does the Internet even permit a do-it-yourself approach to zine making? In chapter 1, for example, I described the typical zine as "insistently unprofessional." Is it even possible to *be* unprofessional online? Does the Internet provide either the space or the resources for those who, wishing to make a statement about consumer capitalism, purposefully choose to extol all things amateurish, unrefined, makeshift? Of course, a zine maker might upload and import images of the very materials that she would have otherwise cut and pasted into an actual zine for use in a blog or e-zine. But it is not likely, I believe, that she could do so *innocently*, that is, without a sense of the considerable irony accompanying her action.

It may even be possible to imagine a certain kind of web designer, someone thoroughly steeped in zine aesthetics, who could develop a storehouse of digital images inspired by what the culture at large deems unaccomplished, raw, clumsy, flawed—regardless of whether such images depicted things that actually exist. Reaching this juncture, when virtual images are designed to approximate items that exist nowhere but in the imagination of a designer, then, a further irony becomes apparent—the irony of *simulacra*, an irony even more at odds with the earnestness characteristic of most zines. None of this is to say that the Internet is void of creative opportunities or, for that matter, yet-to-be-realized creative potential. But it is to suggest that the kind of creativity distinctive of zine making does not always square comfortably with the kind of creativity encouraged by the Internet. In drawing a contrast between blogs and zines, for example, Piepmeier observes the following:

> Bloggers certainly do exhibit a great deal of creativity in blog design and content, but available blog templates make it easy for bloggers to focus on the content rather than on the appearance of the blog. Zines . . . are simpler technology, and because no template exists, each element requires choice and each zine is different. The look of zines, then, is individualized and significant in ways that blogs aren't . . . The necessity of making aesthetic decisions with zines, of selecting paper . . . deciding whether to handwrite, typewrite, or word process, is a level of personal involvement that is not as often present in electronic media. This personal, physical involvement means not only intentionality but care. (Piepmeier 2009, 66)

If what Piepmeier says is true, then DIY for a material zine must mean something qualitatively different than what it means for a virtual one. And this difference is not restricted to the kind and number of available resources for each medium. The most important difference may be found in observing, as I suggested earlier, *what else* gets made in the making of a zine. Through the eyes of outsiders, for example, these little publications seem, at best, primitive, slapdash, and careless; for their makers, though, zines are nothing less than labors of love, embodiments of the genuine care and affection with which they were made. This is likely one reason why comments directed toward zines are dramatically less hostile than comments aimed at blogs; there exists a kinship, a felt camaraderie among those who share an appreciation for what goes into the making of a zine. And because most zine readers are (or have been) zine authors too, zine commentary tends to be more *responsive* (in the larger, more generous sense of that word) than reactive.

Does this mean that the idea of DIY must be wholly abandoned when recontextualized for digital environments? Perhaps the Internet has its own forms of do-it-yourself that we have yet to fully appreciate? Certainly, the emergence of various digital or creative "commons" that provide open access to electronic tools, images, files, texts, and so on would seem to be in the spirit of DIY. Eric Raymond (2001), a self-described "accidental revolutionary," has offered what is now a canonical metaphor for top-down (the cathedral) and bottom-up (the bazaar) software design, the latter of which, by analogy, might be thought to constitute a strictly digital version of DIY, or to provide an electronic toolbox for the online bricoleur.[15] Still, to think this way about "making stuff," that there are two separate repositories—one online, the other found in the usual haunts of zinedom (garages, attics, sheds, yard sales, basements, dumpsters, etc.)—is to endorse the conventional notion of an absolute division between the digital and material realms. Such an idea, unfortunately, stands in stark contradiction to what is fundamental to the approach of any self-respecting bricoleur: namely, that to get the job done, one must be free to use whatever tools and resources that are available, handy. Surely, then, zinesters (and all other citizen bricoleurs) must somehow be free to use what the Internet offers.

And this, in fact, is what is actually happening. Many present-day zines incorporate and creatively blend aspects of both the digital and the material. Rejecting the dichotomy that says zines must issue forth from one of these realms but not both, Frederick Wright points out that "the relationship between electronic and print publishing is far more complex than it is commonly characterized" (Wright 2001, 147). Wright provides a thoroughgoing examination of some of these complexities and for him, what seems to be most telling is the dialectic that emerges when material zines meet digital zines. Among other things,

> Zine publishers used the Internet to distribute printed material, zine publishers published material from ezines in print, ezine publishers from their publications in print volumes, and a host of other activities occurred that were unanticipated by most critics . . . In addition, the legacy of print exerted considerable influence on the activities of zine publishers, from organizing their websites using turnpage links to publishing in editions . . . Many zine publishers appreciated being able to publish on an ongoing basis and the ease with which they could use digital technologies to incorporate multimedia into their work. However, the desire by online audiences for immediate gratification as well as the mainstream attitudes of much of the online audience cooled the enthusiasm of zine publishers for online publication. (147–48)

Even though Wright understands that there is no such thing as an unproblematic transfer of zine publications from material to digital formats, or vice versa, he concludes his study with the rather surprising assertion that "often too much significance is attached to these differences rather than to the similarities of the functions they can serve. *In short, the spirit of zines is not bound to print*" (185–86; emphasis added). And while he thinks that zines (and all literature, for that matter) "will flourish in print and online," his arguments, it would seem, effectively separate zine materiality from zine functions, a breach not likely to be endorsed by the majority of zine makers (186).

I, too, believe that the future will bring a continuing interplay between print and online zines and that, generally, this interplay will work against the binary nature of arguments about print versus new media. But where zines are concerned, and unlike Wright, I also believe that the social function of zines is inextricably linked to their materiality. If this premise is granted, the crucial question, then, becomes one of orientation: How do traditional zines position themselves toward the overwhelming ubiquity of electronic media? Are print zines merely an interpellated genre, a genre not entirely conscious of being *hailed* into digital formats, but at the same time, a genre vaguely aware that something important is lost in this translation? Or might it be possible to imagine other orientations? Is it possible, for example, to give *first* consideration to what zines mean in the context of Internet discourse rather than question how best to tailor zines to the special requirements of digital environments? To put this question another way, what if we were to emphasize what zines *do* before we surveyed the wonders of what the Internet *can do*? Consider whether returning to one of the original functions of zines—namely, to *embody* a critical, oppositional stance toward corporate ownership of media— might not still bear some relevance to our own moment, as well as the future of Internet discourse.

That future, in fact, is the overriding concern of Tim Wu, whose *The Master Switch: The Rise and Fall of Information Empires* attempts to chronicle an observable pattern in the emergence and eventual dominance of our new media, regardless of whether the "new" media in question happened to be the telegraph, the telephone, the radio, the television, and so on. Wu's thesis is that in each of these historical examples, a repeatable pattern can be discerned, a trajectory that moves from open to closed information technologies—that is, from frontiers to empires, until such time as (newer) new media emerge to contest the old. Indeed, Wu argues, this oscillating trajectory is not merely a pattern but an inevitability, something he refers to as "the Cycle," and we would be naïve to think that the Internet is immune to this pattern (Wu 2011, 6–7).[16] Good evidence exists that the forces of consolidation and control are moving exactly in this direction, and recent debates about what is commonly referred to as net neutrality ought to be interpreted as merely one index of a larger and more consequential trend. As Wu observes, "If the Internet, whose present openness has become a way of life, should prove as much subject to the Cycle as every other information network before it, the practical consequences will be staggering. And already there are signs that the good old days of a completely open network are ending" (7).

Add to this perhaps something even more worrisome. Because the Internet is rapidly becoming a universal host platform for all traditional media, information technologies are now converging upon, and being subsumed by, a "master network that can support virtually any kind of data traffic." What this means, Wu maintains, is that "with everything [ultimately] on a single network, the potential power of control is so much greater" and further that "the prospect of a new imperial age . . . seems as likely as it has ever been at this point in the Cycle" (Wu 2011, 318). The funneling of all media into a single network—the Internet—will, according to Wu, inevitably result in the figurative "master switch" of his title, the coveted prize of "those who might seek [total] domination of . . . resources we cannot do without" (319). Such a prospect—absolute control of the master switch—ought to be regarded as a sobering prospect, and one that, needless to say, must be resisted. Wu recommends that we apply a "separations principle" to the Internet, using the U.S. Constitution's "separation of powers" model as an analogy. Extending Wu's analogy, then, the digital "branches" of power that must be kept separate are "those who develop information, those who own the network infrastructure on which it travels, and those who control the venues of access" (302). Only by keeping such powerful interests sequestered from one another will we be able to avoid the information dystopia that Wu sketches out as a real likelihood.

Wu does not, however, entertain the possibility that there might be another solution to the problem of centralized power—a solution that, however limited, could be rediscovered in certain media forms that the Internet is thought to unproblematically encompass. In other words, perhaps not all media forms so easily converge into Internet discourse; perhaps some do not get co-opted into the master network without a degree of watchful and, in some cases, recalcitrant discretion.

I am referring to zines, of course—music zines, anarchist zines, grrrl zines, and others—all of which are able to embody a critical opposition through their very materiality. Recall that zines, especially traditional paper zines, appear the way they do not because of aesthetic choices (or rather, not primarily for that reason) but because of necessity. In other words, this is what a publication looks like when you do not have free access to corporate-owned resources; this is what a publication looks like when you intend to make a statement about that fact; this is what a publication looks like when you do it yourself. As I have attempted to demonstrate in the first two chapters, zines are many things and perform many cultural functions, but central to their collective mission is one purpose common among all zinesters: namely, that centralized owner-ship of information media must be both critiqued and actively, passion-ately, resisted.

Although the Internet has been regarded, at least until recently, as something of a wild and wooly frontier, an open space of free and cre-ative expression, that view is changing dramatically. As Wu's jeremiad makes clear, the trend line is moving inexorably toward the consolida-tion of Internet resources in the hands of corporate control. I noted above that Wu offers one strategy by which to keep these currents at bay. But considering the history of modern zines—especially their unwaver-ing opposition to unified control of media (old or new)—perhaps, then, it is not too far-fetched to suggest that these shabby publications called zines will not be so easily co-opted by the Internet. Perhaps zines will experience a renaissance of sorts, especially if what Wu foresees actually comes to pass. If his vision is correct, then a location will be needed to stand outside of the enclosures of digital hegemony. From such a place, zines will do what zines have always done: circumvent and critique, in ingenious ways, official discourses so that resistant discourses might still have their say. And it seems clear that in order to stand outside of a thoroughly regulated Internet, zines must preserve some devotion to their material origins, even as they experiment with and tactically exploit Internet resources. It follows, then, that I disagree with Frederick Wright's claim that "the spirit of zines is not bound to print." I am con-vinced that not only will zines persist in their material forms, but that they will still have much to say, and a future purpose to fulfill, by virtue of that fact.

Yes, much of the foregoing discussion is speculative. But it would be staggeringly naïve to think that the Internet of the last decade will be the Internet of the next, that the openness and freedom of the Internet's early years will continue to prevail. Equally naïve, the notion that the Internet cannot help but forever be on the side of liberation and democ-racy (an idea very popular among cyber-utopians) has been fairly much discredited, despite the much-ballyhooed rallying cry that "the revolu-tion will be Twittered." Authoritarian and oppressive regimes, it turns out, are capable of learning after all, and, among other things, they have learned that the Internet offers enormous powers of surveillance, far more than what was possible before the widespread use of digital technology.[17] Indeed, and perhaps to the surprise of some, it may be the case that paper zines will prove to be much harder to trace than any blog posting or wiki entry.

Unless one believes the Internet to be unchanging and benign, zines will endure because they have a critical purpose to accomplish, the urgency of which is likely to be exacerbated, not lessened, by Internet discourses. Such is why zines merit our attention and why they belong in our writing classrooms, both as objects of our inquiries and as illustrations of how writing might matter in ways that are mostly deemed unworthy of our pedagogical efforts. In the final section, then, I will return to anarchist zines, and examine the situation of Mark, the author of his own zine and a student in a writing class.

A FEW WORDS WRITTEN ON BEHALF OF SOMEONE NAMED MARK

In a recent pedagogical article, Susan DeRosa describes her approach to teaching the literacy narrative, emphasizing, in particular, how literacy narratives allow students to reflect upon their "*continuous literacy experiences*" as these develop "throughout the writing course." DeRosa wants students to understand "literacy learning as continuous and changing, rather than as a fixed experience that once happened as a past isolated event (or has yet to happen *to them* as writers)." Further, she also hopes to develop within her students an "awareness of their 'literacy in action'—the ways that their writing can effect change in their communities—a sense of civic literacy" (DeRosa 2004, 2). To this end, she asks her students to write letters to the editor of the *Hartford Courant* on an issue that matters to them and then reflect on writing that letter. She concludes her article with excerpts from the reflections of several of her students, all of whom demonstrate a sense of themselves as writers in flux, writers who have come to realize something about themselves as writers that they did not know before.

Among the students that DeRosa comments upon is Mark. We learn that outside of the classroom, Mark publishes his own anarchist zine, *Us Against Them*, but that the requirements of this assignment have led him to realize that "*it's not always best to go for the 'all or nothing' approach of angry, exclamatory writing which leaves you with few supporters and 'preaching to the converted'*" (DeRosa 2004, 7). Mark further explains,

> Since the anarchist movement has always been small and isolated, doesn't it make sense that in order to get our ideas out to more people we'll need to how [sic] it can affect them? All this talk about the evils of capitalism won't bother someone who's benefiting from it, nor will it affect those who could care less. Literacy narratives help me to find other ways of using language and expressing my opinion to those who might not necessarily buy into the typical anarchist rhetoric. (7)

While this sounds something like a conversion narrative in the making, DeRosa takes care to point out that Mark "remains loyal to his intentions and political beliefs but considers other ways to present himself to his audience." For Mark, DeRosa explains, "Literacy narratives give him a space to negotiate his multiple roles as a writer" (7). By virtue of this course (in general) and this assignment (in particular), Mark has thus acquired much more rhetorical flexibility as well as a much more informed understanding of audience and the various roles that writers may effectively perform.

I would not dispute DeRosa's claim that Mark, as well as her other students, broadened "their visions of themselves as writers" and thus made noticeable progress in their development as rhetoricians too (DeRosa 2004, 7). As Mark himself says, "I now ask myself questions as I write that before I never would have considered at all, and I am even more secure that others will be able to see the writing in the way that I do" (8). Not surprisingly, both Mark and his teacher believe important gains have been made in Mark's journey toward a fuller repertoire of available literacies.

But when I first read this account, I experienced a sense of loss. I first questioned the assumption that Mark's development as a writer was merely cumulative, was simply one that offered Mark opportunities to do more and different kinds of writing. Rather, it seemed to me that Mark's growth as a writer, implicitly at least, asked him to repudiate his anarchist writing, that it necessitated a momentous turning away from the oppositional discourses that Mark identified with as the author and publisher of *Us Against Them.* Mark was instead asked to embrace the school-sanctioned rehearsal genre of the "letter to the editor."

Now, to be required to write in any genre is to likewise be required to endorse, however temporarily, a certain point of view about the world, and how textual genres organize recurrent social actions proper to that worldview.[18] By virtue of being asked to write a letter to the editor of the *Hartford Courant,* I want to suggest that Mark was asked to endorse a vision of publicness very different from the one expressed in his anarchist zine. Mark, as most students (including my own) realize, probably had little choice in the matter, or at least believed that he did not. Yet, because the assignment sequence is framed in developmental terms, readers are left to conclude that Mark's growth as a writer required that he set aside, or worse, abdicate—if only for a while—his extracurricular pursuits as a zine maker. Thus, a shift in Mark's understanding of what defines meaningful writing can, I believe, be discerned in a couple of ways.

First, based on what Mark says in his reflections, it is obvious that he realizes something more is at stake here than merely having the opportunity to compose in other genres. Mark's newfound eagerness to critique his zine writing can be evidenced in his realization that "angry, exclamatory writing . . . leaves you with few supporters" and ultimately amounts to little more than an exercise in "'preaching to the converted'" (DeRosa 2004, 7). The same observation could, of course, be voiced by any mainstream critic of zine discourse; and the fact that Mark directs this rather severe judgment toward himself suggests that, in some measure, he has repudiated his earlier avocation as a zinester and now identifies with views that could easily be construed (by zinesters anyway) as a mainstream (and not very friendly) perspective on zine discourse. Perhaps Mark could have voiced an anarchist critique of the letter to the editor genre, pointing out how such a genre perpetuates the myth of citizen agency for individuals who obviously believe in the power of such letters to effect real change and who write such letters in earnest, pleasantly unaware of the overwhelming constraints on discourse under consumer capitalism, even at the local level. Or maybe Mark could have written a different kind of letter to the newspaper, one that critiques the very genre of the letter to the editor or parodically mocks its aspirations. Such an approach to the prompt would have been more faithful to the anarchism Mark once espoused.

But what's more likely is that Mark did not feel he had the liberty to express his views this way. (DeRosa does not share with us what Mark's letter was actually about.) What we do know, however, is that Mark was pleased with, and learned a great deal from, the assignment. I am obviously in no position to dispute that claim. But it seems clear to me that the assignment was not simply a neutral addition to Mark's growing repertoire of genres. Rather, and to put the matter bluntly, it was an unspoken request that Mark *change his attitude about what counts as real writing*, a request that, judging by what we are told, he obliged.

Another indicator of this shift can be found in what appears to be a lack of interest in Mark's experience as a zine writer and publisher. I have no way of knowing all the classroom discussions that ensued from this assignment, but based on what knowledge I do have, there is little curiosity about Mark's experience. I wondered if certain questions had been asked of Mark? For example: "What did you learn as a writer from your experience with anarchist zines?" "What do you think your classmates could learn from your experience?" Or "As a maker of zines, Mark, we're interested to know what advice you'd give to others about knowing how to write to an audience very different from the one in this assignment?" I assume the reason such questions were not asked of Mark was because the anticipated response might have been a distraction or something irrelevant to the teacher's purposes. But it is also likely that, compared to the school-sponsored letter to the editor (and follow-up reflection), Mark's zine writings represented a discourse utterly lacking in any recognizable *legitimacy*, not only outside the classroom walls but within them as well.

I hasten to remind, again, that my perspective is not a fully informed one (how could it be?) and that I enjoy a certain privilege because of that fact. It is, in one sense, too easy to frame this situation as simply one that occurred between one student and one teacher while ignoring the institutional constraints under which this course took place. A quick list of the many things I do not know would have to include the following: Did the instructor teach from a common syllabus? Was she required to meet standard program goals? Did she choose her own textbooks, her own room, her own assignments? How many other courses did she teach this semester? How many students were in this particular course? How many other departmental and university commitments did she have this semester? All such questions point to factors that can have a determinative effect upon any curriculum and pedagogy. As for Mark, I do not know his class standing, his major, his motives, his aspirations, or his particular strengths and weaknesses as a writer. To repeat what should be obvious: my point of view is not, and cannot be, a fully informed one.

And yet, from my admittedly limited perspective, I cannot help but wonder if what Mark brought to this class was an unrecognized opportunity, a missed moment that might have been pedagogically illuminating and useful. If such is true, then we would be well advised to ask a different set of questions: What could *we* learn from those students in our classes who already write, publish, and circulate their own texts? What could *we* learn from those street authors like Mark, who enroll and participate in our classes? What could *we* learn from such students about how writing might get taught—or rather, get taught differently? What could *we* learn from Mark about what writing is or what it could be? In taking leave of Mark, then, allow me to attempt some provisional answers to these questions.

First, in our public writing pedagogies, when rhetorical purpose is built into writing assignments, it usually takes the form of asking students to stake a position toward some issue or controversy and then to marshal arguments on behalf of their position. The assumption here is that the author will be able to persuade the reader to embrace the same position, and then act on that position. One feature of discourse that this kind of assignment promotes—and that zines reject—is, once again, the strict division between production and consumption, between writers and readers. Zine authors, however, have another rhetorical purpose in mind, one that happens to contest this familiar binary. The zine writer also wants you to become a writer, wants you to make your own zine, wants you *not* to receive passively what other people produce but "make things" yourself. Indeed, for the zine writer, there is no better measure of rhetorical success than this: that the reader of *your* zine was inspired to become the writer of *her* own.

I want to suggest that when this occurs, those who might otherwise be said to constitute an audience tend in the direction of something else: a public—a particular kind of public, to be sure, a counterpublic whose identity is contingent upon a reader's decision to author and publish her own texts and whose membership in that counterpublic is performed through self-authoring and publication. We may not have many Marks in our own classes, but surely we have a number of students who embrace an array of identities and affiliations, many of which exist in an uneasy, if not openly conflictual, relationship with the perceived norms of official social life. If such is the case, we can surely find innovative ways to cultivate self-publication in our assignments and classroom projects, emphasizing to students that one goal of their projects is *to motivate others to write and publish as well.*[19] This, too, is a rhetorical purpose, but it is one that very seldom gets incorporated into traditional writing assignments. And yet it may prove to be a timely one, since with the availability of new digital resources, we now have renewed interest in the relationship between writing and self-publication. Indeed, it is not far-fetched to suggest that writing and self-publication will, in the not-too-distant future, be inseparable.

Second, and as should be obvious, zines are highly stylized publications, both in their presentational and textual aspects. What can we teach students about visual and typographic rhetoric through examples provided by zines? What can we teach students about how zines say much more than the content of the writings found within their covers? Among other things, we can show them, in Warner's phrase, how "style performs membership," how style participates in the making of identities, communities, and publics (Warner 2005, 142). Zines embody a purposefully oppositional style, arising out of negation, of resistance to those other discourses that enforce an official or professional view of language and its uses. For many students, then, zines have the potential, at least, to make style into something proximate, nearby, far less sacrosanct than our traditional understandings of style, which generally tend either to classical forms or handbook prescriptions. Zines offer the possibility that students can make style into something their own. Zines, after all, were never meant to be included among the vaunted, respectable genres of texts that usually appear on our syllabi. Indeed, if anything, zines were intended to be an affront to such genres—genres whose first (if not singular) requirement is that they be read, studied, and appreciated from a safe distance.

For writing teachers, then, zines could serve as a useful reminder that school discourse need not be limited to what Mikhail Bakhtin calls *authoritative discourse*, namely, discourse "located in a distanced zone" or of the "lofty spheres" that permits "no play with its borders . . . no creative stylizing variants" (Bakhtin 1981, 342, 343). We owe our students more than this, and indeed many in composition studies have recently urged that we more closely attend to nonacademic discourses. Diana George, for example, observes, "we have only begun to investigate how the circumstance—what John Trimbur identifies as the 'call to write'—works itself out beyond the walls of our classroom" (George 2010, 50). And Bronwyn Williams has recently argued, "If the claim of rhetoric and composition is to study student writing, it must be in conversation about how writing happens before and after students step on to university campuses" (133). Both George and Williams ask us to notice the overlooked and extracurricular writing that occurs elsewhere.[20] Should we do so, it is certainly the case that our classrooms may become sites where previously unacknowledged discourses, even zine discourses, are granted a pedagogical legitimacy they have not traditionally enjoyed.

Finally, there is a tempting suggestion here, one that proceeds by metaphorical extension. In line with Mark's example, what if we regarded our writing classrooms as DIY projects? In a very real sense, the present-day writing classroom has already been written by others, for others. I am hardly the first to observe that the composition course is something of an occupied site, a site subject to any number of institutional constraints and determinations and a variety of administrative controls and impositions. But what if that hegemony were resisted, circumvented in makeshift ways by teacher and student alike? What if writing instruction itself were rewritten in the way a zine author might? What would that look like?[21]

I do not know, but I am aware that others are critically examining university instruction, and the university itself, from an oppositional, alternative viewpoint. A very recent collection edited by Zack Furness (2012), *Punkademics*, includes selections by academics who are, or once were, punks; many of the book's contributors reflect on how punk informs their teaching and scholarship. Along these same lines, Anya Kamenetz's (2010) *DIY U: Edupunks, Edupreneurs, and the Coming Transformation of Higher Education* endeavors to look at higher education through a do-it-yourself lens, asking how it might be possible to cobble together, wrest control of, or otherwise freelance, one's own continuing education. This motive informs another recent work as well, an anthology by the Edu-factory Collective (2009), *Toward a Global Autonomous University: Cognitive Labor, the Production of Knowledge, and Exodus from the Educational Factory*. All of these writings speak to a certain restiveness, a widespread dissatisfaction with the promise and purpose of higher education. It should not be surprising that some of those (unarticulated) frustrations will find their way into English 101. It would be far more surprising if they were contested there, at least in the way that Mark might.

In sum, by introducing zines into our writing classrooms, we create an opportunity to introduce students to an alternate vision of democratic participation, a different understanding of *publicness* that they are unlikely to find in our institutions, our textbooks, and, for the most part, our pedagogies.[22] What follows is that we also create an opportunity to both recognize and promote another kind of citizen—that kind of nameless citizen situated on the outskirts of official public life, distinguished by the fact that he or she is not distinguished at all. What might it mean to acknowledge such citizens?

ZINES AND ALTERNATIVE CITIZENSHIP

In her 2009 NCTE report, *Writing in the 21st Century*, Kathleen Blake Yancey urges writing scholars and teachers to "help our students compose often, compose well, and through these composings, *become* the citizen writers of our country, of our world, and the writers of our future" (Yancey 2009, 1). In her gloss on Yancey's call, Amy J. Wan observes that this call for teachers to turn out "good citizens" is a venerable one, a recurring theme of much progressive pedagogy, and for that reason, something all too familiar because, as a challenge that is routinely invoked, good citizenship "remains an uncontroversial stronghold in the rhetoric of educational objectives" (Wan 2011, 28). One reason these appeals endure, no doubt, resides in the fact that the very term *citizenship* is such an insistently positive one that Wan likens it to what was once said of the term *community*—namely, that because it has no "negatively charged opposite, citizenship becomes completely and unquestionably acceptable" (30). I would also point out that Yancey's phrase, "citizen writers," echoes, in a faintly contentious way, Rosa Eberly's (2000) "citizen critics," since Eberly wants to attend to those *who read texts as citizens* while Yancey wants to encourage those *who write texts as citizens*—or, perhaps more exactly, someday will write such texts. In light of these observations, then, how is it that zines might enable writing teachers to answer Yancey's "call to action" (Yancey 2009)?

Zines do so by offering our students a larger sense of what a citizen is and, at the same time, a glimpse of what a citizen may be. I want to suggest that should writing teachers introduce zines into our pedagogies, we might be able to respond to Yancey's entreaty but do so in ways that she may not have anticipated, and in ways that dispute and revise our commonplace ideas about citizenship. Where, for example, Yancey summons those who produce texts as *citizen writers*, and Eberly invokes those who consume them as *citizen critics*, I am more drawn to those who do both and more—namely, those who *make* texts, those I call *citizen bricoleurs*. To make a zine, for example, does not mean that one has merely written short personal essays, rants, how-to pieces, reflections, notices, reviews, etc. for a certain kind of narrow audience. In other words, to make a zine does not mean that one has simply authored the texts that go into one's zine. Rather, it means that (among countless other things) one finds cheap, available materials to work with; one conceives and designs what the zine will look like; one imagines the kind of reader that will be attracted to this particular zine; one figures out an inexpensive (or devious) way to reproduce, collate, and staple multiple copies; and one circulates said copies through all the usual venues and distribution channels. And yes, not to overlook the obvious, it also means that, typically, one writes the entire content of one's zine.

Zinesters, then, not only read and write zines; they also dream them, plan them, construct them, print them, disperse them, trade them, and talk about them—put simply, they *make* them. Zinesters publish their own handiwork (yes, literally *handiwork*), often from materials that have been used and discarded by others. In doing so, and in their own characteristic way, zinesters enact what de Certeau anticipated several decades ago—namely, they transform consumption into alternate forms of production, even if such production goes unrecognized by the culture at large. And if, as I contend here, we are alert to their broader significances, then we may come to realize that when zines get made, so do other forms of democratic participation, so do broader understandings of publicness, so do other visions of citizenship.

For by bringing zines into our classrooms, we introduce our students to those mostly anonymous citizens, the ones I refer to as citizen bricoleurs—those who understand that the most challenging do-it-yourself project facing us is the ongoing, unfinished project of democracy; those who perform a brand of citizenship that aspires to be neither safe nor respectable, believing that a domesticated citizenry is, figuratively speaking, a housebound one, a dominated one; and, not least, those who make and belong to certain kinds of publics—cultural publics—that resist, critique, and seek to transform the prevailing social arrangements of our time. By dint of their inconspicuous efforts, zinesters lend a helping hand to the task of enlarging our understanding of what democratic citizenship means. But it is a hand that has gone unnoticed and unappreciated. My hope, then, is that our classrooms might be a place where our students become acquainted with these "other" citizens, these citizen bricoleurs, and inquire into the important work they do for us all.

NOTES

1. An obvious question, then: What are examples of other cultural publics? Based on what I have argued thus far, punk surely qualifies as a cultural public (despite its varied expressions) as does third-wave grrrl feminism, also examined in this chapter. Other oppositional identities, such as those that coalesce around camp, street art, culture jamming, etc., often interrogate what counts as legitimate public space and do so through an array of ludic and often spontaneous tactics. These social formations, as well, perform double duty as both (sub)cultures and (counter)publics, and they may be understood as one or the other—or, as I prefer, simultaneously both. On this matter, I should note that Michael Warner, too, sees an affinity between subcultures and counterpublics; however, even though Warner sees these social formations as related, he is more interested in the differences between them, what makes them distinct from one another. Apparently for Warner, a counterpublic, unlike a subculture, not only "enables" but necessitates "a horizon of opinion and exchange." Moreover, a counterpublic has "a critical relation to power," and its membership is not circumscribed by a "precise demographic" (Warner 2005, 56). Nowhere does Warner claim, however, that subcultures cannot possess the same defining features as counterpublics and yet still retain their status as subcultures. In focusing on the differences between the two, Warner overlooks where subcultures and counterpublics intersect, overlap, and duplicate—where, in other words, they are capable of hybridizing into what I refer to here as cultural publics.

2. For a historical discussion of anarchist counterpublics, see Ferguson (2010). While Ferguson alludes to key publications in the early anarchist movement, her focus is not on specific texts (or genres of texts) themselves but on how recent theories of counterpublics can be retroactively applied to historical movements—in her example, the late nineteenth- and early twentieth-century anarchist counterpublic as exemplified by Emma Goldman and Alexander Berkman. Although Ferguson's specific analysis has nothing to do with zines per se, I am not aware of any other work that looks at anarchism, historical or contemporary, through the lens of counterpublic theory.

3. This received view of poetics is challenged by Mikhail Bakhtin who, arguing that the novel is the most dialogic of literary genres, sees in poetry a monologic genre, one of whose many achievements is to suppress and constrain any dialogic orientation toward other genres and the world that such genres aspire to represent (Bakhtin 1981, 273, 286, 298). It is interesting, then, that Warner takes up the genre of lyric poetry in his examination of publics. Even though he concedes that "public speech is no more addressed to a particular person than is lyric" and that both genres came into "ascendancy with print," we would be wise to understand that "one seems to be formed by the negation of the other" (Warner 2005, 81). Specifically, public speech simply cannot afford the transcendence of lyric, "now understood," Warner says, "as timeless self-communion" (82). If it is true, as Bakhtin claims, that poetry is a monologic genre, then Warner seems to go Bakhtin one better when he claims that lyric "displaces all other poetic genres (epic, poems on affairs of state, georgic, satire). It [lyric] is now thought of simply as poetry" (82). It is important to realize, however, that later, when Warner discusses publics in terms of "poetic world making," he is not speaking about any particular poetic genre, lyric or otherwise. Rather, he is referring to an expressive or aesthetic function performed by certain kinds of discourses, a function that cannot be separated from the publics created by those discourses.

4. Warner observes that there are, indeed, occasions when the "transcendence" of lyric poetry is seemingly compromised. One such instance can be discovered in poetry slams, occasions that "sometimes create a counterpublic hybrid discourse, where poetry is pressured into embracing its scene of address (with, however, a corresponding loss of lyric transcendence)" (Warner 2005, 82).

5. It seems that there is more than a little dissatisfaction with the terms *public* and *counterpublics*. In addition to my two offerings in this work—cultural publics and disciplinary publics—there exist any number of proposed alternatives or refinements to our repertoire of names. I am thinking here of Gerald Hauser's (1999) *reticulate* publics, Linda Flower's (2008) *local* publics and *mestiza* publics (see Ackerman and Coogan, 2010), Catherine Squires's (2002) *enclave* and *satellite* publics, and, perhaps the most recent contribution, Richard Gilman-Opalsky's (2008) *transgressive* publics—all of which, taken together, serve as illustrations of a search for an alternative lexicon by which we might revise the public/counterpublic tandem.

6. Two websites, in particular, serve as clearinghouses for all things punk: AbsolutePunk.net and Punknews.org. Global punk was the theme of a recent opinion piece by Jessica Bruder (2012), "Real Punk Belongs to Fighters," which appeared in *The New York Times*. Bruder's thesis is that "punk today belongs more to Russia and Iraq, Myanmar and Indonesia, than it does to its birthplaces." Her lead example is the recent controversy in Russia involving the all-female punk band Pussy Riot, whose members delivered a "punk prayer" in a Moscow cathedral to protest the reelection of Vladimir Putin. Three members of the group were arrested on charges of "hooliganism" and are now imprisoned. At the time of this writing, they have just been convicted and sentenced. See also Bryanski (2012).

7. See, for example, two frequently referenced obituaries by Chris Yorke (2000) and John Marr (1999), the latter of which is available online.

8. It would be hard to dispute the momentous importance of the Riot Grrrl movement and the influence of this particular event on third-wave feminism. That said, it is likewise indisputable that there are feminist continuities here that often get overlooked. From its earliest inception, a number of women punk bands made their musical (and political) influence known. Long before Bikini Kill, bands such as The Slits and The Innocents often played alongside such iconic punk groups as The Clash. Later post-punk groups, such as Siouxsie and the Banshees, especially, featured female bandleaders or singers. In Alice Bag's recent interview with Chicana punk musician Susana

Sepulveda, Sepulveda asserts, "I think feminist ideas have always been a part of punk. Women helped create the punk scene as equal partners and in equal numbers to men. Women empowered themselves to do everything that men had traditionally done. That's not feminist theory—it's feminism in action. Feminism was there at punk's inception" (Sepulveda 2012).

9. For readers interested in how a specifically feminist account of self-publishing in America relates to zine publishing, I highly recommend Piepmeier's opening chapter and suggest that it be read in conjunction with the historical material that I have presented in this first section. Our emphases are distinct but very much related, and her account is crucial to understanding how zines emerged from a skein of historical threads.

10. It should be noted here that Comstock's prescient essay appeared well before the publication of Warner's *Publics and Counterpublics*.

11. As further evidence of their common lineage, one need only observe the distinct "whiteboy" and "whitegirl" affinities between the two phenomena. Despite the overwhelming whiteness of zine and punk culture, Riot Grrrl certainly fostered an emerging gender awareness between both zinesters and punks that also extended to racial identities and intersectional identities, as described here. I have mentioned (in an earlier note) feminist Chicana punk musician Susana Sepulveda, but other identities have been represented as well. African American presence in punk, for example, while hardly dominant, has never been entirely absent. "Afro-punk," as it is sometimes called, has recently emerged into its own movement of sorts, complete with its own roster of new bands, websites, and a 2003 documentary. Insofar as zines are concerned, subgroup affiliations have mostly clustered around gender and sexuality identities. An early advocate for more awareness of identity concerns, Mimi Nguyen has helped to bring a feminist sensibility to zine publishing along with Asian American and African American ones. In an article that recently appeared in *Library Journal*, Celia C. Perez (2009) reviews "zines by people of color," among which she includes *Paco, No History, No Self;* and *Borderlands*. A list of zines specifically by African American women is available at the website for the Barnard College Zine Library. See Freedman (2009).

12. But despite the laudable contributions that grrrl culture made to third-wave feminism, as well as to zine discourses, it must also be pointed out that the movement was successfully marketed and co-opted—offering young women an alternative identity, yes, but an identity as *consumers* who bought repackaged identities from those able to profit from the commodification of oppositional styles. This is nothing new, of course. Even though beats, hippies, punks, zinesters, grunge fans, grrrls, hip-hop artists, etc. may all have originated in expressions of authentic opposition to the culture at large, that culture inevitably commodified such expressions, thereby depleting them of whatever revolutionary promise they may have once possessed. One possible explanation for the volatility of subcultures and counterpublics might be because such formations must continually undergo shapeshifting, transforming themselves to avoid not so much any direct confrontation with the culture at large but rather the more devastating effects of co-optation by that culture. For discussions of how grrrl culture became increasingly commodified, see Sheridan-Rabideau (2008) and Bleyer (2004).

13. This is a revision of the question that appears in Numbers 22:23 and thus a revision of the first telegraphed words that Samuel Morse sent from Washington, DC, to Baltimore, Maryland, in 1844. His posing of this question to demonstrate the telegraph suggests that Morse may have had a sense of the profound changes to come as a result of this new technology. My revision of this question echoes that same sense, emphasizing, in particular, the likelihood that we do not know exactly where the Internet is taking us, though there is abundant speculation about possible directions.

This, I believe, is Wu's central point, and one that if applied to zines, ought to sound a cautionary note about premature eulogies for zines.

14. There might be a surprising reversal at work here, nonetheless. Ordinarily, digital media would likely be considered indestructible—theoretically, at least, imperishable—while paper media would reasonably be assumed to degrade, decompose, and ultimately disappear. Thus, one of the rationales for archiving and preserving zines derives from this physical fact alone. Among some zinesters, however, when comparing the digital zine to its paper version, the latter is considered much more likely to endure. (If this is true, then, the online zine is rendered a more authentically ephemeral artifact than its paper counterpart.) As one grrrl zinester explains, "I'm not convinced that what's written on a blog, that it's still gonna be there if you don't print it out, you know? In ten years, is it just gonna be sucked into the ether? Whereas maybe a hundred years from now somebody's going to go into an attic or basement and find a copy of *The East Village Inky* rattling around, and that, to me, is very exciting" (Piepmeier 2009, 16–17). For this zinester, and many others, the so-called digital "ether"—that impossible-to-find location where digital texts simply vanish—poses a far greater threat to the permanence of zines than any natural decay that will occur to paper zines.

15. There are any number of open source sites and repositories that might provide the wired bricoleur with all he or she needs for a virtual toolbox. The most encompassing and far-reaching tool is likely the Linux operating system, which offers free, open source software to all its users. The recent emergence of THATCamps, licensed under Creative Commons and intended for those working in the digital humanities, encourages a nonproprietary, collaborative, and open approach to solving problems and may likewise provide another kind of toolbox for the online bricoleur. THATCamps are typically presented as *unconferences*, a term that emphasizes their unplanned and mostly nonhierarchical format.

16. Wu's examination of this pattern would serve as an excellent illustration of Bakhtin's notion of centripetal and centrifugal forces, even though Bakhtin's focus, unlike Wu's emphasis on media technologies, is primarily on language and culture. Bakhtin observes how the joined "verbal-ideological" forces of consolidation and dispersal oscillate throughout the history of languages but are also present in the everyday, individual utterance (1981, 272). If this comparison were to hold true, then it would be reasonable to expect that users of new media, like users of language, would similarly participate in a struggle of larger forces that they may or may not be aware of, but which are present in each instance of use.

17. A crackdown on (the mostly youthful) London rioters by British authorities has been well documented. Denying that neither conditions in neighborhoods where the rioting occurred nor the recent austerity measures imposed by the current regime have anything whatsoever to do with the present unrest, many spokespersons for the conservative government of Prime Minister David Cameron blame social media (e.g., Facebook, Twitter, et al.) for the destruction that has occurred. However predictable it may be, this blaming strategy effectively diverts attention away from existing structural inequalities and redirects it toward various other supposed causes, one of which, apparently, is social media. Apart from the question of exactly how important a role social media actually played in the current riots (in my personal opinion, much less than what is reported), the fact that social media can be blamed for widespread unrest is useful to justifying even more repressive measures. As Cameron said, "when people are using social media for violence we need to stop them. So we are working with the police, the intelligence services and industry to look at whether it would be right to stop people communicating via these websites and services when we know they are plotting violence, disorder and criminality" ("Cameron Proposes Social Media Ban,"

2011). In the United States, *terrorism* (a problematic term at best, but an exceptionally convenient one too) has likewise supplied a useful pretext for the curtailment of civil liberties under both the George W. Bush and Barack Obama administrations. My larger point, though, is that, despite our beliefs to the contrary, the Internet serves the forces of repression as much as it does organized resistance and liberation. To think otherwise is dangerously naïve. This, in fact, is the central argument of Evgeny Morozov's (2011) *The Net Delusion: The Dark Side of Internet Freedom.*

18. Just as Bakhtin (1986) reminds us that speech, even in its most innocuous expressions, is always generically cast, genre theory reminds us that written texts are always generic as well. While it may be possible for teachers to assign writing prompts that do not give any special attention to genre considerations, it nonetheless remains *impossible* for writing teachers to assign prompts that allow students to write essays that are somehow "genre free." Such writing does not exist. I do not mean to suggest, then, that there is anything unusual about DeRosa's assignment. I am, rather, inquiring into how the assumptions that inform this prompt, and especially its specified genre, might differ from the assumptions that inspired Mark to author and publish his own zine.

19. As might be expected, there exists a fairly ample literature that explores the use of zines in the classroom—and not only in the composition classroom. See Alexander (2002); Helmbrecht and Love (2009); Piepmeier (2009); Congdon and Blandy (2005); and Wan (1999) for a small sampling.

20. Even though our very young discipline, at various junctures in its brief history, has expressed interest in nonacademic writing, our most abiding interest in "extracurricular" discourses was inaugurated by Anne Ruggles Gere's influential chair's address to the 1993 CCCC. As with all such addresses, a published version appeared soon after in *College Composition and Communication* (Gere 1994). This often-cited essay opened up an important line of inquiry, of which I hope this book is a small contribution.

21. I am grateful to one of my anonymous reviewers for this insightful suggestion.

22. My discussion places emphasis on how teachers might import and use zines in their writing classrooms. However, Piepmeier reminds us that zines themselves perform a teaching function as well, a function she refers to (after bell hooks) as "a pedagogy of hope." Piepmeier contends that zines are instructive not because they have the potential to "eradicate corporate culture." No such quixotic goal is seriously entertained by zine culture. Rather, according to Piepmeier, zines teach that democracy may be cultivated in "local, small-scale, ephemeral ways" through the purposeful enactment of a micropolitics of everyday life" (Piepmeier 2009, 163).

PART TWO

Disciplinary Publics

3

ON THE VERY IDEA OF A DISCIPLINARY COUNTERPUBLIC
Three Exemplary Cases

> *If I should take a notion*
> *To jump into the ocean,*
> *T'ain't nobody's business if I do.*
> *If I go to church on Sunday*
> *Then cabaret all day Monday,*
> *T'ain't nobody's business if I do . . .*
> *I swear I won't call no copper*
> *If I'm beat up by my papa,*
> *T'ain't nobody's business if I do,*
> *Nobody's business,*
> *Ain't nobody's business,*
> *Nobody's business if I do.*
> —Four verses from *Ain't Nobody's Business If I Do*
> by Porter Grainger and Everett Robbins
> (Billie Holiday version)

In her efforts to revise our understanding of what constitutes a public, Nancy Fraser finds herself disputing not only the theoretical assumptions that inform Jürgen Habermas's idea of the public sphere but also conventional ideas about what is deemed private, and what public. One of these conventional ideas is that the public may be defined simply as that which is "of concern to everyone" (Habermas 1990, 71). But who, exactly, constitutes "everyone"? After all, US citizenship has never been an all-inclusive status, and even if one were to reply that, despite this fact, citizens are those who act responsibly on behalf of *all persons* (even noncitizens), one would have a very difficult case to make. The historical evidence does not support such a claim, and in our own nation's past, it seems hardly necessary to point out that many people have not even been granted the status of persons, much less citizens. Everyone, it turns out, does not mean everyone.

Fraser thus rightly concludes that insofar as who constitutes a public, only those persons qualify who have been *extended access* to publics and public participation, for it is they, and only they, who may exercise the privilege of naming precisely that which is of "concern to everyone." What must be done, then, is to expand our available publics, and thereby multiply the available opportunities for public participation. But in doing so, Fraser observes, we cannot escape (nor should we want to escape) the necessity for what she calls "discursive contestation." Obviously, as publics broaden, more and more disputes will emerge about agendas and policies. But just as obviously, more and more disputes will emerge about what counts as a legitimate public concern. To illuminate this point, she returns to her central example of the feminist subaltern counterpublic:

> [U]ntil quite recently, feminists were in the minority in thinking that domestic violence against women was a matter of common concern and thus a legitimate topic of public discourse. The great majority of people considered this issue to be a private matter between what was assumed to be a fairly small number of heterosexual couples (and perhaps the social and legal professionals who were supposed to deal with them). Then, feminists formed a subaltern counterpublic from which we disseminated a view of domestic violence as a widespread systemic feature of male-dominated societies. Eventually, after sustained discursive contestation, we succeeded in making it a common concern. (Fraser 1990, 71)

From being a private concern—one traditionally cordoned off from the scrutiny of others—to being a matter that ought to be a "concern for everyone," domestic abuse was transformed into a public issue, largely because of the efforts of those who belonged to a late twentieth-century, feminist subaltern counterpublic. From a retrospective vantage point, it seems astonishing that, for many, the real scandal was not domestic violence committed against women but rather the fact that such violence was exposed at all, that it was made public by others. I want to suggest that, in varying degrees, a kindred revulsion can be found in numerous other examples of laying bare that which had once been protectively enclosed, quarantined, out of sight (or should I say, *bracketed?*). In other words, I maintain that there is something irrevocably transgressive about the act of going public and that some sense of violation, whether articulated or not, will most likely accompany any such act.[1]

More tailored to my purposes here, I want to extend this claim to intellectuals, scholars, and researchers—those who traditionally locate their work within the academic disciplines but who nonetheless desire influence in larger publics.[2] In this chapter, I offer an alternative to our existing models. That is, I elaborate the idea of a disciplinary counterpublic, and to this end, I review three examples provided by other scholars, each of whom has entertained the very same notion. Drawing from what they write, I construct a provisional description of what a disciplinary counterpublic might look like, and I argue that once enacted, disciplinary counterpublics provide an optional form of democratic participation for academics.

If going public is always scandalous to begin with—even for the academic disciplines—then it might be better for scholars and intellectuals to gain public access through the turnstile of disciplinary counterpublics. Since all counterpublics are, by definition, oppositional, then going public this way means crossing the line without apology, since whatever transgressions might be committed are more likely to be embraced than denied. First, though, I want to examine how and why "going public" is such a vexed phrase.

GOING PUBLIC REDUX

I believe it would be hard to dispute the claim that *going public* is a loaded term, one inhabited by a number of subtleties, connotations, resonances, undertones, and overtones.[3] I also think it would be hard to dispute the likelihood that these associative meanings might tell us a good deal about how the public is regarded in our current social imaginary. Consider first what the phrase says about location and direction. If it is reasonable to assume that one has no need to go where one already is, the public then must be a destination, some place where one hopes to arrive. That being the case, an obvious question occurs: Where, precisely, is the traveler arriving from? Where is the point of departure for those headed in a public direction? In light of how enduring the public/private binary remains, I think we can safely assume that one "goes public" only when one already inhabits a private sphere of some sort. But of what sort?

If, as this book argues, the public is actually constituted of multiple publics, may we not stipulate the likelihood of multiple privacies too? A menu of available privacies might include intimate and family spheres; assorted sites of neoliberal capitalism; membership in exclusive clubs and organizations; enrollments in learned and professional societies; the numerous array of charities, endowments, and philanthropical agencies; the phenomenon of gated communities as well as territorialized neighborhoods; and the many fleeting, unrecorded occasions of everyday free association.[4] In light of the sheer multiplicity of privacies and publics, it might seem that the public/private binary (a binary reinscribed by the very phrase "going public") cannot account for the heterogeneity of present-day social life, that our all too familiar binary is actually much more of a continuum, albeit a somewhat fractured one. To support this claim, one need only notice that certain hybrids have emerged in our recent mappings of public and private. In scholarly contexts, Lauren Berlant, for example, provides a close examination of what she calls the "intimate public sphere," a conservative and "familial politics of the national future [that excessively] came to define the urgencies of the present" (Berlant 1997, 1).[5] In more topical contexts, it should be observed that the now iconic Zuccotti Park, birthplace of the Occupy Wall Street movement, is but one illustration of a burgeoning trend in urban spaces, namely, the "privately owned public space" (POPS), a space where public availability may ultimately be determined by private interests, and where blended purposes, needless to say, raise a number of challenging civil rights issues.[6]

Going public, then, can be a rather complicated matter, not only because there are many publics from which to choose but because there are many privacies from which to depart. Notwithstanding these complexities, going public appears, for the most part, not to be favorably looked upon. Who goes public, after all? Whistle-blowers, to be sure. But it is telling to observe that whistle-blowers tend to be simultaneously celebrated and despised. Indeed, it is hard to think of any whistle-blower who has not been both. One need only recall the vehement indignation and anger directed toward Julian Assange and WikiLeaks—outrage that, not too surprisingly, ensued from governmental departments and spokespersons but that also found expression in our mainstream media as well. The idea that Assange might have been performing a service for the greater good of democratic transparency seems, in retrospect, not to have been the conventional wisdom even—and surprisingly—among institutions that might be assumed to be passionately dedicated to First Amendment freedoms.[7]

And what of the intimate sphere, where daily revelations of some sexual indiscretion or misdeed are commonplace and expected? Such events occur with such routine predictability—especially, it seems, among our political class—that one wonders if a jaded electorate can still muster any surprise, much less outrage, about such behavior. And what about celebrities? Don't they likewise get routinely exposed for infidelities and various sexual exploits? Indeed, an entire journalistic subgenre—the print tabloid—is devoted to (and profits from) the lifestyles of the rich and infamous. In fact, and as has often been observed, it may be that when celebrities go public, they actually increase their audience draw. Or, in other words, that being exposed for this or that transgression is actually something to be wished for, perhaps in line with that venerable dictum that there's simply no such thing as bad publicity. In the two examples mentioned here—politicians and celebrities—going public can destroy careers or advance them; but in either case, what remains constant is a sense of revealed wrongdoing, the shared agreement that a widely sanctioned norm of ethical behavior has been violated. It is illuminating, though, to observe that in nearly all of these examples, another widely endorsed (and for many, revered) norm also gets breached—namely that, as the song goes, it "ain't nobody's business" how one conducts one's sexual affairs. Indeed, this is a common first line of defense for those who have been exposed as well as for those who remain loyal to the exposed party (e.g., "I really don't care what he does in his private life; he's been a damn fine senator").

But even among "ordinary people"—by whom I mean those who do not enjoy great fame or conspicuous wealth—going public is still received with considerable approbation, often in the form of advice conveyed through an abundance of commonplace expressions. Who, after all, has not been told to avoid "airing your dirty laundry" in public; or that an amorous indiscretion is a "family affair" and will remain so; or that "loose lips sink ships" (a fine double entendre). Who has not been advised by close friends not to "kiss and tell" or not to "let the cat out of the bag" or not to "miss a good chance to shut up"? And perhaps there are even some who have been on the receiving end of proverbial wisdom that can be discovered in, of all places, an actual proverb: "Even a fool," Solomon declares to his people, "when he holdeth his peace, is counted wise: and he that shutteth his lips is esteemed a man of understanding" (Prov. 17:28, Authorized [King James] Version).[8] As the blues lyrics in my epigraph illustrate, when the public/private dichotomy gets translated as people's wisdom, the latter term, *private*, is always the dominant one.[9] Indeed, it is hard—maybe impossible—to think of any idiomatic saying that celebrates the virtue of publics, publicity, or going public.

My brief survey is meant to be neither exhaustive nor indisputable. Rather, in sampling a variety of contexts in which the phrase "going public" might actually be heard, I only wish to point out that often the phrase tends to carry with it unsavory associations: hints of a crossed boundary line, a violated norm, a broken promise, a revealed confidence, a trespassed space, and so on. In other words, and as I noted earlier, "going public" is tinged with an assortment of transgressive meanings, even when the phrase itself is meant to convey something right, proper, or desirable. No doubt there are complex social and historical reasons why going public is not typically cast in very flattering tones, but there are more immediately obvious reasons as well. One of these is the common-sense belief that we are originally private beings, born into the intimacies of family life, typically swaddled in the protective comforts of those responsible for our rearing. In other words, we experience privacy first in our lives, then later, and in varying measures, we cultivate a sense of ourselves as public beings. But this developmental trajectory, if it is true, is fraught with difficulties and hazards.[10]

For by granting experiential priority to the intimate, the familial, the proximate, we are encouraged to look upon the private as something natural and, correspondingly, the public as something fabricated, something impersonal, something that necessarily happens in the wake of our essentially private condition as human beings. Going public, therefore, entails a certain loss, a possible surrendering of much in our lives that we may know to be affirming, humane, perhaps even inspiring. Going public, in other words, is the renouncing of certain privileges—specifically the privilege of privacy.[11] And because going public usually means that we must depart from that which is private—which is to say, unseen and unknown by others, sequestered, undisclosed—the act of going public itself is burdened with the always present potential of betrayal, of divulging what had once been deemed properly concealed from others, whether these be state secrets, company secrets, family secrets, or personal secrets.

But are the same troubling resonances present when scholars, intellectuals, and researchers go public with their knowledge and opinions? In other words, do academics likewise experience the act of going public as a betrayal of sorts—a violation of disciplinary norms, institutional norms, social norms, or intellectual norms? I believe this is precisely what occurs, even if a collective sense of violation is seldom articulated or recognized. This means that when academics go public, they seek to do so in ways that lend legitimacy to the act of going public itself. Apart from whatever issues or controversies that academics may wish to engage, and that serve as a motivation for going public, the act itself, at least for academics, is concomitantly a search for the forms by which going public may be legitimized.

I think it fairly obvious that academics typically go public in one of three ways. They gain entry as public intellectuals, those whose role is to think critically (and comment generally) about the public at large;

or they assume the mantle (and the responsibility) of experts and con-sultants, those whose duties include advising decision makers about the most informed course of action to take on particular issues; or they define their public work in terms of socially committed activism, usu-ally occurring within their local communities but sometimes in larger regional, state, and national contexts as well. The borderlines between and among these domains are sometimes crossed, and the boundar-ies that mark them off from one another are thus quite permeable. Nonetheless, each serves as a distinct strategy for those academics who desire to go public in ways that go beyond what is offered by our dis-ciplinary journals and conferences; our institutional policies and our (eternally recurring) strategic plans; our consortiums, societies, and associations. And while it is true that each of these approaches offers an entryway into a larger public (or realm of multiple publics), each also comes with its own anxieties and concerns in doing so.

Of course, I do not intend to suggest a wholesale rejection of any or all of these models, but I do think we are in urgent need of another. Yes, public intellectuals still matter, but I am inclined to agree with Michael Bérubé (2002) that our public intellectuals have, in large degree, out-lived their heyday.[12] While I think the functions they enact still matter, the idea of the public intellectual as a cultural figure seems far less com-pelling than it once did. And while I continue to think that specialist knowledge has great power to influence important policy and legisla-tive issues, I also believe that expertise is in critical need of redefinition. As Michael Warner reminds us, "expert knowledge is in an important way non-public; its authority is external to the discussion." That is, "it can be challenged only by other experts, not within the discourse itself" (Warner 2005, 145). I am not sure this is an entirely accurate descrip-tion, however, since in our moment, expert knowledge is routinely questioned, disputed, misrepresented, ignored, and, in some instances, mocked.[13] The sort of experts we need are those who understand that knowledge is always implicated in values and interests, and that if expert knowledge is to influence public culture, it must not disparage rhetori-cal facility but embrace it. In other words, rhetorical facility must be a constituent aspect of what any redefinition of the term *expert* means, or ought to mean, in our moment.[14]

But what, then, of activist scholars? Is such work not a legitimate entry point, a proper avenue for colleagues who wish to go public—not as public intellectuals or experts but rather as activists intent on mak-ing their communities more democratic places to live? Yes, of course.

Composition studies has a flourishing history of activism, and a short catalog of our efforts would have to include the literacy and advocacy work of Linda Flower (2008) and Elenore Long (2008), along with Wayne Peck, Lorraine Higgins, and others at the Community Literacy Center in Pittsburgh; the literacy and advocacy work conducted by Paula Mathieu (2005) with homeless populations in Chicago and Boston; the literacy and advocacy work of Beth Daniell (2003) with Al-Anon women in a mountain community; the literacy and advocacy work of Ellen Cushman and Erik Green (2010), especially in the preservation of the Cherokee language; the literacy and advocacy work of David Jolliffe (2010) in rural Arkansas, and the literacy and advocacy work of Kim Donehower, Charlotte Hogg, and Eileen Schell (2007) in rural Appalachia—all of these projects exemplify, but do not exhaust, what is most likely *the* typical mode of civic engagement for compositionists who go public with their work.

What is clear, though, is that scholars who choose to "go public" through their activism will likely run a gauntlet of disparagements and criticisms. In a sense, this is rather paradoxical. Compared to the public intellectual and the expert, the activist scholar is the least conspicuous figure of the three, someone who needs no advance recognition or public acclaim and, in fact, may prefer that her work be done anonymously. Yet the activist scholar is also the one figure most vulnerable to the harsh denunciations of others—administrators and colleagues, fellow activists and community partners, and, in some cases as well, their students. From some peers and fellow faculty, the activist scholar will likely encounter a point of view best captured in the title of a recent work by Stanley Fish (2008)—*Save the World on Your Own Time*—a title whose paternal-managerial tones are unmistakably clear. Disapproving tones are one thing, of course, but implicit threats are another. One activist scholar, Dana L. Cloud, was warned by her dean that her protest activities, "made the College controversial among potential donors and contributors," and that "having tenure was not license to say and do anything political in public" (Cloud 2011, 19). Some may even experience a high price to pay among one's fellow activists, not to mention criticism from those on whose behalf social action is undertaken. As with public intellectuals and experts, but perhaps even more so, the activist scholar "goes public" in especially risky ways—ways certain to offend others, ways certain to be read as transgressive—though, to be sure, the specific transgression in question may vary widely depending on who's making that judgment.

As I hope the forgoing discussion makes clear, I think we have good reason to inquire into alternate forms by which academics, intellectuals, and scholars may contribute to the public life of our democracy. One scholar has expressed this desire rather succinctly. Frustrated by the requirement to perform dual roles that sometimes seem to have little to do with one another, this academic concedes, "I am still left with a search for an alternative model, one that navigates between the opposed perils of academic elitism and political disengagement" (Blomley 1994, 385). I, too, am in search of such a model, and in the next section, I will offer a somewhat unorthodox possibility.

THREE DISCIPLINARY COUNTERPUBLICS

As I have attempted to demonstrate in the first two chapters, there are a number of subtle and nuanced meanings associated with the concept of a counterpublic. Nonetheless, the basic idea is not especially difficult to understand, and this is due in large part to the availability of so many concrete illustrations from which to choose—feminist subaltern, riot grrrl, and third-wave counterpublics; hip-hop counterpublics; anarchist counterpublics; transgendered counterpublics; queer counterpublics; scenester counterpublics; hipster counterpublics; and, as I elaborated in part 1, zine counterpublics. All of these examples, and too many others to mention, help illuminate our understanding of counterpublics and thereby help render it an intuitively approachable idea.

But what if the idea of counterpublics (and by implication, counterpublicity) is applied to the academic disciplines? As I have just observed, many in the academy do not believe scholarly disciplines should concern themselves with public matters at all, that the public sphere is not our proper domain. It seems reasonable to assume that these same people would object to the notion of a disciplinary counterpublic, and vehemently so. But even among those colleagues who have found ways to engage in public discourses—as public intellectuals, experts, and activists—even among this coterie, I anticipate that the notion of a disciplinary counterpublic will not be warmly received. Why? The answer to that question is doubtless a rather complicated one, but suffice it to say that even among academics who have fashioned their own forms of public participation, the idea of disciplinarity remains generally unassailable and sacrosanct. Positioning archaeology or microbiology or nineteenth-century American literature alongside punk, anarchist, or hipster counterpublics is still a fairly provocative thing to do. To suggest some manner of conceptual affinity between, say, science and technology studies and grrrl culture counterpublics will be, for many, something of a travesty.

And yet, in what follows, I will argue that there may be unrealized benefits in thinking about disciplines in this manner. Therefore, I want to make the case for the idea of disciplinary counterpublics and suggest that such formations might offer an alternative way of public engagement for academics, scholars, intellectuals, and teachers—those who locate their work within the "groves of academe" but who desire that their contributions not remain there. To assist me in making this case, and to enlist the support of others who are thinking along the same lines, I will examine three textual cases from three separate disciplinary literatures. The author of each reflects upon how his or her specialties might be understood, in whole or in part, as disciplinary counterpublics. After reviewing each, I will conclude with what I believe generally may be said about the characteristic features of disciplinary counterpublics.

Architecture

It hardly needs to be pointed out that some academic disciplines have more of an explicitly public orientation than others. Public administration, by virtue of the object of its inquiries, is a more public discipline than, say, medieval history. Along the same line, it seems reasonable to assert that sociology is a more public discipline than, say, analytic philosophy. I hazard these claims with a necessary qualification in mind: I am not saying that specialties such as medieval history or analytic philosophy have no public implications or resonances. I am only saying what I think is obvious—namely, that some disciplines have a decidedly more public orientation than others. To add yet another qualification, I would hasten to say that this does not mean that more public disciplines necessarily have any interest in counterpublics, or in conceiving of themselves as counterpublics, or in fostering counterpublic discourse. But some do.

One such discipline is architecture (or architectural design), and one scholar who reveals the counterpublic discourses at play and circulating within this discipline is Shannon Mattern (2011). In her recently published article, "Click/Scan/Fold: The New Materiality of Architectural Discourse and Its Counter-Publics," Mattern examines three recent architectural exhibitions and how each grapples with the question of materiality in architectural discourses, especially in the contexts of new media and the potential that such media might have to transform architecture's current self-understanding.

She begins by reporting on an architectural exhibition held in New York City in the fall of 2006. Organized by Princeton University grad students and faculty, that exhibition came to be known as Clip/ Stamp/Fold: The Radical Architecture of Little Magazines, 196X–197X. Displayed at this event were "reprints of decades-old architectural magazine covers" for publications that, taken as a group, were once described by an early commentator as

> "often scurrilous, irresponsible, and subversive of the existing order"; "badly distributed and marketed (although perhaps intentionally so) and . . . short-lived"; usually "hand-made and . . . ill-kempt in appearance, but with a certain flair. They [attempted] to follow in layout and graphics the same style that they preach in their content." (Brown 1968, 223; quoted in Mattern 2011, 330)

Sponsors of the event invited the founders of these little magazines to discuss their motivations, struggles, and hopes for the publications they imagined and eventually brought to life. Many of these "once . . . restive" figures were now established lions in their field and were thus able to "draw standing-room-only crowds" to Clip/Stamp/Fold. For Mattern, the true significance of this event was that it drew attention to "experimental and subversive forms of architectural publication" and thereby inspired other exhibitions of a similar kind (Mattern 2011, 330). Because Clip/Stamp/Fold had already received abundant critical comment, Mattern informs us, she prefers instead to turn her full attention to two subsequent exhibitions, A Few Zines and Postopolis!.

Nearly three years after Clip/Stamp/Fold opened in New York City, another exhibit appeared in Manhattan, this one sponsored by Columbia University's Studio-X. A Few Zines: Dispatches from the Edge of Architectural Production opened in January of 2009, and like its more celebrated predecessor, it sought to draw notice to unofficial forms of publication that once flourished, and still circulate, within the arena of traditional architectural discourse (even though the heyday of architectural zines is generally thought to have occurred in the 1990s). In any case, a number of the more prominent architectural zines—*Monorail, Infiltration, loud paper*—were featured on display, and the makers (editors?) of these little publications engaged each other, as well as exhibit attendees, in panel discussions and informal conversation. What the organizers of this event hoped to accomplish, according to Mattern, can be found in the exhibition's subtitle—namely, its invitation to regard zines as a marginal form of *architectural production itself*, a kind of making that "stand[s] in stark contrast to [the] *built* architectural sub-ject, whose production is institutionalized, expensive, and highly overde-termined" (Mattern 2011, 334). But once zines are regarded as a kind of architecture, a host of questions emerge about materiality and, relatedly for Mattern, the counterpublics at play within architectural discourse.

In the previous chapter, I suggested that one virtue of zines is that collectively they have the power to invite consideration of some (not always welcome) questions about the materiality of discourse. Mattern reports that this is exactly what occurred at A Few Zines and that one particular idea attracting a great deal of attention was the possibility that zines themselves embodied a kind of architectural object. Certainly, it is easy to see why such an argument could be made. Zines are not merely written but rather are built or made; they include aesthetic and design features; they aspire to a certain kind of public notice and appreciation; and, just like the most imaginatively conceived architectural structure, they endeavor to promote a specific kind of human contact and are quite conscious of doing so. Obviously, there are limits to how far this metaphor may be extended and not everyone will grant such a meta-phor any legitimacy whatsoever. Zines, nevertheless, place front and cen-ter the question of materiality and discourse, and this is a question that Mattern wishes to pursue.

Drawing upon many of the same sources noted in my first two chap-ters (e.g., Duncombe, Piepmeier, Radway), Mattern makes a case for the larger significance of zine materiality and does so by placing zines in juxtaposition to their supposedly digital counterpart, blogs. In mak-ing such a move, however, what becomes immediately apparent is that stark differences exist between these two discursive forms, and those dif-ferences are not to be located exclusively in the content published in each. A (paper) zine and a (virtual) blog could, of course, publish the exact same text, but that text would obviously not mean the same thing to all readers. And why? There are several ways to account for such dif-ferences, but nearly all center upon the basic fact of zine materiality. A few examples will suffice.

Mattern observes that, among other things, *how* zines are circulated matters—and matters a great deal. She argues that "a zine . . . is defined in part by its being 'outside the distribution apparatus' of mainstream publications"—mainstream here understood to be officially endorsed rather than located marginally within or outside of a disciplinary litera-ture (Mattern 2011, 335). This provides zine makers the opportunity to participate in often surreptitious forms of distribution, from drop-offs at familiar bus stops, concert halls, and music stores to the more devious act of sliding copies of zines "between the pages of mainstream publications on the shelves of *Barnes & Noble*" (336). While the zinester is busy crafting an "underground presence" in this manner, the blogger can do very little to create a defined readership and is considerably limited in ways to keep "his or her site from reaching a worldwide audience indiscriminately" (336). Second, Mattern notes that zines have a unique temporality, distinct rhythms that differ markedly from online publications. Thus, while a number of those in attendance lavished praise on blogs for their "exciting sense of immediacy and urgency," others pointed out that the "always on" quality of blogs resulted in a rather compulsive and jaded sense of "exhaustive immediacy" (335). Zines, in contrast, take time—to make, distribute, "take in." This "taking in," claims Mattern, "requires more than just a quick glance." It demands another kind of reading, a more "reflexive reading practice" than what blogs typically encourage (335).

And finally, according to some panelists at this event, zines offer far more "opportunities for formal experimentation" than do "blogs and other online platforms" (Mattern 2011, 336). This will doubtless come as a surprise to many, but in light of the multiple decisions and possibilities confronting the zine maker (e.g., "paper quality, size, shape, binding, etc." to name just a few), it seems likely that there may be more expressive options available to the zinester than the blogger (336). In an overview of architectural websites, Mattern points out that "many of the notable design sites use major blogging services or software" (336). One result is a surprising uniformity among such sites, a seeming readiness "to adhere to established protocols and the normative structures of software and hosting services" (337). On those limited occasions when architecture sites do, in fact, take advantage of what would seem to be the infinite resources of web design, they tend to become what Tim Abrahams identifies as repositories for "a huge host of visual effluvia, a flotsam and jetsam of jpegs," the accumulation of which often seems to be little more than "an end in itself" (Abrahams 2009; Mattern 2011, 337). Indeed, Mattern asks us to consider this: "Could it be that the graphic and infrastructural *form* of the blog somehow promotes play and irony for its own sake, rather than posing serious challenges to normative modes of production or the aesthetic or political status quo?" (337). In contrast, there is hardly any need to ask of zine design whether it is intended to pose "serious challenges" to the various status quos identified in Mattern's question. That intent is simply assumed.

In light of these criticisms, it might seem that Mattern has reiterated an all-too-familiar and (for many) not very enlightened argument, a simple binary that rejects all things virtual in favor of all things material (at least material as it is conventionally understood). But this is not the case at all, as she makes clear in the third exhibition she discusses, Postopolis!

Occurring between Clip/Stamp/Fold and A Few Zines, another kind of exhibition was held in New York City, this one devoted to blogging (in particular) and Internet discourse (in general). Postopolis!, according to Mattern, was intended to "emulate the round-the-clock production cycle, the immediacy, and urgency of the Internet" (Mattern 2011, 340). Like its forerunner, Clip/Stamp/Fold, Postopolis! featured exhibits that displayed an assortment of hard copy texts—especially blog entries, posts, and websites—as well as panels, guest speakers, multimedia presentations, informal conversations, "and, of course, perpetual live blogging of the event itself." Mattern speculates that Postopolis! might have been "an attempt to atone for the acknowledged shortcomings of blogs and other web publications." In other words, could it be that by "convening an embodied community, and materializing their conversations on the gallery walls," bloggers, too, might come to know the kinds of closeness and familiarity that transform zine makers into zine communities? (340). As another reviewer of this event, Bryan Finoki, observed, the true significance of Postopolis!

> has been in somehow bridging the virtual world of bloggerdom with an actual node in physical space where people could come together out from behind their anonymous virtual identities and just talk, and listen, and smell each other, and raise a glass to some shared idea and space. (Finoki 2007; quoted in Mattern 2011, 340)

Particularly compelling for Mattern is that "old-fashioned materiality . . . reasserts itself here," but it does so in an almost superseded, mediated way (Mattern 2011, 342). In many respects, Postopolis! "was about pushing against the imperatives of the digital," and yet it was simultaneously about "exploiting the opportunities digital media provide for collective authorship, accessibility, and widespread distribution." And Mattern reminds us, "it was digital networks that brought these folks together" to begin with (345).

The "new materiality" that Mattern pursues, then, is something more than nostalgia for traditional forms of architectural publication, something more than an unthinking rejection of all things virtual. It is rather how existing forms of materiality can interanimate one another in such a way so as to inspire further experimentation in material publication—not for its own sake but for larger and more critical purposes, the most important of which is the construction of alternative discursive spaces, counterpublics where "transformative scene making" might occur. For Mattern, it ultimately matters very little whether these new publications turn out to be "hand-sewn or hand-coded, material or virtual, custom designs or mash-ups," or for that matter, any yet to be realized combination of approaches. What matters instead is whether the counterpublics invoked by new publications will encourage a critical interrogation of architecture's position within the larger "encroaching forces of commodification" at any given time (Mattern 2011, 347). And what that means, for Mattern, is that while certain kinds of counterpublics emerge within architectural discourses, they are not obliged to stay there. Their significance, in other words, surpasses the discipline of architecture itself, at least as it might be commonly understood. Thus, while some architectural designers conceive of new fabrications, new structures, new buildings, observes Mattern, others "design discursive forms and publics" (338).

Teacher Education

In the ample literature on counterpublics, it has become routine to credit Rita Felski with the first English usage of the term. As noted in my introduction, the concept itself was originally introduced and discussed (however elusively) by Negt and Kluge (1993) in their *Öffentlichkeit und Erfahrung*, a work not translated from German into English until 1993, some two decades later. However, in *Beyond Feminist Aesthetics: Feminist Literature and Social Change*, Felski (1989) introduces English readers to the term and does so by arguing for a distinctly feminist counterpublic sphere, an idea that is the apparent inspiration for Fraser's later feminist subaltern counterpublics. In any event, Felski cites Negt and Kluge's original German publication, and it can only be assumed that their work is the source of her influential appropriation of the term.

As it turns out, though, Felski seems not to have been the first author to introduce English readers to the term *counterpublic*. Two years prior to the publication of *Beyond Feminist Aesthetics*, Henry Giroux and Peter McLaren (1987b) published an article titled "Teacher Education as a Counterpublic Sphere: Radical Pedagogy as a Form of Cultural Politics," a piece that appeared in the journal *Philosophy and Social Criticism*.[15] It is not exactly clear, however, what Giroux and McLaren mean by their particular use of the term or what the primary source might be for their appropriation. Unlike Felski, they do not reference Negt and Kluge, nor do they define their key term for readers, and so it remains something of a mystery as to how they intend their use of the term *counterpublic* to be understood.[16] That meaning can, at best, be merely surmised from a close reading of their text, which I will try to provide here.

Giroux and McLaren's (1987b) essay is a complex argument for the claim (or claims) announced by its title, and its argumentative complexity originates from the fact that it endeavors to address and synthesize a number of distinct but related concepts. Not only is the idea of a counterpublic broached here, but so are a number of other weighty themes— themes that range from Gramscian hegemony to discourses of everyday life; from Ernesto Laclau and Chantal Mouffe's "radical imaginary" to an emphasis on social processes rather than social reproduction; from the politics of voice to teacher education *as* cultural politics. And as if to increase the many layers of complexity already at play here, Giroux and McLaren identify a number of purposes beyond their announced focus on the possibility of rethinking teacher education programs as counterpublic spheres (Giroux and McLaren 1987b, 52–55). As I said, theirs is a complicated argument, and perhaps the best way to appreciate their project is to understand what the authors are responding to.

For Giroux and McLaren, "teacher education has rarely occupied a critical space, public or political within contemporary culture" (Giroux and McLaren 1987b, 53). Rather, such institutionalized programs have, more often than not, been notably complicit in reproducing the dominant values of the culture at large, and this is because, in part, "educational bureaucracies" have been successful in defining

> teachers as primarily technicians—that is, as pedagogical clerks who are incapable of making important policy or curriculum decisions such as adapting state-mandated programs to the everyday contexts, contexts, and particularities of their own classrooms. The derision and contempt directed by professional bureaucrats toward teachers, who demand and exert the right to link the practical to the conceptual in an effort to gain some control over their work, continues to haunt the discourse of the contemporary educational enterprise. (61)

Although these words were written some twenty-five years ago, they seem to be as trenchant now as they were when they were originally published. The "derision and contempt" directed toward teachers (and the teaching profession) has, if anything, been exacerbated by an increase in state-mandated testing as a result of such comprehensive federal legislation as the No Child Left Behind Act of 2001 (NCLB), legislation that still remains in force today. It should come as no great surprise, then, that in their later work, both Giroux and McLaren have vehemently criticized this program.[17]

To contest this vision of teachers, and ultimately, to contest a vision of schools as little more than "agencies of social reproduction which manufacture docile and obedient workers for the state," the authors propose to "recast teacher education as a political project, as a form of cultural politics that defines student teachers as intellectuals whose function is to establish public spaces" where students can acquire the resources and aptitudes necessary for democratic action, "for the realization of a more just and human world" (Giroux and McLaren 1987b, 53, 61). And how is this to be accomplished? As their title suggests, one way is by rethinking the field of teacher education as a counterpublic sphere. But, then, what does *that* mean? The answer to this question is not precisely clear, but some features of what they intend may be ascertained from the ways in which the term is used.

At various junctures in their argument, Giroux and McLaren point out the limitations of two durable staples of left critical thought (generally) and radical pedagogy (specifically). These two mainstays are *resistance* and *critique,* and while the authors recognize the necessity of each, they also recognize that, together or alone, these concepts are insufficient for what they have in mind. It is possible, after all, to resist *what is* without offering any positive vision of *what might be.* It is also possible to critique, with admirable insight and clarity, the operations of power and domination and yet not put forward an alternate idea of how the world might otherwise be. As a corrective to these limitations, Giroux and McLaren invite readers to consider teacher education programs as counterpublic spheres, locations where possibility is the watchword, spaces where, it should be assumed, teachers and students alike can "seriously engage *with and in* articulations and practices of radical democracy" (Giroux and McLaren 1987b, 54). In this normative aspect, the term *counterpublic* bears a striking resemblance to the term *counter-hegemony,* and the authors take some pains to explain how they see the relationship between the two terms.

A bit surprisingly, the term *counter-hegemony* is more formally defined and elaborated than the term *counterpublic*—a fact that may speak to the close kinship the authors see between the two terms. Initially, counter-hegemony is introduced so that a contrast may be drawn with *resistance,* a term that, in its most basic sense, "often lacks any overt political project" and that often "reflects social practices that are informal, disorganized, apolitical, and atheoretical in nature" (Giroux and McLaren 1987b, 55). Resistance, strictly understood, may thus lack any ambition whatsoever to propose alternative social arrangements. Counter-hegemony, on the other hand, "speaks to the creation of new social relations and public spaces that embody alternative forms of experience and struggle" (56).[18] Indeed, there is a clear intimation here that counter-hegemony works as a kind of fulcrum, a concept that "shifts" the "terrain of critique . . . to the terrain of the counterpublic sphere" (56), as if to suggest that counter-hegemony is both necessary and preliminary to counterpublicity.

However that may be, what seems indisputable is that in their usage of both, Giroux and McLaren perceive these two concepts to be inextricably linked. Does this mean, then, that their use of the term *counterpublic* originates more in Gramscian-inspired scholarship than it does in Habermasian inquiries, even though the authors reference both? After all, and as already noted, Giroux and McLaren did not have at their disposal any of the major statements of counterpublic theory, particularly those articulated by Felski, Fraser, Warner, and others who published after this article. Nor did the authors have any apparent familiarity with the work of Negt and Kluge, since no mention of *Public Sphere and Experience* appears in their text. What seems most likely is that Giroux and McLaren, acquainted with Habermas's *Structural Transformation* and well-versed in materialist scholarship on hegemony and counter-hegemony, offered what might have been, at the time anyway, a term quite possibly of their own invention: the counterpublic sphere. Any self-respecting dialectician, after all, does not need Habermas, Gramsci, Laclau and Mouffe, or Negt and Kluge to imagine and entertain the idea of a *counter*public sphere. Such an idea would already be nested in the concept of a public sphere to begin with. Does it matter, then, the source of the authors' use of the term *counterpublic*?

In one sense, yes, but in another, no. Because Giroux and McLaren provide, at best, scant information about what they mean by counterpublics, some knowledge (perhaps any knowledge) of sources might help readers clarify how Giroux and McLaren imagine teacher education as a counterpublic sphere. On the other hand, a cursory look at the history of this term, as well as its intellectual migrations, will readily confirm that it is resists easy definition and that the term is, in fact, endlessly appropriated and revised, sometimes contested, occasionally extended and repurposed. It is usually accompanied by more than its fair share of uncertainties, and in this respect, Giroux and McLaren merely fall in line, retroactively, with much of the scholarship on counterpublics to

follow in their wake. What seems likely is that the miscellaneous ambi-
guities that attend counterpublic inquiry cannot be considered apart
from its richness and flexibility as a theoretical construct.

Giroux and McLaren, like many who come after them, make good
use of the elusiveness of the concept itself, and this can be discerned
not only in their seeming reluctance to define their key term for readers, or to identify its sources, but also in the ways that counterpublic
gets subtly redeployed in the course of their argument. As the title
suggests, the authors are most interested in asking readers to consider teacher education institutions as counterpublic spheres. Before
long, however, it appears that counterpublic spheres may also emerge
within a new locus, as the authors implore "radical educators" to
become active in "the construction of new, *counterpublic spheres within
school sites*" (Giroux and McLaren 1987b, 53; emphasis added). Further
along, readers are invited to consider the possibility that not only is
teacher education a counterpublic sphere in itself but that it is, at the
same time, also "part of an extended counterpublic sphere that might
work in some coordinated fashion to educate intellectuals . . . in the
broad struggle for democracy and social justice" (55). This point is
later reprised when the authors argue that "counterpublic spheres
cannot be created solely within teacher training institutions or school
classrooms but must eventually merge with other communities of resistance," presumably other allied counterpublics (67). In the course of
their discussion, the following sites, then, have all been named as possible counterpublic spheres: teacher education programs, teacher education institutions, schools, sites within schools, school classrooms, and
unspecified other counterpublics with which educational counterpublics might establish solidarity.

I do not mean to imply that this apparent slippage of terms somehow
discredits Giroux and McLaren's argument. One obvious way to answer
that criticism would merely be to point out that while teacher education
is the author's central example of a counterpublic sphere, such programs cannot be severed from other educational counterpublics and
indeed bear a material and determinative relation to them. That said,
the seeming ease with which counterpublics beget counterpublics may
eventually invite us to wonder whether the way we conventionally speak
of counterpublics—as entities, formations, or even locations—is an adequate one. I will return to this problem in my closing, but for now I will
turn my attention to the last of three disciplinary counterpublics.

Science and Technology Studies

Emerging in the 1970s, largely out of earlier interdisciplinary scholarship and inquiry, science and technology studies (STS) has, arguably, made its own disciplinary status; its official legitimacy is conferred by such predictable features as its own conferences, journals, professional societies, grant sources, academic luminaries, and, perhaps most important of all, institutional sponsorship. An increasing number of major research universities offer graduate programs in STS, among them Harvard University; Rensselaer Polytechnic Institute; Cornell University; Brown University; MIT; the University of Wisconsin; the University of California, Davis; Virginia Tech; and many others. Clearly, science and technology studies has arrived. But where did it come from? What were its origins?

While its history is somewhat complicated, most observers acknowledge the work of Thomas Kuhn as foundational to the development of STS, along with the earlier work of Ludwik Fleck. Donald A. MacKenzie and Judy Wajcman, Steve Fuller, and Carl May have all made contributions, and Bruno Latour has been a major theoretical influence in the field. While numerous others have made important contributions, these thinkers share a predisposition to consider science and technology as legitimate objects of philosophical inquiry and, ultimately, as phenomena embedded in social and cultural practices that neither science nor technology can elude or transcend. The implications of this approach are rather wide-ranging, but what should be obvious is that science and technology, once understood this way, have public significances that have not always been acknowledged or realized.

David Hess is one of the prominent figures in science and technology studies and the author of an early introduction to the field (Hess 1997). More recently, he has authored the essay I wish to discuss here: "To Tell the Truth: On Scientific Counterpublics."[19] This essay was originally published in the journal *Public Understanding of Science* and concerns itself not with the question of whether STS is a disciplinary counterpublic but rather whether such entities as scientific counterpublics actually exist, and if so, whether they ought to be the objects of inquiry by scholars working in science and technology studies. Hess's answer to both questions would be a resounding yes.

Hess begins by noting that insofar as science and technology are concerned, the "public" is generally thought of in two ways—first, as a mostly haphazard assortment of individuals who hold opinions about science and technology, or both; and second, as individuals whose collective understanding of science is usually characterized as "lay knowledge," knowledge lacking in any specialized expertise. These two assumptions about the public, taken together, constitute what is often referred to as the "deficit model" of the public, a definition that is widely endorsed in the literature and one that Hess seeks to challenge—not so much by launching a frontal assault on this model himself but by indirectly offering two alternative versions of what a scientific public might be: *counterpublics* and *official publics*.[20] The former contest the reigning orthodoxies of scientific knowledge and the latter promote those same orthodoxies. Drawing especially upon the work of Pierre Bourdieu, Hess further points out that counterpublics and official publics both serve as examples of "mobilized public opinion." Although it is easier to think of counterpublics this way, official publics, too, are mobilized publics, albeit of a different kind. Official publics, in other words, are mobilized publics "constructed by political, economic, and, in some cases, intellectual and civil society elites" (Hess 2011, 629). Their very ubiquity, their established dominance, may be one reason why official publics are typically not perceived to be mobilized at all.

Before arguing the case for scientific counterpublics, Hess must challenge and extend our common understandings of what makes a counterpublic. He therefore finds it necessary to revise the models offered by Fraser and Warner and to do so by advancing three "main shifts of focus" (Hess 2011, 629).

The first of these is *not* to limit counterpublics to social categories defined exclusively by "race, class, gender, or sexuality." Instead, Hess announces, "I will assume counterpublics can emerge in any social field: civil society, the polity, and the economy" (Hess 2011, 629). Second, he desires to shift attention away from an overweening concern with texts and discourse to the larger panorama of organizational and associative networks that "have the capacity to generate both interactional and contributory expertise" (630). Third, Hess wants to embrace the personal as a constituent feature of a new understanding of expertise, so that "objectivity [need] not depend on . . . a self-effacing *moi commune*" (630). Having enunciated these stipulations, Hess then provides us with a definition:

> Regardless of institutional location, a scientific counterpublic is formed when scientists who are located in subordinate positions in their respective research fields generate publicity by addressing a broader public audience

about the public-interest implications of agenda conflicts in their respective research fields. (630)

One inference that may be drawn here is that scientific counterpublics operate not only *within* a given scientific discipline (or, as one might expect, on its margins), but also, and simultaneously, *external to* that given field's "analytical terrain" (Hess 2011, 630). A scientific counterpublic, then, seems to have something of a rather unsettled, wavering location, situated inside and outside of its home discipline all at once. Because scientific counterpublics are typically concerned with matters of "broad public interest," they form "cross-field linkage[s]" with other "subordinate networks" in other fields, as well as civil society itself (630).

Realizing how easily scientific counterpublics might be dismissed as nothing more than the predictable "grumbling of researchers whose work has not survived the empirical scrutiny of their peers," Hess hastens to point out that the genesis of scientific counterpublics is not traceable to "bad science" or "failed science." For this reason, STS researchers who conduct inquiries into scientific counterpublics usually avoid "pronouncing a verdict on a technical controversy," even though they often draw attention to areas of "undone science," and more generally, propose ways that the views of subordinate networks can be taken into account (Hess 2011, 631–32). Similarly—the crucial axis here—the best determinant of where and how a scientific counterpublic is likely to emerge is not to be found in "superior or inferior knowledge" but rather in autonomy (632). According to Hess, "scientific counterpublics emerge with the greatest frequency in the low-autonomy fields, such as the social sciences and medicine"—those fields, in other words, that are highly dependent on external, public funding, as opposed to (to borrow his example) mathematics (632).

Having offered a provisional definition for scientific counterpublics, as well as several qualifications to that definition, Hess then proceeds to discuss his two examples: bacterial theories of cancer and "import substitution" as a strategy for local economic growth. I will review the first of these to illustrate his argument.[21]

At the turn of the twentieth century, encouraged by impressive progress in bacteriological science, many biologists entertained the hypothesis that the etiology of human cancers could be traced to bacterial infection. This hypothesis held sway for some time, but by the 1920s, it had been largely discredited in favor of what eventually became the orthodox view of cancer as "a diffuse, multicausal" condition with origins that could be attributed to a host of factors, including (but not limited to) "inheritance, genetic damage, and viral infection" (Hess 2011, 632). Needless to say, this rather layered explanation has been rendered even more complex in recent years by the inclusion of environmental factors, lifestyle choices, etc. That noted, some researchers have challenged the prevailing consensus on cancer's etiology and returned to bacteriological theories of cancer's origins. Foremost among such researchers is Virginia Livingston, who, beginning in the 1950s, "led a network of researchers" committed to testing this hypothesis, the end result of which was her announcement "that she had isolated a bacterial agent for cancer" (632). The larger scientific community, however, remained unconvinced and generally has not taken her work seriously. But should they have?

For some, to even ask that question is sheer impertinence. But Hess reminds us that not too long ago, established opinion on the etiology of gastric ulcers was dramatically reversed. Where it once was thought that stress was the primary cause of ulcers, two unknown researchers from Australia successfully convinced fellow researchers that a bacteriological cause exists for this condition. Like Livingston, these two researchers promoted a "subordinate position" in their specialty, one that "was controversial among bacteriologists and medical researchers" (Hess 2011, 632). But unlike Livingston, they eventually persuaded other researchers of the validity of their hypothesis, an occasion that resulted in marked changes for the treatment of gastric ulcers. Why were these two researchers successful and Livingston was not? First, the Australian researchers were able to find a "single, stable bacterial agent" to which the cause of ulcers could be attributed, whereas Livingston's research had posited the likelihood of bacterial variation and change (632–33). And second, the Australian researchers' findings were highly compatible with the dominant medical view of ulcers and could thus be easily adapted to what was already known. As Hess points out, it was settled opinion that "psychosocial stressors" rendered the immune system susceptible to "chronic infections" (632). Explanations that attributed gastric ulcers to stress or bacteria could therefore be linked. Such linkages mitigated any real or perceived threat to the established paradigm.

On the other hand, the Livingston research group did not fare so well. Already situated in "lower-status positions in the academy," their research appeared, as one might predict, in "lower-status journals that tended to minimize the potential for wider awareness" (Hess 2011, 632). Occupying a subordinate position within her own research community and "frustrated by the lack of funding and recognition for her approach to cancer etiology and treatment, Livingston's network became part of a broader scientific counterpublic . . . [one] that emerged in the field to protest the focus of cancer treatment of chemotherapy, surgery, and radiation therapy" (633). Was this scientific counterpublic, by any measure, successful? Hess points out that Livingston's challenge peaked in the 1980s and notes that her influence waned only "with the growth of 'integrative' cancer care in the 1990s" and the subsequent appearance of the National Center for Complementary and Alternative Medicine (633). So it appears that, yes, Livingston bequeathed a legacy of needed changes that reflected her scientific commitments. But could she have done so had she not "gone public" with her concerns, had she not entirely circumvented her research community in order to craft alliances with other marginalized groups and thereby form a scientific counterpublic intent on publicizing an alternative viewpoint to a broader audience?

Obviously, Livingston was unable to persuade the larger scientific community that human cancers possess a bacteriological etiology.[22] But she and her colleagues were successful in "articulating an alternative view of the public interest" and suggesting that "area[s] of undone science" remained to be investigated, areas that could possibly prove to be of "great social benefit" were such areas not blocked by powerful "organizational interests" that had a clear stake in protecting orthodox approaches to cancer research, diagnosis, and treatment. For Hess, then, the truth told by bacteriological etiology advocates does not have to be "correct," at least not in a purely scientific sense. Theirs is "a different, more sociologically nuanced kind of truth," one that asks if the public interest might be better served "by devoting more resources" to competing hypotheses, alternative technologies, to those areas of "undone science" that could eventually prove to be beneficial (Hess 2011, 634).

What ought to be clear is that scientific counterpublics typically emerge out of correctly apprehended inequities in power, regardless of whether such power originates in governmental, institutional, or disciplinary realms—or, as is usually the case, in the orchestration of all three. Hess is scrupulously attentive to the workings (subtle and overt) of such power and asks if the public interest is best served when *official* (that is to say, dominant) scientific publics can easily silence, or otherwise marginalize, any disputing perspectives, hypotheses, theories, or research. Hess obviously thinks not, and he proposes two ways that contending scientific opinions can receive a fair hearing and be taken more seriously that they are.

First, Hess argues that one policy model by which to "bring more attention to the work of scientific counterpublics" would be to designate some measure of "public research funding to a competitive funding process that would seek to identify areas of undone science." As indicated above, undone science is marked by an interest in research questions that might potentially have "broad public interest but receive systematic inattention" within particular scientific fields (Hess 2011, 638). To allocate some quota of public monies to undone science, then, could result in scientific advances that, in turn, could prove felicitous to the public health. Hess goes on to imagine and articulate the details of how such a program might work and what criteria might apply for those who wish to receive such funding, after which he offers a second proposal.

Having earlier observed that while certain kinds of scientific conferences purposefully include laypeople, Hess notes that, typically, the usual definition of *laypeople* does not include activists and advocates or members of scientific counterpublics. Thus, Hess concludes, "by separating the lay opinion public from mobilized counterpublics, the lay opinion public is more easily aligned with official publics" (Hess 2011, 638). What results is that lay public opinion gets enlisted in warranting the existing consensus on any given scientific question. As a counter to this orchestrated state of affairs, Hess proposes that we ought to hold "dissensus" conferences, meetings that steer "attention to and analyze the perspectives of a scientific counterpublic" (639). Not only would such meetings draw notice to undone science, as well as unorthodox scientific opinion, they would also serve to thematize "power-knowledge issues in a given scientific field" (639). The great danger for such conferences, according to Hess, is that they could be vulnerable to co-option, or what he calls "bureaucratic capture," by established interests and official science (639).

Have either of these proposals been adopted or, for that matter, seriously considered? Not to my knowledge, but it may be too early to tell, since Hess's article is quite recent. For my purposes, more important is the recognition that among those scientific fields with inquiries that have a public interest at stake, contending views sometimes emerge that likewise have, or could have, public implications. It follows, then, that if a scientific field has a public orientation to begin with, disputed opinion within that field will likely have a public orientation too. It should come as no great surprise that scientific counterpublics could exist and indeed, for Hess, do exist.

WHAT, THEN, IS A DISCIPLINARY COUNTERPUBLIC?

I have just discussed three illustrations of what I call disciplinary counterpublics. While there are significant differences between and among them, my purpose in reviewing these illustrations is to determine what may be said in general about disciplinary counterpublics. What might we infer from the examples I provide here? What are the defining characteristics, if any, of certain academic formations that emerge to contest official discourses, but in unofficial and often contentious ways? What, after all, is a disciplinary counterpublic?[23]

First, let me begin by observing that what these three examples reveal is that the idea of disciplinary counterpublics is not as far-fetched or counterintuitive (I have earlier used the term *outrageous*) as it may seem. What these three illustrations confirm, I believe, is the possibility to think of academic disciplines as having some bearing upon, identity with, or participation in counterpublic discourses. If this premise is granted, then a number of questions immediately arise: What, for example, does a disciplinary counterpublic look like? What does it do? What exactly is it in opposition to? How long does it endure? Who are its members? Why is one needed in the first place? Does it matter, and if so, for whom? My hope, of course, is that the disciplines examined here— architecture, teacher education, and science and technology studies— provide some partial answers to these large questions as well as some insights into an admittedly elusive concept to grasp.

The question I wish to address in closing, however, centers upon the kinds of disciplinary counterpublics available and the various expressions they may assume. What I have discerned from my discussion above is that disciplinary counterpublics generally take one of three forms, and in the remainder of this chapter, I will elaborate on each in hope of further clarifying the nature of disciplinary counterpublics.

Internal Disciplinary Counterpublics

Judging by my examination of architectural and scientific counterpublics, I am aware that many, if not most, counterpublics emerge from *within* the discipline itself, from internal disputes about whose texts matter, whose research dominates, whose projects receive funding, whose points of view are deemed representative of the disciplinary community at large, and so on. But is this not a rather commonplace occurrence in academic disciplines? Is it not the case that *any* scholar working within *any* established academic discipline will likely be (and will need to be) thoroughly familiar with her field's internecine disputes and assorted points of contention? Yes, of course. But some disciplinary conflicts have a more public face than others and, therefore, take on a different resonance entirely.

Consider the disciplinary counterpublics discussed here. All of these counterpublics emerge out of disciplines that have an already established public orientation; or that conduct scholarly inquiries in the name of public interest; or that sometimes possess a public visibility and import that many other disciplines simply do not enjoy. In other words, while the fields out of which disciplinary counterpublics emerge may have already "gone public," those fields will have done so in all of the approved of ways, using one (or more) of the permissible routes I mapped out earlier. However, when internal disputes emerge within specialties that already have a public bearing, it is reasonable to assume that such disputes may have public implications as well (though this will not always be the case). Still, it is unlikely that when disciplinary counterpublics go public, they do so in the same way official publics do. Disciplinary counterpublics, in other words, usually do not have available to them the same structures of legitimacy as do those larger disciplinary publics from which they derive. If they wish to have any public influence at all, they are forced to establish alliances with other counterpublics outside the existing boundaries of their discipline proper, even as they articulate disagreements within that same discipline. I think it safe to say that disciplinary counterpublics are somewhat Janus-faced, of necessity turned toward (at least) two audiences at once: those situated within the field and those situated away from it. Even though they may originate within a particular discipline, they commonly form alliances outside of that discipline, and from their medial location, disciplinary counterpublics advocate for their point of view to those most likely to effect the change they desire.

By their willingness to air disciplinary grievances in a public way, make transparent what some might regard as family matters at best, and form alliances with other counterpublics, it is not too hard to see why one characteristic of disciplinary counterpublics would be their apparent tendency to violate norms, to cross lines, to trespass spaces, to break rank—in a word, to *transgress* what others have deemed to be normal and proper behavior. I have earlier argued that any instance of going public is inevitably tinctured in multiple shades of transgression. But where disciplinary counterpublics are concerned, those hues are deepened, saturated in color—vivid, full, dramatic—and unapologetically so.

While officially approved of disciplinary publics typically seek ways to ameliorate and lend further legitimacy to the mere fact of going public, disciplinary counterpublics tend to savor their unofficial status, delight in their outsider perspectives, and freely confess their transgressions, even though they have no need to be forgiven for their wayward ways. To be a disciplinary counterpublic means never having to say you're sorry—at least not for going public with your inquiries and arguments.

Autonomous Disciplinary Counterpublics

In their discussion of teacher education counterpublics, Giroux and McLaren (1987b) posit an equivalence between teacher education and its status as a disciplinary counterpublic. In other words, the authors seem to argue that the discipline itself is (or ought to be) a counterpublic in its own right. Indeed, by virtue of what their subtitle implies, Giroux and McLaren ask us to consider if disciplines themselves, in their entirety, can be regarded as counterpublics. Is what the authors advocate even possible? That is, could teacher education be a counterpublic and nothing other than that? And if such might be true of teacher education, what about, say, microbiology? Or media studies? Or anthropology? Or English? Is it even possible to think of some academic disciplines as not merely provoking counterpublics into existence but rather as counterpublics in and of themselves? As autonomous counterpublics?

It is a question others have considered. In a recent collection, Daniel C. Brouwer entertains the possibility that communication studies might be regarded as a counterpublic in itself. And yet, in his opening paragraph, Brouwer announces that the term *counterpublic* "is insufficient to capture or characterize all of communication," and that the term is better thought of as a "conceptual lens through which to examine certain types of communication structures and practices," or, more exactly, to see them "in a certain way." But even as a conceptual lens, the counterpublic frame, "may be neither valuable nor appropriate" (Brouwer 2005, 195). Having made these qualifications, he then goes on to explain how counterpublic inquiry can enrich the discipline of communication studies "by *expanding our objects of inquiry beyond rational-critical norms of public deliberation*" (198). This is an exceptionally valuable discussion, but, ultimately, Brouwer decides that it is mistaken to think of communication as a counterpublic. Attention is better directed, he argues, toward examining *what counterpublic theory can do for communication studies*.

This is understandable, of course. It is relatively easy to point out the many ways that counterpublic theory can inspire new directions in scholarship, new inquiries, new research possibilities. It is a bit harder to show that certain disciplines, especially those with a public orientation, can occasionally bring into being certain oppositional formations—disciplinary counterpublics—within their own discourses. (Difficult, yes, but not impossible, as should be evident from my discussion of architecture and cancer research.) But it is a different matter altogether to make the claim that a given *discipline is a counterpublic.* Indeed, what could that possibly mean? If a discipline can be understood as a counterpublic, what, then, is a disciplinary counterpublic counter to?

The answer is that such formations can only be in opposition to a public rather than a larger or more encompassing academic discipline within which they are situated. While it is no doubt true that some academic disciplines have as their object of study public debate and deliberation, public policy, public administration, and so on, it is almost impossible to conceive of a discipline founded upon and successfully maintained solely through its oppositional relationship to other publics or the public at large. Counterpublics, as Warner has already informed us, are rather mercurial formations, volatile and precarious at best. It seems improbable that any discipline would endorse a self-definition that embraced concerns about whether that discipline's expiration date was imminent. There may prove to be some critical or normative value in thinking about one's home discipline as a counterpublic, but beyond such conjectures, the actuality of such a thing seems not merely remote but impossible.

Rhetorical Disciplinary Counterpublics

And yet, there remains another way to think about this question. Maybe we have been all wrong in looking upon counterpublics as entities, as actually existing social formations. Some counterpublic theory, in fact, is moving in this direction. Robert Asen has argued that we may be too enthralled with the idea of counterpublic as an "analytic" (or perhaps worse, essential) category. In our theorizing of counterpublics, we may have become too focused on whether an "advocate's call [for publicity] falls inside or outside" this or that counterpublic (Asen 2009, 266). In the process, we may have turned our attention away from more rhetorically interesting questions, such as "how an advocate calls for publicity" or how "individuals and groups construct identities, shape needs and interests, and build forums and networks" (283). Asen wants us to move away from our preoccupation with definitional concerns to more rhetorically founded ones.

Eric Doxtader offers a similar rethinking of counterpublics along rhetorical lines. Much like Asen, Doxtader turns our attention to "the question of *how* oppositional communication works" (Doxtader 2001, 64). In order to answer such a large question, we would do well to cease thinking of *counterpublic* in all our fossilized ways—as a fixed category, an entity, a thing. Instead, Doxtader suggests, let us say, "*counterpublic* is a verb . . . a series or process of speech-actions that (aim to) replace (public) violence with speech and action" (65). Regarded this way, then, Doxtader maintains that our proper object of inquiry ought to be not *counterpublics* but rather *counterpublicity*. For Doxtader, this shift in point of view is momentous, if only because the "rhetorical study of counterpublicity is concerned to plot the . . . turns by which counterpublics identify themselves, challenge the conventions of dominant discourse, and recover the productive contingency of speech and action" (66). The focus turns now toward rhetorical acts rather than defining characteristics.

Or to frame this shift as a request: both Asen and Doxtader ask us to suspend (or productively interrupt) the endless reification of the term *counterpublic*—that is, to think of it (following Doxtader) as a verb rather than a noun.[24] Once we do so, our inquiries will be more rhetorically informed, as well as more rhetorically interesting, at least in the view of these two authors. And once we stop thinking of counterpublics as fixed entities, something else happens too, something that bears upon the argument I make here.

For while it seems improbable that any discipline could actually *be a counterpublic*, it seems very likely that, in certain moments and situations, any discipline could *act as one* and, in fact, may find it necessary or useful to do so. To think this way about disciplinary counterpublics is to place emphasis upon the ways that *some* disciplines on *some* occasions establish a needed presence in the larger public sphere by virtue of their cumulative rhetorical acts and strategies. It is to direct attention to *the counterpublic function* rather than the (less compelling) question of whether any particular discipline is or is not a counterpublic. From this performative angle, any given discipline may, at any given time, function as a counterpublic. But that does not mean that it will always continue to do so, or even for that matter, ever do so.

In this light, it may be illuminating to think about composition studies as a counterpublic—a strategic and rhetorically motivated counterpublic, a liminal counterpublic, as I will explain. While it is no doubt true that occasionally counter formations have emerged *within* composition (say, for example, the "abolitionist" movement that emerged in the 1990s), it can be reasonably argued that composition studies' more vexing disputes are with the larger public, and especially with the matter of how composition studies gets represented in public discourses. Composition need not do away entirely with such familiar roles as public intellectuals, experts, and activists. But by taking a bricolagic point of view, it will look upon these roles as tools, uses, and possibilities rather than fixed identities.

Having established that it is possible (indeed useful) to entertain the idea that scholarly disciplines can function as counterpublics, I wish now turn to an examination of composition as a counterpublic, albeit a counterpublic of a certain kind.

NOTES

1. In the opening pages to his *Publics and Counterpublics*, Michael Warner (2005) recounts the story of the Greek philosopher Diogenes, of whom it is reported that to satisfy his sexual urges often "walked into the central marketplace and masturbated," thereby provoking the disgust of his contemporaries. According to later commentators, however, this behavior was not especially unusual for Diogenes, for it seems that, as a matter of principle, he did "everything in public" (21). Diogenes, Warner tells us, intentionally refused to acknowledge the distinction between public and private and, through his many routine behaviors, lived life as if no such distinction existed. Understood this way, Diogenes was a "performance critic" of sorts, someone who, through his actions, called into question the extent to which conventional morality was based upon what he regarded as an artificial distinction between public and private (Warner 2005, 21). At the risk of obvious understatement, it is not very hard to see how in his particular way of "going public," Diogenes was performing a transgressive act. It is more challenging, though, to discern how every act of going public entails some sense of violation, some transgression. As Warner notes, public and private do not merely constitute the terms of a distinction; they also constitute a hierarchy. One term, that is, usually dominates the other. For Warner, the privileged term in this binary is *public* because, as he reminds us, "being in public" is a privilege in itself, one "that requires filtering or repressing something that is seen as private" (22–23). And yet, to claim that "being in public" is a privilege is not the same thing as claiming that *public* is the privileged term in the public/private binary. This chapter assumes the reverse to be true—that etymologically, historically, and politically (especially in the neoliberal moment we now share), *private* is the dominant term, and any movement away from its dominance will be read as transgressive.

2. I conflate these terms, mindful of the important distinctions between them and of other terms that could be added to my list—investigators, teachers, professors, and so on. While others may be better suited to parse the differences among them, it is enough for my purposes to observe that each of the figures I identify here falls under a general category that might be called "academics who go public." As will be seen in this chapter, I am more interested in the *ways* that academics go public than the various names for those academics who do.

3. The phrase "going public" continues to enjoy wide usage in composition studies, its popularity derived, at least in part, from Peter Mortensen's 1998 article by the same name. More recently, Linda Flower (2010) has used the term in relation to what

happens when learning disabled populations make visible their concerns and their embodied selves. Too, Shirley K. Rose and Irwin Weiser (2010) have edited a recent anthology, the title of which is *Going Public*, that tries to understand what happens when writing programs engage public discourses.

4.   The juxtaposition is not my own. Ralph Cintron wonders if these two phenomena might not be somehow analogous by virtue of what they signify to others in their common embrace of fixities, or essential identities, or in the ways they "both signal reductions of abundance" (Cintron 2003, 35).

5.   Lauren Berlant elaborates on this notion in *The Queen of America Goes to Washington City*. Along with other cultural observers (see Robbins, for example), Berlant doubts whether any such thing as a public sphere actually exists. In stark contrast to an influential and vital public sphere, say, the kind imagined by Habermas, what we have in its place is the "intimate public sphere," a highly sentimentalized and clamorously private rendering of democratic life. The model citizen in this substitute public sphere, not surprisingly, turns out to be the fetus, the infant, the toddler, the child, on whose behalf all deliberation must serve, at least emblematically. For Berlant, what has occurred is nothing less than "the privatization of U.S. citizenship," transforming what ought to be a democratic public sphere into one largely defined by a nostalgia for personal and familial values and concerns. It is, in short, a victory for conservative and reactionary ideologies (Berlant 1997, 3)

6.   Because of the overlooked threat such spaces might pose to First Amendment rights to freedom of speech and assembly, some efforts are underway (in both New York City and Great Britain) to map such spaces in order to bring them to the attention of the general public. See, for example, Keller and Almanzar (2011) as well as Vasagar (2012). Privately owned public spaces are but one material example of how enduring the private/public binary is, but also the difficulty in establishing and maintaining clear-cut boundaries between the two. More worrisome, though, for some observers, is the colonizing of public spaces by private interests. For a discussion of how such social mechanisms work, see, in general, the work of David Harvey (2005), but for historical examples, see, in particular, his essay "The Political Economy of Public Space."

7.   Political journalist Glenn Greenwald (2011), perhaps more than anyone else, has questioned what he perceives to be the hypocrisy and blatant lack of commitment of our press to First Amendment freedoms. On this matter, see his column "The Secrecy Loving Mind of the American Journalist."

8.   It should come as no great surprise that the wisdom literatures of many cultures recommend discretion in what private matters one should or should not reveal to others. A famous Spanish proverb, for example, observes, "If you keep your mouth shut, the flies won't get in"; and an African proverb warns not to "take another mouthful before you have swallowed what is in your mouth." The idea that there might be something inviolate about the intimate and familial, or that candor implies danger, vulnerability—these are hardly recent commonplaces.

9.   For the same sentiment expressed through a different musical genre, I refer the reader to the Hank Williams tune "Mind Your Own Business," one verse of which includes the following stanza: "If I want to honky tonk around 'til two or three/Now, brother that's my headache, don't you worry 'bout me/Just mind your own business."

10. While the Russian psychologist Lev Vygotsky (1986) did not put the matter in terms of public and private but rather in terms of social and individual, this insight nonetheless forms the basis of his crucial disagreement with Jean Piaget. Where the latter argued that we are originally individual beings and that our primary developmental task was therefore one of socialization, Vygotsky argued the reverse: we are originally social beings and our developmental task is therefore one of individual differentiation. But while the analogy might be useful to consider, and while there may be overlaps

between these paired terms, it seems obvious that there are limits to the extent to which the "social" can be equated with the "public," or correspondingly, the "individual" with the "private," though the latter pair has more etymological affinities than the former. See Vygotsky, *Thought and Language*, especially chapter 2.

11. I am compelled to point out, though, that while the terms *private* and *privilege* seem to have the same etymological root, and while it may, therefore, seem justified to conflate the two, it is more accurate to say that *privilege* is a term that is both public and private in its origins and meanings, owing to the fact that it is a hybrid of *privus* (L.) for individual and *legis* (L.) for law (*OED*, 2nd ed.). It is generally described as an act that exempts an individual (or individuals) from an existing law. Privilege, therefore, is something that originates in a public institution (the law) and yet at the same time is something that the law announces it will no longer require for this or that person. To go public, then, with matters that have already been extended a private exemption, is to violate not a law but an arrangement, a pact. My use of privilege here is meant to refer to those features of lived life that have seldom been of any special interest to the public or its legal institutions. This privilege, then, is of a different kind—the privilege of living an undisclosed life that "ain't nobody's business" but one's own.

12. Bérubé comes close to delivering what could only be interpreted as a eulogy for the public intellectual, since that figure has transformed into what he calls the *publicity intellectual*. According to Bérubé, "the figure of the publicity intellectual presents a cultural impasse, and the impasse is not going to be finessed by better public relations—since the marketing (and self-marketing) of intellectuals as PR agents is precisely what killed the public intellectual in the first place" (Bérubé 2002, 3). Whether we are witnessing an impasse or a burial, what seems indisputably clear is that the public intellectual, as a cultural player, appears headed for the exits, departing rather noticeably from the public stage as a character that merits special attention or credence.

13. One way that expertise is manufactured, commodified, and strategically warehoused by the entire academic enterprise is to guarantee that it never becomes *too public*, in other words, to assure that its public availability is controlled by shareholders—namely, institutions, disciplines, publishers, libraries, and so on. While many commend the way digital technologies have made knowledge and research broadly accessible to scholars across the globe, the same cannot be said of the general public's ability to access and consult such work. In the words of one blogger, what has resulted is nothing less than a kind of "intellectual apartheid." How, in other words, can an academically disenfranchised citizen afford the cost of that $30 article, or worse, that $503 annual subscription to the journal *Subjectivity*? In the knowledge economy, the author claims, "it works like this: If you wish to enjoy access to the most authoritative information—knowledge vetted by experts—then you must pay for the privilege. Even research which has been funded for 'the public good' by governments or granting institutions is mostly enclosed behind commercial barriers that keep it from those it could benefit most" (Burton 2009). It doesn't have to be this way, the author claims, and offers ideas as to how experts can make their work more publicly available through open access publishing, transfer of copyright ownership, etc. I only wish to point out that the vaunted status of expertise, seemingly at least, requires that it *not be too public*. Perhaps there is some warrant for the skepticism expressed by the public when the distribution of expert opinion seems to be closely managed and inconsistently accessible. On these questions, see Burton (2009).

14. I refer readers to the work of Daniel Sarewitz (2004) and other scholars who make arguments similar to this one. For just a very small sampling of such work, see Goodwin (2009), Oreskes (2004), Hess (1997, 2011), Pielke (2007), Wynne (2006),

and Jasanoff (2012). Some of this work emerges from communication scholars who conduct inquiries into the rhetoric of science, but the larger share derives from scholarship in science and technology studies (STS), discussed in this chapter.

15. All of my references are to the article just mentioned, but I should point out that in the same year, another version of this piece was published as a chapter in an anthology edited by Thomas S. Popkewitz (1987). The title of that version was slightly different— "Teacher Education as a Counterpublic Sphere: Notes Toward a Redefinition"—but the text is largely the same. I have included both versions in my bibliography, but I only cite the journal article.

16. I attempted to contact both Giroux and McLaren for clarification regarding their sources. No response was forthcoming.

17. Giroux's most eloquent criticism of NCLB (in my opinion) can be heard in an online interview available on YouTube titled "Culture, Politics & Pedagogy: A Conversation with Henry Giroux" (Giroux 2006). See also, Peter McLaren and Ramin Farahmandpur's (2006) "The Pedagogy of Oppression: A Brief Look at 'NCLB,'" which appeared in *The Monthly Review* during the same year.

18. A more recent iteration of this point comes from neo-Gramscian theorist Nicola Pratt, who describes counter-hegemony as "a creation of an alternative hegemony on the terrain of civil society in preparation for political change" (Pratt 2004, 332n).

19. Hess (1997) is the author of one of the early introductions to the field, *Science Studies: An Advanced Introduction*. Several other introductory textbooks have become available during the previous decade.

20. While Hess does not take this task upon himself, he does review others who have critiqued the notion of a lay public and its utility to STS. On this matter, see especially, Wynne (2006).

21. Hess's other example addresses a scientific counterpublic that has formed around "import substitution" as a viable theory for economic development. As Hess reveals, "most mainstream economists today view import substitution policies . . . as a failure" and advocate instead for policies that encourage the more dominant approach, "trade liberalization and export-oriented growth" (Hess 2011, 635). With its stress on local, strategically contained growth, along with economic "quality of life" issues, import substitution has, for the most part, not prevailed in contemporary economic thought. But like its bacteriological counterpart, it has developed its own distinct research projects, its own advocates, its own organizational links, all of which are designed to provide import substitution with a legitimacy in the public sphere that it does not enjoy in its own discipline. See Hess (2011), 635–37.

22. Is there any possibility that Livingston might yet be proven right? That would be hard to say, but some recent research might give hope to those who side with bacteriological explanations of cancer. Writing in *The New York Times*, Gina Kolata (2011) reports that two genome studies, conducted separately by Dr. Robert A. Holt and Dr. Matthew Meyerson, each discovered certain bacteria to be associated with colon cancers, although both researchers warned that bacterial causation could not be established.

23. As I have mentioned earlier, there seems to be a general dissatisfaction with the term itself, and a quick survey of counterpublic scholarship will reveal a recurrent desire not only to rethink the concept but to rename it as well. The most recent attempt can be seen in Brouwer and Asen's (2010) *Public Modalities: Rhetoric, Culture, Media, and the Shape of Public Life*. In their introduction to this collection, they argue that we need a new conceptual metaphor to guide our public inquiries. They then reveal the shortcomings of our received metaphors—sphere, networks and webs, publicity, screen, culture—noting the value of each but ultimately finding all to be inadequate when compared to the metaphor they propose—namely, modalities. Using this metaphor, Brouwer and Asen wish to recover a kind of missing *techné*, a rhetorically informed

and motivated approach to investigating the processes of public engagement. Of the chapters included in this collection, the one of special interest to this author (for what should, by now, be obvious reasons) is Brouwer's essay "Risibility Politics," an excellent discussion of "camp humor in HIV/AIDS zines" (Brouwer 2010, 219).

24. There is no need to review here the basic features of all counterpublics, as my purpose in this concluding section is to show what is unique about disciplinary counterpublics. That said, the general characteristics of what makes a counterpublic has likely been best captured by Brouwer (2005). In his article "Communication as Counterpublic" (discussed here), Brouwer observes that most counterpublics "share these key features: *oppositionality, constitution of a discursive arena,* and a *dialectic of retreat from and engagement with other publics*" (Brouwer 2010, 197). Each of the three disciplinary counterpublics discussed in this chapter share these features, but emphasizes each one differently.

4

COMPOSITION STUDIES AS A KIND OF COUNTERPUBLIC

Style performs membership.
—Michael Warner, *Publics and Counterpublics*

A few years back, in a review of *The Trouble with Principle*, Terry Eagleton (2000) opens with a scathing (albeit tongue-in-cheek) appraisal of Stanley Fish's liberal credentials. "It is one of the minor symptoms of the mental decline of the United States," writes Eagleton, "that Stanley Fish is thought to be on the Left." This statement is followed by a pronouncement wherein Eagleton unceremoniously dubs Fish "the Donald Trump of American academia, a brash, noisy entrepreneur of the intellect who pushes his ideas in the conceptual marketplace with all the fervor with which others peddle second-hand Hoovers." Eagleton wonders how it happened that Stanley Fish came to be seen, at once, as street fighter and boardroom bully, as revolutionary provocateur and latter-day Churchillian defender of the realm. As Eagleton views things, this apparent balancing act between Little Fish and Big Fish—between "the saber-rattling polemicist" and "the respectable academic"—is rather something of a smokescreen. For what's being juggled here is not a left-wing Stanley Fish versus a right-wing Stanley Fish but rather two renditions of conservative thinking that, in the end, do not differ all that much from one another.

For those of us who recall his lively debates with Dinesh D'Souza, the Stanley Fish sketched by Eagleton could only be a caricature. Fish, after all, was something of a culture hero for many of us, if only because he could ward off (with such enviable dispatch, I might add) what was then the latest front in the conservative assault on the university: political correctness. Never mind, as Eagleton (2000) points out, that Fish does not seem particularly interested in such global issues as "forced migration, revolutionary nationalism, military aggression, the depredations of capital," and so on. Never mind, as Eagleton further observes, that the neopragmatism embraced by Fish seems to countenance, at best, a kind of parochialism, an interest in matters strictly limited to the domestic and, especially, academic realms. No, at the end of the day, such incongruities simply did not matter as much as the fact that we in the academy had, at long last, discovered a compelling spokesperson, a champion who could effectively address right-wing criticisms of the work we do. Fish even seemed able to ease our worries that D'Souza's criticisms might be ones shared by the public at large.

I was reminded of those debates, and of Eagleton's comments, in reading Paul Butler's (2008) "Style and the Public Intellectual: Rethinking Composition and the Public Sphere." Butler opens with his own Fish story, this one ensuing from a 2005 op-ed that Fish wrote for *The New York Times*, "Devoid of Content." In his piece, Fish advances the notion that content has absolutely no place in the composition classroom. What matters—and the only thing that matters to Fish—is form, by which he apparently means grammatical form, especially form defined as syntax. Anything beyond form is pretext and pretense, a "lure and a delusion" that must be gotten rid of if we are to teach students how to write "a clear and coherent sentence" (Fish 2005). And for Fish, learning how to write that sentence is, apparently, the only legitimate reason for composition courses to exist in the first place.

Still, Butler is not so much interested in arguing with Fish about the nature of the composition curriculum. Butler's questions are larger and, I think, ultimately more revealing ones: How is it that Stanley Fish—along with Louis Menand, Heather MacDonald, and others—speaks for composition studies in the public sphere when those of us trained in the discipline do not? By what authority? To what purpose? And exactly who is it that Fish is writing for? This last question proves especially interesting, for, as Butler points out, Fish had basically made the same argument three years earlier in *The Chronicle of Higher Education*. Why, then, did the first article elicit so little comment but the second provoked considerable indignation, especially among compositionists?

The obvious explanation, and one that Butler acknowledges, was that Fish was writing for two very different audiences—the first composed of fellow academics; the other composed of the readership of *The New York Times*. Butler reports that one contributor to the WPA (Writing Program Administrators) listserv, Jeff Galin (2005), posted a comment that attributed the vigorous response of the later op-ed to its wider, more public circulation. But that explanation seems to leave some unanswered questions. If, for example, it is reasonable to assume that compositionists make up a significant portion of the readership of *The Chronicle*, why was no offense taken at how we were represented to the larger academic community? Is our outrage reserved only for (mis)representations of our work to a general public?[1] Galin's post would seem to suggest as much. The problem with Fish's *New York Times* op-ed, according to Galin, is that "it circumvents the entire academic community and speaks directly to an audience that already believes that academics don't know what they are doing, especially when it comes to writing." But have we compositionists not also heard some version of the same complaint in our departments, in our universities? Do we really need to travel *outside* the academic community to encounter the view that we have absolutely no clue as to what we're doing, "especially when it comes to writing" (quoted in Butler 2008, 55)?

If it is true, as some of us believed, that Fish was once a firebrand of the left, fending off reactionary attacks on the university, we might now be forced to revise those earlier judgments. For something of a reversal has occurred since his debates with D'Souza. Fish now seems to have warmed up considerably to popular denunciations of the academy, at least insofar as writing instruction is concerned. What seems to have emerged is an unlikely partnership between an uninformed general public and, typically, an esteemed professor (or two or three) of literature, all of whom regard present-day writing instruction with deep skepticism, if not outright disdain. The basis for this curious alliance is a shared linguistic conservatism that tends to limit writing pedagogy strictly to considerations of form, that tends to conflate written style with prescriptive grammars, and that tends to dismiss as irrelevant any genuine motivation our students might have to write well. It's as if the perfect student in Fish's classroom is one who, upon receiving her assignment, mutters to herself, "Thank God! At least one of my professors has given me the opportunity to write some excellent sentences!"

I believe it no small coincidence that the kind of student idealized by Fish would delight George Will (1995) as well, who would surely heap abundant praise upon said student—not to mention the teacher who had the good sense to steer her on the right path. To be fair, it might seem that Will, in *his* lambasting of composition, looks much more favorably upon course content than does Fish. In a snapshot history of our discipline, for example, Will seems to rail against the fact that somewhere along the line, " 'process' became more important than content." Before too long, though, we learn that by "content," Will means exactly what Fish teaches, an admiration of prescriptive formalism: "Rather than studying possessive pronouns," Will grouses, "students are learning how language silences women and blacks" (Will 1995). At this point, it is hard not to wonder about the relationship between conservatism in language and conservatism in politics—not to wonder if, maybe, Eagleton might be right after all.

So then, rifling through the file drawer of these composite sketches, composition finds no image of itself that is recognizable; instead, it finds itself to be mostly vanquished to a sort of representational place within a place, a liminal or threshold site located betwixt and between the constructions of others regarding the vocation we profess, the work we do.[2] We seem to find ourselves confined to the local lockup, poised for release, ready to make our way into the public, yet all the while remaining outsiders to dismissive conversations *about us*, that *concern us*—but conversations, it should be noted, that are never addressed *to us*. Nor does there seem to be any urgency on the part of those who represent the work of composition to allow us in, to include us in their conversations.

COMPOSITION IN THE PUBLIC SPHERE

Paul Butler, then, is right to ask, "[W]here are composition's public intellectuals, and why does the field need them so urgently today" (Butler 2008, 59). Butler offers two possible reasons for the absence of public voices on behalf of composition. First, our "disciplinary associations based on gender,"—that is, our status as those who perform the academic equivalent of "women's work"—does not recommend us to the role of public intellectuals (as confirmed by, among other things, Richard Posner's [2001] listing of public intellectuals, only 16 percent of whom are female) (Butler 2008, 61; Holbrook 1991, 201). Butler notes, similarly, our discipline's contentious, if not presumed secondary, relationship to literary studies. Given our lowly status, it seems that we will need to face some hard truths about ourselves: We do not have within our ranks any Pulitzer prize–winning authors such as English professor and cultural historian Louis Menand. We do not even have any luminaries as celebrated for their public wrangles as Stanley Fish (or, for that matter, Harold Bloom and, more recently, Michael Bérubé). In short, owing to our disciplinary youth, or perhaps the nature of our work, we simply do not possess the artistic or intellectual cachet that would provide us with an ongoing public forum in such vaunted outlets as *The New Yorker*, *Harper's*, or *The New York Times*. And if the present social imaginary does not allow our disciplinary work to be considered intellectual to begin with, it hardly seems likely that we will gain admission as legitimate *public intellectuals*.

Why not just walk away, then, from what would seem to be, at best, a quixotic pursuit? Why not return to our research projects, our scholarly debates, our classrooms, and rest content in the knowledge that our work matters, if not to *The New York Times* then to our students and colleagues? Why do we need to go public anyway?

For Butler, one answer can be discovered in the fact that the public itself is very much engaged in issues pertaining to language and language instruction—usage, grammar, literacy, style—and that, of these, style is of most interest to the general public. Unfortunately, for composition, it is also style that we as a discipline have, over the last two decades, "disdained or ignored" (Butler 2008, 62). As Butler puts things, "our disciplinary abandonment of style has precipitated the incursion of the public intellectual into composition studies." Put a bit differently, "in its neglect of style as a topic of serious scholarly inquiry . . . the discipline of composition and rhetoric has ceded the discussion to others outside the field" (62). Of course, and as I noted above, there are other reasons why composition has not made its presence felt in the public arena. Nevertheless, according to Butler, our reluctance to engage stylistic issues within the field has mostly left us "powerless to refute popular, and often reductive, characterizations for which there is no public counterargument" (62). To address this situation, Butler encourages us "to take back the study of style . . . to reanimate stylistic practices in composition" so that we might "dispel pejorative constructions of the field . . . from outsiders who treat composition as less than the transformative field that it is" (63). According to Butler, our field needs to "go public with a renewed emphasis on style and to employ its disciplinary expertise" (62).

I am heartened by Butler's "call to style" and inspired by his argument that we might possibly rehabilitate style and, at the same time, answer the misleading characterizations of our field. As should be obvious from my previous chapter, I am less convinced that our disciplinary expertise will provide us a needed entryway into the public sphere where these disparagements routinely occur. After all, Fish and Menand provide for their readers not expertise but an affirmation of popular commonplaces regarding, among other things, what the public believes to be the wretched state of writing instruction. And when style is yoked to the supposed travesties of present-day writing instruction, style, too, proves itself to be an especially durable and enormously appealing target—of far more interest to the public than, say, a column devoted to *Samson Agonistes* or the complexities of Peirce's semiotics. Fish and Menand know this and know that their readers will grant them an expertise to speak with authority on these matters, regardless of whether they actually possess that expertise. Unlike Fish and Menand, however, composition will be required to get its papers in order and produce evidence of its bona fides should it ever entertain any hope (ironically enough) of speaking on its own behalf. Butler, then, is right to point out that some kind of demonstrable expertise will prove useful, if not necessary, in our efforts to find a public voice. But, I wonder, is that enough? And if not, well, what's a discipline to do?

I do not have *the* answer to that question, but I will try to offer *one* answer.

I think it obvious that composition's public efficacy—its capacity to speak influentially in publics beyond the one we already inhabit— is inseparable from the politics of representation. A good measure of Butler's article, and the entirety of this chapter, attempts to understand how it is that we are on the receiving end of so much, well, bad press. And yet, perhaps more baffling than the sheer number of unflattering representations we receive is the odd fact that such constructions go unanswered. As a discipline with a specific disciplinary identity, we do not "write back" to those who represent us; we do not (for the most part) take advantage of the public forums available to us for this purpose (e.g., letters to the editor, guest columns, etc.); and we do not, as individuals, seem to be inclined to speak for everyone in our specialty. And yet, we *do* care about how we get represented; we *do* write to one another—on discussion lists, in emails, papers, articles, reviews, and the like—about this or that recent outrage; and we *do* incorporate outside portrayals of our discipline into our scholarship. Some of us—most recently, Butler, in his article—have tried to offer models of how we *might* respond to public characterizations of our work, but, alas, these tend to be dress rehearsals for our colleagues rather than actual performances for a public. In sum and at present, we do not answer those who have among their resources the power to shape public attitudes about us. But this need not always be the case.

Before embarking on my larger argument here, I wish to be clear. I am not suggesting that we take on the role of the public intellectual; it seems to me that such a figure is, at present, a hopelessly belated one— or rather (and at the risk of being ungracious), a ghost from our recent past. Nor am I suggesting that we eagerly look for additional opportunities to publicly display what we know about writing and the teaching of writing. Yes, doing so would certainly allow us to put a more public face on our scholarship and would, at the very least, result in a more conspicuous presence than we have now. But ultimately, gaining public access strictly through expertise is undesirable because, in my view, such a strategy will soon reveal the several ways public discourses limit and manage that expertise. To volunteer but one example: experts tend to be, figuratively speaking, *summoned* into public life, and thereafter *remanded* into arenas of specialist knowledge. I will concede that this is an improvement on our present status, insofar as it goes. It just doesn't go very far, especially for those who wish to exercise a genuine agency within a larger public sphere. Finally, I view our activist models of public participation as the ones most immediately available to us, and the ones where we are likely to discover the best opportunities to contribute to the public good within our local communities. And yet, despite our admirable successes in this arena, I want to suggest that our activist models are insufficient for the kind of democratic participation that I think might yet be available to us.

Such is why I want to make the case for another model, a model that sees composition as a counterpublic: a special kind of counterpublic—a disciplinary counterpublic—that has the power to bring to the fore, in compelling ways, the public importance of the work we perform. To think about composition as a counterpublic, as I noted earlier, does not require us to think about composition as a counterpublic *exclusively* or *essentially*. It only requires that we acknowledge that in some situations, on some occasions, composition may find it useful *to act in counterpublic ways*—to function as a counterpublic among larger publics, most of which, as is increasingly obvious, do not understand us the same way we understand ourselves. Once we accept this premise, where then to begin?

As a starting point, I believe we would be wise to adopt the following credo: *that every public representation of us is, at the same time, a public address to us; that every public word spoken about us is a public word spoken to us.* Such a position does not obligate us to respond to every negative appraisal that gets published, just as every conversational utterance does not demand a rejoinder (silent answers, for example, often communicate more than voiced ones). I am simply arguing that we position ourselves differently than we have thus far toward the many public representations of us, that we embrace a new starting point where these matters are concerned. In other words, I think it might be time to insinuate ourselves into discourses that were never meant to include us to begin with.

I am well aware that for several (if not most) of my colleagues, this prospect will seem unsavory at best, and just plain wrongheaded at worst—one more unwanted distraction from our true calling, scholarship and teaching. But with the advent of the "public turn" in composition, we should be reminded that the sheer breadth of composition's public involvement is already quite extensive, encompassing an array of practices that range from public writing classrooms to community literacies, from service-learning pedagogies to the rapidly shifting contexts of new media, from ethnographic studies of writing in public contexts to activist scholarship committed to social change. No matter how we define the nature of our scholarship and teaching, it would seem difficult, if not impossible, to separate our disciplinary work from public concerns. The question, then, is this: If we go public, as Butler would like us to do, will journeying forth into the public sphere complement our disciplinary work? For Butler, of course, the answer is an unequivocal yes, since the cumulative knowledge we possess about style is obviously relevant to public discussions about what style is, who teaches it (or not), and why it matters. Our ventures into the public arena need not require us to take on the roles of public intellectuals or experts or activists. Rather, our ventures instead require that we rethink those roles in a profoundly new way—not so much as character performances, but as a repertoire of uses, methods, and functions by which we gain access to larger publics.

FROM AUDIENCES TO COUNTERPUBLICS

In the early to mid-1980s, roughly about the same time that, according to Butler, scholarly interest in style began to wane, a revived interest in audience appeared as a vital and exciting line of composition inquiry. Douglas Park's (1982) "The Meanings of 'Audience,'" Lisa Ede and Andrea Lunsford's (1984) landmark "Audience Addressed/Audience Invoked: The Role of Audience in Composition Theory and Pedagogy," and Barry M. Kroll's (1984) "Writing for Readers: Three Perspectives on Audience" were followed by important contributions from Peter Elbow (1987), James E. Porter (1992), and others. And while it may be true that the heyday of audience scholarship has now passed, it has not disappeared entirely, as evidenced by important contributions from Kay Halasek (1999) and, much more recently, John Schilb (2007). One common thread running throughout all of these studies, though, is an overwhelming focus on audience from the point of view of the writer or rhetor. Certainly, it is that perspective which is most reflective of our field. But I would offer that we have not considered thus far the possibility of *audience agency*. Of course, for an audience to exercise agency, it must first have a sense of itself as a collective body rather than a group of discrete individuals more or less haphazardly gathered for a specific rhetorical occasion. So how, then, do audiences acquire this collective consciousness and, further, how is audience agency then manifested?

One of the surest ways to make an audience is to publicly represent a group to others but not include members of the represented group as part of the intended audience. *Contra* Ede and Lunsford, this is a different kind of "audience invoked," one wherein an audience is brought into existence by a refusal on the part of a representing party to acknowledge a group's *rightful status as an audience*. I do not want to overstate my case here, but it is apparent that some considerable portion of the civil rights movement, the women's movement, and the gay and lesbian rights movements can be explained in terms of audience agency. For it is obvious that each of these groups, in distinct moments and ways, organized themselves as audiences for discourses that sought to exclude them, even while those same discourses were preoccupied with representing the groups they excluded. As I said, I do not want to overstate my case, nor do I want to suggest a facile equivalence between the historical situation of those groups and the current predicament of composition. In most important ways, they simply do not compare.

But composition might learn from the historical examples mentioned here that gaining legitimacy in a broader, more general public is a difficult process, one typically fraught with various modes of discursive struggle. In her discussion of multiple publics, as I noted earlier, Nancy Fraser observes that "subordinated social groups—women, workers, peoples of color, and gays and lesbians" have found it useful and necessary to form what she calls *subaltern counterpublics*, "parallel discursive arenas" organized to create a cultural location from which to circulate counterdiscourses. Using the feminist subaltern counterpublic as her primary example, Fraser calls our attention to the remarkable array and vitality of "journals, bookstores, publishing companies, film and video distribution networks, lecture series, research centers, academic programs, conferences, conventions, festivals, and local meeting places" that make up a "parallel discursive arena" where identity is affirmed and solidarity maintained (Fraser 1990, 123).

Yet more than this, according to Fraser, the feminist subaltern counterpublic served a larger "contestatory function" as well. She points out that the very notion of a "counterpublic militates in the long run against separatism because it assumes a *publicist* orientation." While not denying that such counterpublics "function as spaces of withdrawal and regroupment," she is equally interested in the fact that they also function as "bases and training grounds for agitational activities directed toward wider publics." Or to be more exact, Fraser notes, "it is precisely in the dialectic between these two functions that their emancipatory potential resides" (Fraser 1990, 124). The same description would apply to any of the movement counterpublics identified above.

I would like to draw attention to two aspects of Fraser's work that are seldom noticed or discussed. The first is that publics—in some measure, however indefinable—are also audiences.

To contest public representations made of them, those who identified with feminist subaltern counterpublics had to understand those representations first as an *address*—to be sure, an address to that mythical "public at large" but also, and perhaps more importantly, an address to that group whose identity was being represented and, therefore, an address that could and (for this group) had to be answered. It is significant, I believe, that as long as representations go unanswered, they have the uncanny quality of seeming to be *addressed to no one* (or, if you prefer, being addressed to a universal audience, a "general public" perhaps, which arguably, because of its assumed ubiquity, equates to no audience at all). Only when representations are disputed are we able to illuminate them as discourses with real audiences, discourses that possess genuine addressivity because they are no longer thought to address everyone. Fraser does not broach these questions, for that is not her purpose. But there is within her work an invitation to examine publics in their more obviously rhetorical dimensions. Fraser's writings, in fact, could serve as a starting point for inquiries into the specific question of audience agency as well as the broader question of the relationship between audiences and publics.[3] Considerable work is needed on this latter question and, as with style, composition may be suited to conduct such inquiries.

The second point I wish to draw attention to is that nowhere does Fraser assume that counterpublics must wait until a requisite knowledge is achieved. Entry into the larger public sphere, in other words, is not always the result of simply acquiring the proper credentials, of gaining additional expertise on the matters under discussion. For the counterpublics Fraser describes—and, I would argue, for composition as well—if representing oneself publicly to others were strictly a matter of superior knowledge, composition would, on the matter of style, already have a strong voice in the public sphere. It is clear that questions of public access are unavoidably matters of power, and that the task of securing a foothold in public discourses that represent us will likely necessitate some active, tactical, and (for Fraser) agitational efforts. But to what end?

In answer to that question, Fraser (ironically perhaps) endorses a Habermasian vision of publicness (no matter how multiple and contentious publics may be), the ultimate purpose of which is reformed policies or procedures. While she does not explain how counterpublics move from "opposition and contestation" to "dialogue and agreement," she nonetheless implies that they will somehow do so, since a defining characteristic of all counterpublics is that they have a "publicist orientation" (Doxtader 2001, 60). Like Habermas, she imagines the larger public sphere to be essentially a site of rational-critic debate, a location for reasoned deliberation on issues of common concern to all. And while she points out that one major contribution of a feminist subaltern counterpublic was to show how matters of common concern could be redefined—how, for example, it was possible to transform what were thought to be private or domestic issues into public ones—her understanding of subaltern counterpublics shares this much in common with Habermas's bourgeois public sphere: both understand publicness largely in terms of rational-critical debate or deliberation.

In light of this shared assumption, it is noteworthy that Paul Butler speaks favorably of the work of Michael Warner (2005), and especially of Warner's revised notion of counterpublics. I will not rehearse Warner's theory of counterpublics here, as I have already explicated his theory in earlier chapters. Instead, I prefer to draw attention to Butler's remarkable suggestion that it may be possible to regard composition as a counterpublic in its own right, since, among other distinguishing features, composition exists "in tension with a larger public" and possesses "an awareness of [our] subordinate status (Butler 2008, 60)." As a counterpublic, albeit a particular kind of counterpublic, composition shares with all other counterpublics the quality of a distinct and often fiercely defended identity. And while it is manifestly true that other academic specialties have strong disciplinary identities too, it is difficult—maybe impossible—to point to another academic discipline that is so routinely and publicly discredited as our own. Composition's "tensions" with that larger public as represented by Fish, Menand, and others, as well as our "subordinate status" both inside and outside the academy, render us squarely in line, I believe, with Warner's attempt to expand upon what constitutes a viable counterpublic.[4] Warner will take special care to remind readers that dominant publics *and* counterpublics are, first and foremost, *publics*, a term that subsumes both. As publics, they each fall within the purview of a number of characteristics that he uses to illuminate exactly what publics are, how they come into being, and who constitutes their membership, as well as their larger social functions. Of the several rules that Warner sets forth (seven to be exact), it is the first that bears the most relevance to this discussion.

ADDRESSING ADDRESS

Warner's first rule maintains that "*[a] public is self-organized*" (Warner 2005, 67). For Warner, this means that "a public is a space of discourse organized by nothing other than discourse itself. It is autotelic; it exists only as the end for which books are published, shows broadcast, Web sites posted, speeches delivered, opinions produced." A public, in other words, "exists *by virtue of being addressed*" (67). The problem, as I observed earlier, is the maddening circularity that such a claim presents. If a public does not actually exist until it is brought into being through address, why would (or how could) anyone address a public that does not yet exist? Warner recognizes this circularity and, in fact, seems to regard it as a pleasant inevitability, a paradox that must be endured if we are to speak honestly and intelligently about publics and counterpublics.

What happens, though, when we apply this insight to the problem outlined above? What kind of public is invoked, in other words, when Stanley Fish, Heather McDonald, George Will, et al., address their readerships and, in the act of doing so, criticize (if not crudely disparage) the kind of work performed by those whose scholarship is aimed at understanding writing and how it gets taught? Clearly, these authors (and many others) are hoping to shape public attitudes concerning, among other things, the sorry state of writing instruction—and often by implication, the sorry state of the contemporary academy. But is it accurate to say that a public is actually brought into being as the result of a George Will column? This hardly seems to be what actually occurs. More likely, the public imagined by Will is already in place, even if tenuously so, existing by virtue of texts that preceded his, and within which his own column will add to the circulation of texts that define the specific public that is his audience. While Will does not conjure from thin air, so to speak, a brand new public with each new column, he does enact, through his columns, singular and necessary performances of textual maintenance. Thus, says Warner, if publics are to persist, it is only through the reflexive circulation of the texts that identify them as publics:

No single text can create a public. Nor can a single voice, a single genre, even a single medium. All are insufficient to create the kind of reflexivity we call a public, since a public is understood to be an ongoing space of encounter for discourse. Not texts themselves create publics, but the concatenation of texts through time. Only when a previously existing discourse can be supposed, and when a responding discourse can be postulated, can a text address a public. (Warner 2005, 90)

Some readers will, I think, hear in this passage a very Bakhtinian understanding of addressivity, of how texts respond to already exist-ing texts and yet, simultaneously, address possible future texts whose responses they can at best assume and maybe hope to bring into being.[5] For Warner, this process is crucial to how publics—all publics—are cre-ated, sustained, and revised. Publics must be constantly "under con-struction" if they are to persist, and the addressivity of texts is a defin-ing feature of what publics are. For Mikhail Bakhtin (1986), however, addressivity is a condition of all language use, not just language whose central purpose is the making and maintenance of publics. What this means is that, unless one argues that *all address is public address* (and I do not), then we are obligated to recognize that some forms of address are not directed solely or primarily toward publics, that some forms of address are meant for audiences that do not aspire to any measure of publicness whatsoever. Notice that in making this claim, I find it neces-sary to make a distinction between audiences and publics. And indeed, while many others have found it useful to make the same distinction (including Warner himself), the contrast between these two ideas—between audiences and public—is a deceptively complex one.

Warner, for example, reveals a great deal about how he conceives of audiences when he contends that "public discourse, in the nature of its address, abandons the security of its positive, given audience." Seemingly then, unlike discourse aimed at a "positive, given audience," public discourse "promises to address anybody. It commits itself in prin-ciple," if only implicitly, "to the possible participation of any stranger" (Warner 2005, 113). Hence, by its nature, public discourse cannot help but to resist limits, preexisting demarcations of any sort. Yet, by dramatic contrast, Warner will draw attention to the "*bounded* totality of audience," a totality characterized by such restraints as the specific-ity of an event, a purposeful assembly, a "shared physical space," and so on (66; emphasis added). On the basis of this premise—the idea that audiences are bounded and publics are not—it may seem that Warner endorses the common view that understands audiences and publics as absolutely distinct, indeed, that frequently constructs them as a binary opposition. To ascribe this position to Warner, however, would be mistaken. It would be more accurate to say that, for Warner, while publics aspire to surpass the very boundary lines that audiences might welcome, this does not mean that publics cannot encompass or contain particular audiences. Nor does it mean that some audiences can, in varying ways and degrees, function as publics, albeit certain kinds of publics. Such distinctions, as Warner concedes, "are not always sharp," even though the need for "understanding the distinctions better" always remains (66). One reason why the distinction between audiences and publics is irresolvable is because our conceptions of both are necessarily mutable. That is, because our understandings of either cannot escape history, our conceptions of both must elude any attempt at fixed definition.

As I said above, this is an enormously complex question, and I will not pretend that I can answer it here. But for my limited purposes, I wish to make two points. First, like Warner, I do not see audiences and publics as mutually exclusive. Rather more likely, audiences and publics are thoroughly imbricated, dynamic, and at least partially determined by the rhetorical purposes of the speaker or writer, especially that person's decision as to whom, precisely, her words are intended. Those words might be for an actually present, exceptionally well-defined, and (to use Warner's term) *bounded audience*, but they might also be for a specific *public* that the rhetor has in mind or for those even more abstract members of a general public or the public at large. In fact, speakers and writers might aim their words toward either audiences or publics and, as is often the case, both simultaneously. Mapping these differences, as Warner notes, is challenging because "different senses of audience and circulation are in play at once" (Warner 2005, 66).

But what is indisputable, I think, is a shared feature so obvious that it hardly needs to be stated at all: that audiences and publics are both the intended objects of *someone else's address*. My second point, then, is similarly obvious (though maybe its implications are not): that *addressivity* is a defining characteristic of both audiences and publics. True, some forms of addressivity might differ from one audience to the next or from one public to the next. And also true, at least from Warner's vantage point, publics typically offer more reflexive circularity of texts than do audiences, though I think Warner would acknowledge that reflexive circularity is not entirely absent from the latter. In any case, addressivity is a linchpin feature of publics and audiences, and this fact will, as

I hope to show, help us understand how certain kinds of publics are made through exclusions, intended or not.

Returning, then, to those figures mentioned earlier—Stanley Fish, George Will, Heather MacDonald, Louis Menand—we are obliged to ask: When such authors present their individual representations of composition, do they write for audiences or publics? Given what I have just said, I think it clear that I regard these writers to be addressing both at the same time. To reprise Warner, "different senses of audience and circulation are in play at once" (Warner 2005, 66). Thus, in charting the addressees for their individual writings, it is not very difficult to imagine the following: the general (or national) readership of *The New York Times* (or *Harper's* or *The Atlantic*, etc.); the coterie readership that each author, by virtue of acquired reputation, is able to command (Stanley Fish *fans*, George Will *fans*, etc.); the agentive readership whose members might actually be able to bring about needed reforms in the present state of writing instruction; the politically nostalgic readership, for whom hand-wringing denunciations of the academy are commonplace and always, in some measure, *de rigueur*; and finally, the excluded readership, those who read these authors' works and in so doing, realize that they are neither the intended audience nor the intended public for the texts they just read. A compositionist reading George Will, I offer, must work very hard to overcome what could only be described as a profound sense of exclusion. How, then, as a disciplinary identity, are we to respond to such exclusions? Or is it even possible to do so? What is a compositionist to do?

One answer for composition studies, as I have suggested above, is that we must act *as if* we are being addressed, even when we are not. We must stipulate that when we are represented in public discourses, we are effectively, and simultaneously, being addressed by those who represent us. In this way—perhaps only in this way—will we be admitted into public discourses that seemingly exclude us. At the risk of oversimplifying a hoped-for trajectory, I believe our situation provides us the opportunity to move from what seems to be an excluded audience to what might be called a liminal counterpublic. We are liminal because we occupy a threshold moment, liminal, according to Victor Turner (1967), because our position is best described as always somewhere betwixt and between, a threshold that must be understood both temporally and spatially. For us, the betwixt and between refers not only to our location amid the many public representations of us but also to our temporal circumstances—where we have been as a discipline and where we may be going.

We are a counterpublic because, in the moment we now inhabit, we find ourselves in marginal and oppositional relationship to other, more dominant publics that determine how we get represented publicly.

Our present status is a hopeful one, however, because while it will not be easy, we are poised to cross that threshold. We are ready, I believe, to exercise a bit of our own agency—as both audience and nascent public. The obvious question, then, is how so? How do we create a public space for ourselves and, at the same time, contend with those who represent us in ways we do not recognize. Or put differently, once we decide to insinuate ourselves as an audience for discourses that never intended us as such, how do we respond to those whom we now imagine to be addressing us?

COMPOSITION AND BRICOLAGE

For some time now, there has been a standing challenge to the view of audiences as passive consumers of texts (broadly defined). These stirrings hail from many perspectives and disciplines. I have already mentioned that in composition studies, John Schilb's (2007) *Rhetorical Refusals: Defying Audiences' Expectations* points clearly in this direction. In literary studies, Janice Radway's (1991) much-cited *Reading the Romance: Women, Patriarchy, and Popular Literature* suggested that an incipient agency could be found in the widely discredited genre of the romance novel. And in media studies, a large body of scholarship has been devoted to the notion of "active audiences" that, in various ways, perform engagement, negotiation, and, more often than not, resistance. David Morley's (2003) study, "The Nationwide Audience," is often cited in discussions of active audiences, as is the work of John Fiske (2010), who, among other things, has introduced the term *audiencing* to these discussions. In turning scholarly attention away from a common noun (audience) to a progressive verb (audiencing), Fiske asks us to think of listeners, readers, and viewers in explicitly active terms. That is, Fiske asks us to understand audience members as potential agents rather than helpless and hapless receivers of cultural production.

Fiske is especially noteworthy here because he calls upon the ideas of Michel de Certeau (1984) to help explain the kind of audience agency (or resistance) he has in mind. In coming face-to-face with the sheer ubiquity and dominance of commodity culture, Fiske asks how is it possible for ordinary people to enact their own agency. In words that echo de Certeau, Fiske introduces us to his own term, *excorporation*. In contrast to incorporation, "[e]xcorporation is the process by which the subordinate make their own culture out of the resources and commodities provided by the dominant system" (Fiske 2010, 13). By excorporation, Fiske means something nearly synonymous with what de Certeau refers to as bricolage. In fact, Fiske offers a definition of bricolage that not only reiterates de Certeau but likewise reiterates his own definition of excorporation. "In capitalist societies," Fiske observes, "bricolage is the means by which the subordinated make their own culture out of the resources of the 'other'" (115). When Fiske imagines what opportunities might presently exist for exercising audience agency, he sees the arts of bricolage as an important (if not the most important) resource for effecting the kind of resistant agency he thinks is possible. Members of an audience—any audience (we may assume)—have at their disposal the tools needed to transform themselves from a merely consuming audience into a productive one. According to de Certeau, they are able to do this through the many tactical "*ways of using* the products imposed by a dominant social order" (de Certeau 1984, xiii).

But what does this mean when applied to the situation of composition studies that I have outlined here? After all, if what I have said is accurate, what's being imposed on composition are not the familiar and scripted imperatives of how we are construed as a passive audience but exclusion from audience status altogether. Although we are often represented in public discourses, it seems reasonably clear that we are not addressed by those same discourses. The question that emerges, then, is whether the arts of bricolage can assist us in the project of enacting our own version of audience agency, of insinuating ourselves as an audience for discourses that were never meant for us. I think the answer to this question is yes.

In chapters 1 and 2, I examined zine counterpublics and offered the suggestion that, for zinesters, bricolage would be an appropriate methodology for the reflexive circulation of zine texts. But I think it likely, as well, that bricolage might be the methodology best suited for all counterpublics, including, as I argue here, disciplinary counterpublics such as composition studies. This is so because counterpublics, owing to their marginal and oppositional relationship to more dominant publics, are required to be eclectic, improvisational, tactical, and more than a little cunning. To make a public of any sort, especially where none seemingly existed before, is no easy task and requires nothing less than an imaginative use of all available resources, of all the tools in the toolbox, so to speak. Notwithstanding how intimidating this task may be, it is only through the arts of bricolage that certain kinds of publics—counterpublics—emerge and are sustained in the larger public arena.

To be clear, then, what would bricolage look like for composition stud-ies? What kinds of expression might it assume? Are there specific forms of bricolage that correspond to disciplinary publics (in general) and com-position studies (in particular)? These are hard questions to answer, if only because, by definition, where, when, and how bricolage materializes can never be known entirely in advance. That qualification duly noted, allow me to conclude by sketching out what I think may be some possible ways that compositionists might don the mantle of what I refer to as citi-zen bricoleurs.

In the previous chapter and this one, I inquired into three conven-tional ways that academics, scholars, and intellectuals find passage into the larger public sphere. I examined the distinct roles of the public intel-lectual, the expert, and the activist, and I found each of these to be, in some respect, wanting—not entirely up to the task of crafting a viable public presence. I now wish to return to these three roles in order to sug-gest that we reconsider them as a bricoleur might—namely, as a toolbox, a repertoire of methods that, when taken together, may be effectively used to craft for ourselves a public presence.

While the public intellectual, as a recognizable figure, may be fading fast on the present cultural landscape, this does not mean that the *func-tions* performed by the public intellectual are required to vanish as well. The bricoleur, in other words, might be inclined to revise our received understandings of public intellectuals by shifting attention away from celebrity figures to what those figures contributed to public discourses, what those figures actually did in the contexts of public discussions. Any self-respecting bricoleur would, I believe, reject the honorific of *public intellectual* but would not reject any situational exigency to perform that function as needed. In other words, intellectual work would still question the questions placed before us, interpret the interpretations imposed upon us, and represent the representations that shape public life in our time. Yet the bricoleur would enact these functions only when circum-stances compel her to do so, and in a manner best described as improvi-sational, tactical, and, most likely, unheeded. By refusing the celebrity sta-tus that accompanies the title of public intellectual, we are (ironically per-haps) better equipped to do genuine intellectual work in the publics that reflect the nature of our disciplinary inquiries—in our institutions; our local and regional communities; our extracurricular, language, and writ-ing groups; and even possibly other counterpublics we have yet to notice.

What, then, of the compositionist as expert? What is the likelihood that we can parlay our scholarly expertise into a public presence that we have yet to enjoy? Is this, then, our best ticket for admission into the public arena? And should we take that ticket, even if the seats aren't that good?

In Paul Butler's discussion of how style is broached in the public sphere, he observes that those most disenchanted by the putative demise of written style are, curiously enough, those least interested in what composition studies might have to say about the matter. Either those who write publicly about style (and, more generally, who write about writing) are unaware that a discipline such as ours exists, or they do not grant to our work the status of legitimate expertise. I think the latter is more likely, but I am not especially vexed by this fact. As Warner has observed, and as I noted previously, "expert knowledge is in an important way nonpublic: its authority is external to the discussion. It can be challenged only by other experts, not within the discourse of the public itself" (Butler 2008, 145). In addition, the expert precedes her reputation, so to speak, announces her status *as expert* before her arrival. It's reasonable to assume, then, that the public's advance knowledge of an expert's presence may very well have a preemptive, silencing effect on public discussions, if for no other reason than the one Warner mentions. Such is why the role of expert must be both limited and contained. If, on certain occasions, public intellectuals are humorously referred to as "free-range intellectuals," the opposite is certainly true of experts. Cooped and corralled, experts enjoy very little range at all, and their participation in public discourse must be domesticated and circumscribed. In a sense, then, George Will, Heather MacDonald, and Stanley Fish are perfectly right *not* to acknowledge composition studies. To admit expertise into public discussions of style, or language, grammar, and writing, would be to jeopardize the desired goal of considering these matters as distinctly public topics.

Does this mean, then, that to have a public presence we must forego the disciplinary expertise that we have acquired over the last several decades? No, but it means that we might do well to abandon the title of expert—that is, unless we aspire only to a very limited kind of public participation. In the spirit of the bricoleur, and as with the public intellectual, we would do far better to use our expertise situationally, creatively, tactically—or, as the doctor's prescription might read, PRN, on an "as needed" basis. Taking such an approach does not require us to, in any way, diminish the importance of the knowledge we have gained as scholars, researchers, and teachers. It only requires us to give thoughtful consideration to when, where, and how this knowledge is to be used in the public sphere.

Finally, does bricolage have anything to suggest to us about the activist and advocacy work that many of us conduct in our local communities, including the various forms of engaged scholarship that we undertake? Our involvement in literacy projects, community service-learning initiatives, extracurricular writing groups, civic deliberations and debates—all of these examples speak to a vital public presence that we have already established in the locales where we live and work. What can a bricolagic perspective possibly add to our understanding of activities that seem already, and of necessity, to make good use of bricolage? Surely those involved in the kinds of projects I mention here know all too well the value of cunning, of ad hoc improvisations and the circumstantial use of less than conventional resources. What, if anything then, could bricolage say to the activist scholars and teachers in our ranks?

Two suggestions commend themselves to our notice. First, and in keeping with what I said about public intellectuals and experts, it seems that activists, too, would do well to avoid the essentializing moniker that could easily be applied to the work they do in communities. Any name, honorific or moniker—any consolidating title that reduces the variety and complexity of the work they do—stands opposed to the insistent flexibility that is a hallmark of bricolage. Activists must be free, in other words, to be more than, or other than, activists. They must be free to draw upon their expertise in situations that call for specialized knowledge, perform the intellectual questioning needed for a deeper understanding of local issues, conduct research and inquiry (however unorthodox), as well as advocate, organize, and write and reflect. Second, as bricoleurs, activists must have some consciousness that while they are busy making and remaking their communities, they are likewise making and remaking a space for composition studies within the larger public—and, as Warner might add, "transforming . . . the space of public life itself" (Warner 2005, 124).[6] I am not recommending that our activist constituencies be distracted from their immediate challenges and purposes. I am only saying that with an awareness of the public importance of their work, activists may conceive and tailor their usual projects in such a way as to enhance the possibility of a more conspicuous public presence for the kind of work we do in composition studies.

As I have tried to show here, the bricoleur is someone who is not as interested in bearing the title of public intellectual or expert or activist. The bricoleur is, instead, someone interested in fulfilling these roles on an as-needed basis. The bricoleur is someone able to find new uses *not* for public intellectuals but for the important critical functions they perform; *not* for experts but for situational uses of their expertise; not for activists but the public spaces they make in the course of their activism, however it may be directed. The bricoleur resists the compartmentalized roles by which public participation is typically authorized and will use all available tools at hand, even if this means (as it does) transforming received, identifiable roles into uses, methods, and tactics. For the bricoleur, the point is to get the job done, to accomplish a task. And if the task is to craft a more significant public presence for composition studies, the bricoleur, in my view, is the most likely figure to accomplish this task.[7]

CONCLUSION

In a comment on the work of John Fiske, Will Brooker and Deborah Jermyn note that in his enthusiastic embrace of Michel de Certeau's idea of bricolage, Fiske "has occasionally been accused of over-optimism" in promoting a micropolitics based on "audiences' powers of 'resistance'" (Fiske 2003, 92). I have no illusions that the same could be said of the argument I make here. The very notion that composition studies might be—or perhaps worse, *ought* to be—regarded as a counterpublic, even a liminal or occasional counterpublic, will strike some as nonsensical and others as simply too divergent from our real calling of inquiry into writing and the teaching of writing. I think it safe to say that many colleagues will, of course, see no particular urgency to "go public" in the first place, believing that our true mission occurs within our disciplinary boundaries, not outside of them. Others might urge us to step outside of our disciplinary bounds but gingerly and in a very limited way, perhaps only for the purpose of fostering relationships with other disciplines, as required, say, by writing across the curriculum programs and perhaps other interdisciplinary projects as well.

But there remain those who believe that our scholarship, our research, and our teaching, considered as a whole, have an obvious public significance and that this significance needs to be cultivated in any way possible. This chapter is one attempt to offer an alternative to the received forms of public participation typically reserved for academics. For compositionists, once we see the extent to which our work is ignored, frequently misrepresented, and routinely disparaged in public discourses, we often retreat back to our disciplinary home and comfort ourselves that such depictions do not matter. Rarely, though, we dispute the representations and restraints that define, and ultimately limit, our public participation. I clearly think the last of these is the most important. Such is why I believe that composition studies will benefit from thinking of itself, on needed occasions, as a liminal (or, if you prefer, a not yet fully realized) counterpublic. It is my hope that once we cross the threshold into a different kind of public engagement we may find that we hold within our power the ability to alter received understandings of what counts, or ought to count, as legitimate public discourse.

This is a tall order indeed, but as citizen bricoleurs of an academic sort, we may yet commence the work of making a different kind of public for ourselves, our students, and other citizens who find themselves, for whatever reason, positioned somewhere on the outskirts of full public participation.[8]

NOTES

1. Throughout this chapter, I will use the pronoun "we" to refer to the compositionists for whom I speak. But who, exactly, are "we" people? Who qualifies as a compositionist in my usage? Does my term include all graduate teaching assistants who teach first-year writing? All lecturers, full- or part-time? All colleagues, regardless of their specialty, who happen to teach English 101? Or is my term meant to encompass only those who have been professionally trained as composition scholars and researchers, some of whom (remarkably enough) may or may not teach any sections of composition whatsoever? Obviously, the definitional questions I pose are rather complicated ones, but I will try to hazard an answer. By "compositionists," I mean those who have an interest in, and an abiding dedication to, composition studies as a legitimate field of intellectual inquiry *and* who teach composition as well, regardless of how often or how much. My hope is that this definition, while certainly provisional, allows for the term to encompass full-time, tenure-track scholars and researchers trained in the field (as would be expected) *as well as* lecturers, teaching assistants, and other colleagues— anyone who would self-identify as a compositionist because of a commitment to it as *both* a scholarly pursuit and a teaching subject, at once.

2. The term is a famous one borrowed from the work of anthropologist Victor Turner (1967), who gave currency to the concept of liminality, a concept later appropriated by postcolonial theory, chiefly through the writings of Homi Bhabha (1994). My use of the term here, and later in this article, owes more to Turner than to Bhabha but, in any case, does not capture the more nuanced meanings of liminality. My purpose is simply to point to our present location amid public discourses and suggest that our present location, thankfully, is not a fixed one.

3. It should be noted, however, that some important work has been done that attempts to clarify this distinction. I direct readers to Richard Butsch's (2007) *The Citizen Audience: Crowds, Publics, and Individuals* and Sonya Livingstone's (2005) *Audiences and Publics: When Cultural Engagement Matters for the Public Sphere*, a collection that, among other things, offers an excellent parsing of the possible relationships between the two terms as well as some insight into their historically situated meanings.

4. As I have noted previously, Warner rejects Fraser's use of *subaltern* counterpublic because he finds her term to be too limiting, inextricable as it is to the motive of policy reforms that Warner believes are characteristic of Fraser's understanding. In other words, Warner does not want to limit his understanding of publics or counterpublics to a Habermasian model of rational-critical debate (Warner 2005, 118–19). The question, however, is whether he finds any place whatsoever for rational-critical debate in his "poetic world making" model.

5.   Bakhtin (1986) examines addressivity most fully in his theory of the utterance, best explained in the titular essay "The Problem of Speech Genres" that appears in *Speech Genres & Other Late Essays.*

6.   Harry C. Boyte (1992) has called attention to the pragmatics of public problem solving, to the many historical reforms, for example, that ensued from citizen activism. These, too, argues Boyte, must be considered in any full discussion of what constitutes a public or public sphere.

7.   I use the verb "craft" advisedly here, because the term, it seems to me, is not precisely the equivalent of bricolage. No doubt, there are strong affinities. Like the bricoleur, the craftsperson supposedly possesses a "lower" kind of knowledge generally discredited by the academic disciplines. And due to our "historical prejudices," argues Robert R. Johnson, "a craftsperson is just simply not an artist, let alone a thinker" (Johnson 2010, 674). Among other things, Johnson tries to disabuse us of antiquated notions about craft so as to "bring the concept of craft to bear upon the problem of disciplinarity in writing studies" (679). Although he does not explain the distinction between craft and bricolage, he does seem to imply that one exists. Perhaps one difference lies in the source of materials out of which things are made. Scraps, refuse, discards—such items are not always the materials of the craftsperson. And while Johnson takes pains to associate *craft* with a breadth of talents, uses, and knowledge, the term cannot seemingly help but evoke images of specialized expertise—weaving, pottery, woodworking, quilting, smithing, and so on.

8.   An obvious question occurs: Why does the bricoleur appear to be exempt from what could be the essentializing perils of his own title? My answer is that because the bricoleur has no official status within the public sphere, his title is not a fixed, preordained, or clearly defined one. As I have tried to show, the nature of the bricoleur's activities have a guerrilla quality to them—wavering, inconsistent, situational, unpredictable, even occasionally volatile. Once the bricoleur is named in such a way that his activities are perfectly codified and defined—in other words, is essentialized—he or she no longer exists.

Epilogue
WHEREABOUTS UNKNOWN
Locating the Citizen Bricoleurs among Us

In this work, I have sought to examine two general kinds of publics—what I call cultural publics and disciplinary publics. Within these broad categories, I have discussed two counterpublics, the first of which corresponds to zine discourses, and the second of which corresponds to academic discourses—specifically the field of composition, at least on those occasions when composition finds it useful or necessary to act in counterpublic ways. The startling contrast between these two counterpublics is as purposeful as it is unlikely. In the introduction, I stated that I wanted to place in tandem two very different kinds of publics: one official, the other unofficial; one of the street, the other of the institution; one highly respectable, the other highly disparaged, at least when it is noticed at all. More than this, though, I suggested that both of these discursive worlds could, when looked upon in a particular way, be understood as counterpublics: oppositional social formations that have a stake, however defined, in widening or altering public life as we know it, that have a commitment to understanding democratic culture as something always under permanent construction.

The citizen bricoleur, as I posit this figure, is the *agent par excellence* of counterpublic making. To understand why this emphasis on *making* might be important, I ask readers to notice that in our theories, scholarship, pedagogies, and discussions about publics, the one verb form seldom heard to describe our activities is *to make*. We routinely *go* public, we *study* publics, we *address* publics, we *theorize* publics, we *serve* publics, we *teach* about publics, we *write* about publics, we *argue* about publics, we *participate* in public life, and we often *engage* in public debate. What we do not do, however, at least not to any noticeable degree, is express an interest in *making* publics or public life. There may be good reasons for why this is so. It could be that we are so utterly wedded to received notions of *the* general public, or *the* public sphere, that the idea of making a public seems too daunting, too overwhelming to even entertain. But to be waylaid by the enormity of such a task seems to require that we forget there are *other* publics besides that one assumed to be general, singular, all encompassing. The other publics I refer to, of course, are counterpublics—multiple, distinct, impermanent, wildly various in scope, reach, influence, and membership but utterly essential to democratic culture. If, as I claim, the citizen bricoleur is the one figure most responsible for making counterpublics, the reverse is also true: counterpublics *make possible* the figure of the citizen bricoleur. And while the citizen bricoleur, like others, may similarly teach, study, address, serve, engage, and otherwise wrangle with the meanings of public life, her foremost concern is making new kinds of publics and counterpublics and making better those that already exist.

* * *

There were no trumpets, no proclamations, no official announcements. There were no parades, no banner headlines, no celebrations whatsoever. And really, why should there have been? Linguistic transformations are hardly the stuff of great moment. They take too long and happen too ponderously. They do not allow one to indulge that disquieting sense one sometimes gets when experiencing an historic event as it occurs.

Nonetheless, it seems that at some point in our recent past, the term *citizen* became less a noun and more an adjective. A catalog of examples is rather easy to generate. Among other such figures, we now have in our midst the following: citizen scholars, citizen soldiers, citizen critics, citizen journalists, citizen hoboes, citizen scientists, citizen employers, citizen advocates, citizen police, citizen artists, and numerous others.[1] To this already burgeoning list, I have added my own contribution—the citizen bricoleur—in the hope of recognizing those mostly unsung figures who, in a multitude of unnoticed ways, participate in the creation of counterpublics and what I think to be a richer, more authentically democratic culture. But does this reordering of terms—this transformation of citizen from noun to adjective—does it bear any significance in itself?

I believe so, if only because, however innocuously, it turns our attention away from what a citizen is to what a citizen does. Rather than rest easy with citizen as a fixed category, a status, a legal definition, when the term *citizen* is used to modify a different term, the yoked pair tends to highlight a function, an action, or something done in the name of citizenship. In other words, compounds (like the ones just listed) allow for the possibility that even those who are not citizens can act as citizens, can perform in citizenly ways. Furthermore, by expanding the range of who might legitimately be considered a citizen, such paired terms ask us to think about citizenship in a far less conventional light—that is, in vastly more encompassing ways. *Citizen hoboes?* Are you serious? Can you give me some examples of *citizen critics?* Remind me, then, how does a *citizen scientist* differ from ordinary scientists? What exactly do you mean by *citizen bricoleur,* and please tell me, where might one be found?

And yet, might not this lexical shift reveal something of an unacknowledged privilege? Might it not be that only those who possess citizenship can relish the luxury of entertaining such fascinating hybrids as citizen scholars or citizen journalists or citizen artists? For those who are not (or not yet) citizens, I wonder: Is it not more likely that *citizen as noun,* citizenship as a legal designation, has far more profound implications than any interesting hybrid that I or anyone else can imagine? For some, citizenship is a matter of some urgency, and I speak here not strictly of immigrant populations but also of those persons (citizen and noncitizen alike) whose habeas corpus rights have been suspended, or whose status as citizens has been compromised by voter registration laws meant to disenfranchise specific populations. Citizenship still matters, not just to those who are not citizens but to those who are, to those who see their citizenship rights as compromised or increasingly threatened. In the midst of these controversies, the very notion of citizenship is undergoing critical reexamination.

* * *

Of the counterpublic theorists discussed in this book, the one who has most engaged the daunting task of reexamining citizenship, if only implicitly, is Nancy Fraser. Nearly two decades beyond her highly influential essay "Rethinking the Public Sphere" (Fraser 1990), Fraser rethinks the public sphere once again, this time taking into account material and historical changes occurring not only culturally but globally too. In this later essay, "Transnationalizing the Public Sphere: On the Legitimacy and Efficacy of Public Opinion in a Post-Westphalian World," Fraser reminds her readers that scholarly examinations of the public sphere have, at least since Jürgen Habermas, always been founded on the public's relationship to the state—but, to be exact, only to a particular kind of state, the Westphalian state. Such a state, Fraser observes, "has tacitly assumed the frame of a bounded political community with its own territorial state"—in other words, a traditional nation-state, as one would be commonly understood (Fraser 2007, 8). Even scholarship that has challenged Habermas on other points, including Fraser's own, has proceeded on this same assumption.

But that assumption can no longer go unquestioned. In a time when it has become routine to speak of the *global public sphere* or *diasporic public spheres* or, to use Fraser's favored term, *transnational public spheres*, it has likewise become increasingly clear that the modern state is entering a "post-Westphalian" moment. By that Fraser means that the contemporary state cannot help but be a leaky enterprise, a spillover phenomenon, a territory that can no longer stay within the sovereign lines it draws for itself. Put in more concrete terms, Fraser holds that "whether the issue is global warming or immigration, women's rights or the terms of trade, unemployment or 'the war against terrorism,' current mobilizations of political opinion seldom stop at the borders of territorial states" (Fraser 2007, 14). To this list, Fraser adds the imbrications of global capital, the rapidly increasing multilingualism of national populations, and the (mostly) unimpeded reach of new technologies. If, as Fraser argues, public sphere theory is predicated on the kind of bounded, self-identical state that no longer exists (or is fast fading), then we have to question if the public sphere itself remains a viable construct—and if public sphere theory itself retains any critical force at all. Fraser answers yes to both of these concerns but argues that each must be rethought, and that is what she does in this article.

Of course, Fraser knows that to rethink the public sphere through a post-Westphalian lens also demands rethinking what a citizen is. Although she does not elaborate a new definition of citizenship, she does realize what's at stake. She anticipates how our received thinking about what defines a citizenry will need to be revised. Traditional public sphere theory, as Fraser points out, sets forth on the assumption "that a public coincides with a national citizenry, resident of a national territory, which formulates its common interest as the general will of a bounded political community." Such a conception, however, is no longer serviceable. It is too readily belied "by such phenomena as migrations, diasporas, dual and triple citizenship arrangements, indigenous community membership, and patterns of multiple residency" (Fraser 2007, 16). What may have once existed as an identifiable, national citizenry is now quickly becoming "a collection of dispersed interlocutors, who do not constitute a *demos*." Correspondingly, public opinion was once thought to address a state, which in turn was thought to be responsive to that opinion. A more accurate description, claims Fraser, is that the current addressee of public opinion is now "an amorphous mix of public and private transnational powers that is neither easily identifiable nor rendered accountable" (Fraser 2007, 19). What do these new conditions mean, then, for the traditionally assumed equivalence between a public and a citizenry?

Fraser thinks they have profound consequences, because the long-standing identification of the public with a democratic citizenry must now be jettisoned, especially if our theories of the public sphere are to have critical force. We must now construe the public to be something larger than a national citizenry, and our warrant for doing so can be discovered in a premise of classical public theory itself—namely, the "all-affected principle." Fraser observes that public sphere theory regards public opinion as legitimate "if and only if all who are potentially affected are able to participate as peers in deliberations concerning the organization of their common affairs." It has traditionally been assumed that those "potentially affected" in this phrase were equivalent to the citizens of a Westphalian state. But now this is manifestly untrue, since it is clear that "one's conditions of living do not depend wholly on the internal constitution of the political community of which one is a citizen." Fraser suggests that we might still retain the all-affected principle "without going through the detour of citizenship" (Fraser 2007, 20), and that we would be well advised to do so:

> [T]he all-affected principle holds that what turns a collection of people into fellow members of a public is not shared citizenship but their co-imbrication in a common set of structures and/or institutions that affect their lives . . . Where such structures transgress the borders of states, the corresponding public spheres must be transnational. Failing that, the opinion that they generate cannot be considered legitimate. (16)

The legitimacy of public opinion, then, can no longer be determined by, or inextricably bound to, national citizenship, at least not in the post-Westphalian world we all now inhabit. Publics, public opinion, and public participation must now, of necessity, surpass any facile equivalence with political citizenship. They cannot afford to do otherwise.

As mentioned above, Fraser's latest rethinking of the public sphere has considerable implications for what citizenship means in our times. Notice, though, that her purpose is not to rethink citizenship but to rethink the public sphere. She is not especially interested in citizenship per se, other than to point out that it can no longer be conflated with the public sphere. In fact, she does not broach the topic of what a revised understanding of post-Westphalian citizenship might entail. It would be hard, though, to come to any other conclusion but this: that in a post-Westphalian state, citizenship, as usually understood, must now be a radically altered concept, as well as a status depleted, rather than enhanced by the material and historical transformations that are currently underway. If we are to rethink the public sphere once again, as Fraser would have us do, then we are obliged to rethink citizenship as well. But even our doing so will likely prove inadequate. For citizenship must not be merely rethought but reimagined. And it is to this project that the citizen bricoleur, I believe, can make a contribution.

* * *

Early on in this work, I argued that we need another kind of citizen, an alternative citizen who, in making certain kinds of publics—counterpublics—also constructs more democratic ways of being in the world, with or without the certifying apparatus of the traditional nation-state. Such figures I named citizen bricoleurs, not only to draw attention to the valuable making functions they perform but to honor such figures as citizens, particularly when that title, at least for some, is not the first descriptor that comes to mind. Because the term *citizenship*, as Amy Wan (2011) points out, has such a relentlessly positive aura, it is not usually bestowed upon punks, zinesters, anarchists, grrrls, and others who pitch camp on the outskirts of public esteem. Citizen bricoleur, then, is a title that is meant to enlarge our commonplace ideas as to who counts as a citizen and indeed what citizenship means for our time and place. It is a title the purpose of which is to invite such questions. Distinct from Fraser, though, it desires that such questions emerge *not* from a transnational perspective but from a pedestrian one—a somewhat out-of-the-way point of view, street-bound, looking here and there, around and about.

In *The Practice of Everyday Life*, Michel de Certeau compares two visions of New York City—one from the perspective of someone looking down on Manhattan from the 110th floor of the once-standing World Trade Center, the other from the point of view of the pedestrian at street level, moving along sidewalks and intersections, through alleys and parks and so on. Neither can see what the other sees; each has his or her peculiar blindnesses. Yet, for de Certeau, it is the walker who has the better vantage. This is because the one spying upon the city from above has been transformed into a "voyeur," distanced from the life of the city, possessing an abstract, totalizing view of what appears to be an immobilized world below. From his perch, the elevated viewer can (and surely will) read the city as a facsimile of itself, a representation in the same way that every text is read as a simulacrum of something else. Yet, for the many who move along those crowded streets, the city is something else entirely. As de Certeau explains,

> The ordinary practitioners of the city live "down below," below the thresholds at which visibility begins . . . [T]hey are walkers, *Wandersmänner*, whose bodies follow the thicks and thins of an urban "text" they write without being able to read it. These practitioners make use of spaces that cannot be seen; their knowledge of them is as blind as that of lovers in each other's arms . . . The networks of these moving, intersecting writings compose a manifold story that has neither author nor spectator, shaped out of fragments of trajectories and alterations of spaces. (de Certeau 1984, 93)

I liken the citizen bricoleur to de Certeau's walker in the city, a practitioner of the quotidian, a maker of new spaces, a rhapsode of the prosaic. Where Fraser offers a transcendental view of publics and citizens, the citizen bricoleur offers us a view of the same from below, from street level, as it were. While I am in no way inclined to gainsay the insights that Fraser offers from her macro perspective, I would argue that a micro perspective is needed as well, if only as a valuable counterpoint to the view from on high. For as it turns out, both the public sphere and citizenship may be interrogated at street level too. And those who enact such inquiries from below, so to speak, those who challenge orthodox definitions of what a public is, and what a citizen is—these are the citizen bricoleurs of this work.

* * *

During breakfast conversations I have had over the last year or so (with, I should add, friends who share my political views), I have often sensed considerable frustration with the Occupy Wall Street (OWS) movement. Much of that frustration, no doubt, derives from the movement's apparent lack of results, from its inability to change anything—to effect new laws or, failing that, new legislative initiatives that might eventually lead to restrictions on the unfettered ease with which corporate wealth influences public policy and electoral politics. The frustration I heard voiced over those morning meals was heartfelt, to say the least, even in those occasional moments when it spiraled into expressions of anger. A particular sore point, as I recall, was the reluctance of OWS leaders to forward a set of specific demands, a program, an agenda. How is it even possible, my friends would ask, that a movement—any movement—could refuse to articulate what it wanted?

Tellingly, I think, the impatience expressed by my friends on the left was surpassed by the impatience expressed in right-wing and conservative opinion and in commentary from our mainstream media as well. It was as if everyone not a part of the movement addressed OWS with an insistent and deceptively reasonable appeal: "Just tell us what you want. How can anything possibly improve unless we know what it is you're after?" For my part, I believe the movement was right to withhold its demands for as long as it could. The task for its leadership was how to keep alive the energy and momentum of OWS for as long as possible, how to hold together a group fundamentally united only by its opposition to the excesses of amassed capital and the ever increasing division of wealth in our country. And yet, beyond that basic opposition, OWS remained a motley group indeed. Among its members were anarchists, celebrities, labor leaders, students, political activists, street artists, the jobless, the homeless, and more than a few sympathetic passers-by. What kind of coherent demands could possibly be wrought from such a group?

Realizing the likely consequences of doing so, OWS leaders refused (at least for a while) to be baited into issuing any position statements, manifestos, or formal set of demands.[2] Put a bit differently, OWS refused to surrender to what I call the propositional imperative, the unceasing call for a specific list of demands that could be made translatable into debate points. Generally speaking, those on the political left desired such a list because, without one, it was hard to see how the OWS movement could effect any meaningful change. On the other hand, the political right wanted a list of demands, too, but for what I assume were very different reasons. In my view, conservative forces understood that the best way to splinter the OWS movement would be to insist upon a statement of demands. Not only would such a statement likely fracture the already precarious unity of OWS, but it would also contain and domesticate the movement by rendering it agreeable to what Michael Warner labels "the ideology of open public discussion" (Warner 2005, 211), an alteration that would, in my opinion, eventually prove to be a factor in the diminishment of OWS.

In many respects, the dilemma faced by OWS and its leadership is one that accompanies other counterpublics, or at least those that express a commitment to social change. Recall that in his discussion of queer politics, Warner maps out the sometimes stark divergences that exist, say, between gays, who usually "invoke a more traditional rhetoric of minority identity," and queers, who typically participate in very nontraditional modes of activism (Warner 2005, 212). While the former are dedicated to changing extant laws and policies, especially through organized advocacy and a discourse of rights, the latter tend to hold in contempt "the traditional debate styles that form the self-understanding of the public sphere: patient, polite, rational-critical discussion" (210). Still, it would be wrong to claim that only the former expresses demands and, therefore, only the former of these matter. Queer activists have demands, too, Warner reminds, demands that do not always fit perfectly on a legislative agenda, "powerful demands that have to do with the organization of social and political life" (221). Those sorts of demands, the kind that seek to alter "the space of public life itself," are demands that are more likely to be performed than articulated, embodied than debated, lived than reasoned (124). For Warner, both must exist side by side, and there is considerable value in them doing so.

Because it is a counterpublic—albeit a complex, multilayered counterpublic, one that is itself composed of multiple other counterpublics—OWS struggled with the same push and pull that most other counterpublics do. On the one hand, it certainly wanted to influence and promote the enactment of laws that might restrain what many considered to be the unbridled financial practices that resulted in hardship for the overwhelming majority of Americans who are not members of the 1 percent. On the other hand, OWS, I think, realized that legislative action was not its first purpose. Its primary mission was to consolidate a loosely wrought and extremely fragile identity of people united by their shared opposition to the disastrous consequences of aggregated capital.

In retrospect, it seems to me that OWS and its leadership chose the latter tactic and, for the most part, were right to do so. OWS, I believe, consciously decided to let others debate and deliberate issues, advance policy initiatives, or engage in court challenges. Because OWS emerged only recently, it did not have any established traditions to fall back upon, traditions that may have allowed it to deliver a policy agenda and, at the same time, function as a mass protest movement. Because of its sudden appearance, and unlike the queer politics described by Warner, OWS did not enjoy the longevity that might have enabled it to balance both purposes at once. Some, including myself, remain hopeful that OWS will return as we embark upon this election season, reinvigorated and a little wiser perhaps, maybe more experienced in street politics and its complicated relationship to legislative politics.

* * *

If Occupy Wall Street qualifies as a counterpublic in its own right (however mingled and elaborately textured it may be), then are we not encouraged to ask if there were citizen bricoleurs present at its birth? In histories now being written of OWS, this indeed appears to be the case. Most trace the movement's origins to a Canadian publication, *Adbusters*, famous, among other things, for its advertising spoofs but having a larger mission than just parody. On its website, *Adbusters* characterizes itself as "a global network of culture jammers and creatives working to change the way information flows, the way corporations wield power, and the way meaning is produced in our society." On July 13, 2011, a blog post appeared on the *Adbusters* website that announced OWS and called for all readers to "flood into lower Manhattan, set up tents, kitchens, peaceful barricades and occupy Wall Street" ("Shift in Revolutionary Tactics"). And in this way, so the story goes, a movement was born.

What is especially interesting about *Adbusters*, however, is that it originated as a zine in the late 1980s. It is not only the case that the crucial role *Adbusters* played in the formation of OWS has been mostly overlooked, so has the publication's origins as a zine. In the words of Levi Asher,

> It's a strange and delightful fact that the Occupy movement which began last month on Wall Street was not born on Twitter or Facebook or a blog. Rather, the idea emerged from a dusty print-based medium that almost nobody cares about anymore (or so we thought), a format that dates back to the days of Husker Du and Pagan Kennedy. Occupy Wall Street was born in a zine. (Asher 2011)

Asher continues, pointing out that in its early paper format, *Adbusters* appeared on shelves next to other famous zines such as "Bitch, Giant Robot, Bust, Maximum Rock 'N' Roll, Craphound and Factsheet Five." While Asher may not fully take into account the transition of *Adbusters* from zine to website, he does recognize the influential presence of a zine spirit and sensibility in the ultimate formation of OWS.

Importantly, Asher notes that the "amazing public acclaim" for the Occupy movement is a "testament to the creative thinking of a few individuals," in particular, *Adbusters*' editors, Kalle Lasn and Micah White. Famous or not, these individuals—whether they be editors, illustrators, writers, designers, and others—are, to my mind, exemplary citizen bricoleurs, people who from the scraps of a widely felt but unarticulated discontent, stitched together a movement, a protest, a counterpublic that came to be known as Occupy Wall Street.

* * *

Where, then, may the citizen bricoleur be found? In organized protests? Yes, certainly, but not always or only there. She may very well be located in Zuccotti Park, but she may also be in an office on a third floor nearby, looking down on Zuccotti Park. She may be in a small-town basement or a faculty lounge reading about Zuccotti Park. She may be stapling a zine or writing an assignment that addresses the issues raised by OWS. The citizen bricoleur, in other words, could be an activist, an expert, a public intellectual—all of these or none of these. There are no prerequisites for the dubiously acclaimed, and not likely sought after, title of citizen bricoleur. In fact, that title is something of an oxymoron.

Yes, the citizen bricoleur may be little more than a face in the crowd, but *her* crowd is a large one indeed, consisting of all those other anonymous citizens with whom, and on behalf of whom, she does her work. She is therefore likely to be found in a classroom or in the streets; in a basement or in a meeting room; in a coffee shop or in an office; in a church or in a tavern; in a concert hall or in a town hall. The citizen bricoleur may be located anywhere, in fact, anywhere there is a desire to *make* or *make better* a certain kind of public—a counterpublic—and to make this counterpublic out of all the tools and materials at hand.

There you will find the citizen bricoleur.

NOTES

1. My list is generated through personal familiarity with many of these terms as well as through casual conversations I have had with friends and colleagues. I also became acquainted with quite a few new combinations through the research conducted for this book.

2. In late September 2011, OWS did compose a declaration and manifesto, organized in the manner of a bill of particulars, itemizing specific charges against banks and other financial institutions and also reasserting the right to peaceable assembly. A number of discussions and ideas appeared on the OWS website, postings that, along with other input, constituted a kind of "work in progress" of OWS demands. Notwithstanding these exploratory first stirrings, there was never an *official* statement of demands issued by OWS. However, a faction of the New York General Assembly, the 99% Declaration Working Group, circulated a document titled "The 99% Declaration" and called for a ratifying convention to be held in Philadelphia on July 4, 2012. In February 2012, however, National Public Radio correspondent Eyder Peralta reported that OWS rejected the efforts of Michael S. Pollok, an early OWS legal adviser, to promote such a declaration or organize a ratifying, national convention. OWS remained staunch in insisting upon its autonomy and informed its members "that any statement

released outside of the movement's official website" should be interpreted to be unaffiliated with OWS (Peralta 2012). This conflict, I think, speaks to the tension I discuss here—the (generally) external call to advance specific demands, and the (generally) internal need to hold a movement together.

REFERENCES

Abrahams, Tim. 2009. "Nostalgia Is No Substitute for Criticism." *Blueprint*, May 12, available at http://www.blueprintmagazine.co.uk.

Ackerman, John M., and David J. Coogan, eds. 2010. *The Public Work of Rhetoric: Citizen-Scholars and Civic Engagement.* Columbia: University of South Carolina Press.

Alexander, Jonathan. 2002. "Digital Spins: The Pedagogy and Politics of Student-Centered E-zines." *Computers and Composition* 19 (4): 387–410. http://dx.doi.org/10.1016/S8755-4615(02)00141-X.

Arendt, Hannah. 1958. *The Human Condition.* Chicago, IL: University of Chicago Press.

Asen, Robert. 2009. "Ideology, Materiality, and Counterpublicity: William E. Simon and the Rise of a Conservative Counterintellegentsia." *Quarterly Journal of Speech* 95 (3): 263–88. http://dx.doi.org/10.1080/00335630903140630.

Asher, Levi. 2011. "Adbusters: The Zine That Created the Occupy Movement." *Literary Kicks: Opinion, Observations, and Research*, October 18, available at http://www.litkicks.com/Adbusters#.UMUUR6XEWhE.

Atton, Chris. 2002. *Alternative Media.* London: Sage Publications.

Avery-Natale, Ed. 2009. "Narratives of Entrance into Anarcho-Punk in Philadelphia." Paper presented at the North American Anarchist Studies Network Conference, Hartford, CT, November 22, 2009, available at http://astro.temple.edu/~tua65420/Narrative_of_Entrance_into_Anarcho-Punk_in_Philadelphia.pdf.

Bag, Alice. 2012. "13 Questions with Susana Sepulveda." *Diary of a Bad Housewife*, January 30, available at http://alicebag.blogspot.ca/2012/01/13-questions-with-uc-santa-cruz.html.

Bakhtin, Mikhail. 1981. *The Dialogic Imagination: Four Essays.* Ed. Michael Holquist. Trans. Caryl Emerson and Michael Holquist. Austin: University of Texas Press.

Bakhtin, Mikhail. 1986. *Speech Genres & Other Late Essays.* Ed. Caryl Emerson, Michael Holquist, and Vern W. McGee. Austin: University of Texas Press.

Berlant, Lauren. 1997. *The Queen of America Goes to Washington City: Essays on Sex and Citizenship.* Durham, NC: Duke University Press.

Bernays, Edward. 2004 [1928]. *Propaganda.* Brooklyn, NY: Ig Publishing.

Berthoff, Ann E. 1981. *The Making of Meaning: Metaphors, Models, and Maxims for Writing Teachers.* Boston, MA: Heinemann.

Bérubé, Michael. 2002. "Going Public." *Washington Post Book World*, July 7, 3–4.

Bhabha, Homi. 1994. *The Location of Culture.* New York: Routledge.

Bizzell, Patricia, and Bruce Herzberg, eds. 2001. *The Rhetorical Tradition.* 2nd ed. Boston, MA: Bedford/St. Martin's.

Blackstone, Lee Robert. 2005. "A New Kind of English: Cultural Variance, Citizenship, and DiY Politics amongst the Exodus Collective in England." *Social Forces* 84 (2): 803–20. http://theanarchistlibrary.org/library/lee-robert-blackstone-a-new-kind-of-english-cultural-variance-citizenship-and-diy-politics-amon.

Bleyer, Jennifer. 2004. "Cut-and-Paste Revolution: Notes from the Girl Zine Explosion." In *The Fire This Time: Young Activists and the New Feminism*, ed. Vivien Labaton and Dawn Lundy Martin, 42–60. New York: Anchor Books.

Blomley, Nicolas. 1994. "Activism and the Academy." *Environment and Planning D: Society & Space* 12 (4): 383–85.

Bookchin, Murray. 2000. "Thoughts on Libertarian Municipalism." *Left Green Perspectives* 41, Institute for Social Ecology, January, available at http://www.social-ecology. org/1999/08/thoughts-on-libertarian-municipalism/.

Borrowman, Shane, and Theresa Enos, eds. 2009. *Renewing Rhetoric's Relation to Composition: Essays in Honor of Theresa Jarnagin Enos.* New York: Routledge.

Boyte, Harry C. 1992. "The Pragmatic Ends of Popular Politics." In *Habermas and the Public Sphere,* ed. Craig Calhoun, 340–55. Cambridge, MA: MIT Press.

Bravo, Kyle. 2008. *Making Stuff and Doing Things: A Collection of DIY Guides to Doing Just about Everything.* 3rd ed. Bloomington, IN: Microcosm.

Brooker, Will, and Deborah Jermyn, eds. 2003. *The Audience Studies Reader.* New York: Routledge.

Brouwer, Daniel C. 2005. "Communication as Counterpublic." In *Communication as . . . Perspectives on Theory,* ed. Gregory J. Shepherd, Jeffrey St. John, and Ted Striphas, 195–208. Thousand Oaks, CA: Sage Publications.

Brouwer, Daniel C. 2010. "Risibility Politics: Camp Humor in HIV/AIDS Zines." In *Public Modalities: Rhetoric, Culture, Media, and the Shape of Public Life,* ed. Daniel C. Brouwer and Robert Asen. Tuscaloosa: University of Alabama Press.

Brouwer, Daniel C., and Robert Asen, eds. 2010. *Public Modalities: Rhetoric, Culture, Media, and the Shape of Public Life.* Tuscaloosa: University of Alabama Press.

Brown, Denise S. 1968. "Little Magazines in Architecture and Urbanism." *Journal of the American Planning Association. American Planning Association* 34 (4): 223–33. http:// dx.doi.org/10.1080/01944366808977811.

Bruder, Jessica. 2012. "Real Punk Belongs to Fighters." *New York Times,* June 8, available at http://www.nytimes.com/2012/06/09/opinion/real-punk-belongs-to-fighters.html.

Bryanski, Gleb. 2012. "Pussy Riot Trial Hurtles towards Verdict in Russia." *Reuters,* August 5, available at http://in.reuters.com/article/2012/08/05/russia-pussyriot-trial-idIN-L6E8J39II20120805.

Burton, Gideon. 2009. "Academia Must Divest from Intellectual Apartheid." *Academic Evolution,* available at http://www.academicevolution.com/2009/03/intellectual-apartheid.html.

Butler, Paul. 2008. "Style and the Public Intellectual: Rethinking Composition in the Public Sphere." *JAC* 28 (1–2): 55–84.

Butsch, Richard. 2007. *The Citizen Audience: Crowds, Publics, and Individuals.* New York: Routledge.

Calhoun, Craig. 1992. "Introduction: Habermas and the Public Sphere." In *Habermas and the Public Sphere,* ed. Craig Calhoun, 1–48. Cambridge, MA: MIT Press.

"Cameron Proposes Social Media Ban." 2011. *Global Post,* News Desk, August 12, available at http://www.globalpost.com/dispatch/news/regions/europe/united-kingdom/110812/cameron-social-media-ban.

Cintron, Ralph. 2003. "'Gates Locked' and the Violence of Fixation." In *Towards a Rhetoric of Everyday Life: New Directions in Research on Writing, Text, and Discourse,* ed. Martin Nystrand and John Duffy, 5–37. Madison: University of Wisconsin Press.

Cloud, Dana L. 2011. "The Only Conceivable Thing to Do: Reflections on Academics and Activism." In *Activism and Rhetoric: Theories and Contexts for Political Engagement,* ed. Seth Kahn and Jonghwa Lee, 11–24. New York: Routledge.

Cogan, Brian. 2008. "Crass, Throbbing Gristle, and Anarchy and Radicalism in Early English Punk Rock." *Journal for the Study of Radicalism* 1 (2): 77–90. http://dx.doi.org/10.1353/jsr.2008.0004.

Comstock, Michelle. 2001. "Grrrl Zine Network: Re-Composing Spaces of Authority, Gender, and Culture." *JAC* 21: 383–409.

Congdon, Kristin G., and Doug Blandy. 2005. "Zines, DIY, and Critical Pedagogy." *Telemedium* 52: 59–63.

Couture, Barbara, and Thomas Kent, eds. 2004. *The Private, the Public, and the Published: Reconciling Private Lives and Public Rhetoric*. Logan: Utah State University Press.

CrimethInc. Workers Collective. 2001. *Days of War, Nights of Love: CrimethInc for Beginners*. Salem, OR: CrimethInc. Free Press.

CrimethInc. Workers Collective. 2008. *Expect Resistance: A Field Manual*. Salem, OR: CrimethInc. Free Press.

Cushman, Ellen. 1999. "The Public Intellectual, Service Learning, and Activist Research." *College English* 61 (3): 328–36. http://dx.doi.org/10.2307/379072.

Cushman, Ellen, and Erik Green. 2010. "Knowledge Work with the Cherokee Nation: Engaging Publics in a Praxis of New Media." In *Public Work of Rhetoric*, ed. John Ackerman and David Coogan, 175–93. Columbia: University of South Carolina Press.

Daniell, Beth. 2003. *A Communion of Friendship: Literacy, Spiritual Practice, and Women in Recovery*. Carbondale: Southern Illinois University Press.

de Certeau, Michel. 1984. *The Practice of Everyday Life*. Berkeley: University of California Press.

DeRosa, Susan. 2004. "Literacy Narratives as Genres of Possibility: Students' Voices, Reflective Writing, and Rhetorical Awareness." *Ethos*: 1–14, available at http://demo2.bd.psu.edu/academic/lrc/ethos/teach/teach.htm.

Dewey, John. 1954 [1927]. *The Public and Its Problems*. Athens, OH: Swallow Press.

Donehower, Kim, Charlotte Hogg, and Eileen Schell. 2007. *Rural Literacies*. Carbondale: Southern Illinois University Press.

Donnelli, Emily. 2008. "Mapping a Post-Process Dialogics for the Writing Classroom as Public." PhD diss., University of Kansas, Lawrence.

Downing, John. 2000. *Radical Media: Rebellious Communication and Social Movements*. Thousand Oaks, CA: Sage Publications.

Doxtader, Eric. 2001. "In the Name of Reconciliation: The Faith and Works of Counterpublicity." In *Counterpublics and the State*, ed. Robert Asen and Daniel Brouwer, 59–85. Albany: SUNY Press.

Duncombe, Stephen. 1997. *Notes from Underground: Zines and the Politics of Alternative Culture*. Bloomington, MN: Verso.

Eagleton, Terry. 2000. "The Estate Agent." Review of *The Trouble with Principle* by Stanley Fish. *London Review of Books* 22, no. 5 (March 2), available at http://www.lrb.co.uk/v22/n05/terry-eagleton/the-estate-agent.

Eberly, Rosa A. 2000. *Citizen Critics: Literary Public Spheres*. Urbana: University of Illinois Press.

Ede, Lisa, and Andrea Lunsford. 1984. "Audience Addressed/Audience Invoked: The Role of Audience in Composition Theory and Pedagogy." *College Composition and Communication* 35: 155–71.

Edu-factory Collective. 2009. *Toward a Global Autonomous University: Cognitive Labor, the Production of Knowledge, and Exodus from the Educational Factory*. New York: Autonomedia.

Elbow, Peter. 1987. "Closing My Eyes as I Speak: An Argument for Ignoring Audience." *College English* 49 (1): 50–69. http://dx.doi.org/10.2307/377789.

Emig, Janet. 1982. "Inquiry Paradigms and Writing." *College Composition and Communication* 33: 64–75.

Farmer, Frank. 2008. "Composition Studies as Liminal Counterpublic." *JAC* 28 (3–4): 620–34.

Felski, Rita. 1989. *Beyond Feminist Aesthetics: Feminist Literature and Social Change*. Cambridge, MA: Harvard University Press.

Ferguson, Kathy E. 2010. "Anarchist Counterpublics." *New Political Science* 32 (2): 193–214. http://dx.doi.org/10.1080/07393141003722040.

Finoki, Bryan. 2007. "Post on 'Post-Postopolis! Blues.'" *Subtopia* (June 4), available online at http://subtopia.blogspot.com/2007/06/post-postopolis-blues.html.

Fish, Stanley. 2005. "Devoid of Content." *New York Times*, May 31, A17.

Fish, Stanley. 2008. *Save the World on Your Own Time*. New York: Oxford University Press.

Fishman, Jenn, ed. 2012. "The Turn to Performance." *College Composition and Communication Online* 1, no. 1 (January), available at http://www.ncte.org/cccc/ccconline.

Fiske, John. 2010. *Understanding Popular Culture*. 2nd ed. New York: Routledge.

Flower, Linda. 2008. *Community Literacy and the Rhetoric of Public Engagement*. Carbondale: Southern Illinois University Press.

Flower, Linda. 2010. "Going Public—in a Disabling Discourse." In *The Public Work of Rhetoric: Citizen-Scholars and Civic Engagement*, ed. John M. Ackerman and David J. Coogan, 137–56. Columbia: University of South Carolina Press.

Fraser, Nancy. 1990. "Rethinking the Public Sphere: A Contribution to the Critique of Actually Existing Democracy." *Social Text* 25/26: 56–80. http://dx.doi.org/10.2307/466240.

Fraser, Nancy. 2007. "Transnationalizing the Public Sphere: On the Legitimacy and Efficacy of Public Opinion in a Post-Westphalian World." *Theory, Culture & Society* 24 (4): 7–30. http://dx.doi.org/10.1177/0263276407080090.

Freedman, Jenna. 2009. "Zines by African-American Women." Barnard College Library Zine Collection. February 26, available at http://barnardzines.livejournal.com/55386.html.

Furness, Zack, ed. 2012. *Punkademics: The Basement Show in the Ivory Tower*. New York: Minor Compositions.

Galin, Jeff. 2005. "NYTimes.com: Devoid of Content." Online posting, dated May 31, available at WPA-L@asu.edu.

George, Diana. 2010. "The Word on the Street: Public Discourse in a Culture of Disconnect." In *Writing and Community Engagement: A Critical Sourcebook*, ed. Thomas Deans, Barbara Roswell, and Adrian J. Wurr, 50–60. Boston, MA: Bedford/St. Martin's.

Gere, Anne Ruggles. 1994. "Kitchen Tables and Rented Rooms: The Extracurriculum of Composition." *College Composition and Communication* 45: 75–92.

Gilman-Opalsky, Richard. 2008. *Unbounded Publics: Transgressive Public Spheres, Zapatismo, and Political Theory*. Lanham, MD: Lexington Books.

Giroux, Henry. 2006. "Culture, Politics & Pedagogy: A Conversation with Henry Giroux." Interview. December 5, available at http://www.youtube.com/watch?v=DgdVCnTTqXA.

Giroux, Henry, and Peter McLaren. 1987a. "Teacher Education as a Counterpublic Sphere: Notes toward a Redefinition." In *Critical Studies in Teacher Education: Its Folklore, Theory, and Practice*, ed. Thomas S. Popkewitz, 267–97. New York: Falmer Press.

Giroux, Henry, and Peter McLaren. 1987b. "Teacher Education as a Counterpublic Sphere: Radical Pedagogy as a Form of Cultural Politics." *Philosophy and Social Criticism* 12 (1): 51–69. http://dx.doi.org/10.1177/019145378701200103.

Goodburn, Amy. 2001. "Writing the Public Sphere through Family/Community History." *Readerly/Writerly Texts* 9: 9–24.

Goodwin, Jean. 2009. "The Authority of the IPCC First Assessment Report and the Manufacture of Consensus." Paper delivered at the National Communication Association Conference, Chicago, IL, November 14.

Greenwald, Glenn. 2011. "The Secrecy Loving Mind of the American Journalist." *Salon*. November 29, available at http://www.salon.com/2011/11/29/the_secrecy_loving_mind_of_the_u_s_journalist/.

Gustafson, Sandra. 2008. "American Literature and the Public Sphere." *American Literary History* 20 (3): 465–78. http://dx.doi.org/10.1093/alh/ajn027.

Habermas, Jürgen. 1991. *The Structural Transformation of the Public Sphere: An Inquiry into a Category of Bourgeois Society*. Boston, MA: MIT Press.

Halasek, Kay. 1999. *A Pedagogy of Possibility: Bakhtinian Perspectives on Composition Studies*. Carbondale: Southern Illinois University Press.

Halloran, S. Michael. 1983. "Rhetoric in the American College Curriculum: The Decline of Public Discourse." *PRE/TEXT* 3 (Fall): 245–69.

Halloran, S. Michael. 1996. "Rhetoric in the American College Curriculum: The Decline of Public Discourse." In *Composition in Four Keys: Inquiring into the Field*, ed. Mark Wiley, Barbara Gleason, and Louise Wetherbee Phelps, 184–97. Mountain View, CA: Mayfield.

Hansen, Miriam. 1993. Foreword. In *Public Sphere and Experience: Toward an Analysis of the Bourgeois and Proletarian Public Sphere*, by Oskar Negt and Alexander Kluge, ix–xli. Minneapolis: University of Minnesota Press.

Harper, Todd, Emily Donnelli, and Frank Farmer. 2003. "Wayward Inventions: He(u)retical Experiments in Theorizing Service-Learning." *JAC* 23 (3): 615–40.

Harris, Joseph. 1996. *A Teaching Subject: Composition since 1966.* Upper Saddle, NJ: Prentice Hall.

Harvey, David. 2005. "The Political Economy of Public Space." In *The Politics of Public Space*, ed. Setha Low and Neil Smith, 17–34. New York: Routledge.

Hauser, Gerald. 1999. *Vernacular Voices: The Rhetorics of Publics and Public Spheres.* Columbia: University of South Carolina Press.

Hawkes, Terence. 1977. *Structuralism and Semiotics.* London: Metheun. http://dx.doi.org/10.4324/9780203443934

Hebdige, Dick. 1979. *Subculture: The Meaning of Style.* New York: Metheun. http://dx.doi.org/10.4324/9780203139943

Helmbrecht, Brenda, and Meredith A. Love. 2009. "The *BUST*in' and *BITCH*fin' *Ethe* of Third-Wave Zines." *College Composition and Communication* 61: 150–69.

Herman, Edward S., and Noam Chomsky. 2002 [1998]. *Manufacturing Consent: The Political Economy of the Mass Media.* New York: Pantheon.

Herrick, James. 2005. *The History and Theory of Rhetoric: An Introduction.* 3rd ed. Boston, MA: Allyn and Bacon.

Hess, David. 2011. "To Tell the Truth: On Scientific Counterpublics." *Public Understanding of Science* (Bristol, England) 20: 627–41.

Hess, David J. 1997. *Science Studies: An Advanced Introduction.* New York: NYU Press.

Hoffman, John. 2004. *Citizenship beyond the State.* Thousand Oaks, CA: Sage Publications.

Holbrook, Sue Ellen. 1991. "Women's Work: The Feminizing of Composition." *Rhetoric Review* 9 (2): 201–29. http://dx.doi.org/10.1080/07350199109388929.

Isaacs, Emily J., and Phoebe Jackson. 2001. *Public Writing: Student Writing as Public Text.* Portsmouth, NH: Boynton Cook/Heinemann.

Jarratt, Susan. 2009. "Classics and Counterpublics in Nineteenth-Century Historically Black Colleges." *College English* 72: 134–59.

Jasanoff, Sheila. 2012. *Science and Public Reason.* New York: Routledge.

Johnson, Robert R. 2010. "Craft Knowledge: Of Disciplinarity in Writing Studies." *College Composition and Communication* 61 (June): 673–90.

Jolliffe, David A. 2010. "The Community Literacy Advocacy Project: Civic Revival through Rhetorical Activity in Rural Arkansas." In *The Public Work of Rhetoric: Citizen-Scholars and Civic Engagement*, ed. John M. Ackerman and David J. Coogan, 267–96. Columbia: University of South Carolina Press.

Kamenetz, Anya. 2010. *DIY U: Edupunks, Edupreneurs, and the Coming Transformation of Higher Education.* White River Junction, VT: Chelsea Green Publishing.

Keller, Michael, and Yolanne Almanzar. 2011. "Rate New York City's Privately Owned Public Spaces." *New York World (Get inside Your Government).* October 19, available at http://www.thenewyorkworld.com/2011/10/19/publicspace/.

Kincheloe, Joe. 2001. "Describing the Bricolage: Conceptualizing a New Rigor in Qualitative Research." *Qualitative Inquiry* 7 (6): 679–92. http://dx.doi.org/10.1177/107780040100700601.

Kolata, Gina. 2011. "Two Cancer Studies Find Bacterial Clue in Colon." *New York Times*. Health. October 17, available at http://www.nytimes.com/2011/10/18/health/18cancer.html.

Kroll, Barry M. 1984. "Writing for Readers: Three Perspectives on Audience." *College Composition and Communication* 35: 172–85.

Kuhn, Thomas S. 1996. *The Structure of Scientific Revolutions*. 3rd ed. Chicago: University of Chicago Press.

Leventhal, Anna. 2007. "Zines, Materiality, and the Question of Preserving Ephemera." Paper presented at the Canadian Association for the Study of Book Culture, Saskatoon, SK. May 30, available at http://media.mcgill.ca/files/imperfect%20bound.pdf.

Lévi-Strauss, Claude. 1962. *The Savage Mind*. Chicago: University of Chicago Press.

Lewis, Kylie. N.d. *Personality Liberation Front* [zine]. http://grrrlzines.net/interviews/personalityliberation.htm.

Lippmann, Walter. 1925. *The Phantom Public*. New York: Harcourt, Brace.

Livingstone, Sonia, ed. 2005. *Audiences and Publics: When Cultural Engagement Matters for the Public Sphere*. Bristol, UK: Intellect Books.

Long, Elenore. 2008. *Community Literacy and the Rhetoric of Local Publics*. Andersen, SC: Parlor Press.

Lynch, Paul. 2012. "Composition's New Thing: Bruno Latour and the Apocalyptic Turn." *College English* 74: 458–76.

Marcus, Greil. 1989. *Lipstick Traces: A Secret History of the Twentieth Century*. Cambridge, MA: Harvard University Press.

Marr, John. 1999. "Zines Are Dead." *Bad Subjects* 46. Bad Subjects Collective. December, available at http://bad.eserver.org/issues/1999/46/marr.html.

Mathieu, Paula. 2005. *Tactics of Hope: The Public Turn in Composition Studies*. Portsmouth, NH: Boynton/Cook.

Mattern, Shannon. 2011. "Click/Scan/Bold: The New Materiality of Architectural Discourse and Its Counter-Publics." *Design and Culture* 3 (3): 329–53. http://dx.doi.org/10.2752/175470811X13071166525298.

McLaren, Peter, and Ramin Farahmandpur. 2006. "The Pedagogy of Oppression: A Brief Look at 'NCLB.'" *Monthly Review: An Independent Socialist Magazine* 58 (3): 94–99.

Morley, David. 2003. "The Nationwide Audience." In *The Audience Studies Reader*, ed. Will Brooker and Deborah Jermyn, 95–104. New York: Routledge.

Morozov, Evgeny. 2011. *The Net Delusion: The Dark Side of Internet Freedom*. New York: BBS Public Affairs. http://dx.doi.org/10.1017/S1537592711004026

Mortensen, Peter. 1998. "Going Public." *College Composition and Communication* 50 (December): 182–205.

Negt, Oskar, and Alexander Kluge. 1993. *Public Sphere and Experience: Toward an Analysis of the Bourgeois and Proletarian Public Sphere*. Minneapolis: University of Minnesota Press.

Nguyen, Mimi, ed. 1997. *Evolution of a Race Riot*. http://mimithinguyen.com/artwork/1948804_EVOLUTION_OF_A_RACE_RIOT.html.

Nguyen, Mimi. 2000. Untitled column. *Punk Planet* 40, available at http://threadandcircuits.wordpress.com/2010/03/28/58/. This site reprints the earlier article.

Nicholas, Lucy. 2007. "Approaches to Gender, Power, and Authority in Contemporary Anarcho-Punk: Poststructuralist Anarchism." *eSharp* 9, no. 7 (June).

Oreskes, Naomi. 2004. "Science and Public Policy: What's Proof Got to Do with It?" *Environmental Science & Policy* 7 (5): 369–83. http://dx.doi.org/10.1016/j.envsci.2004.06.002.

Park, Douglas. 1982. "The Meanings of 'Audience'." *College English* 44: 246–57.

Peralta, Eyder. 2012. "Occupy Wall Street Doesn't Endorse Philly Conference." *The Two-Way: NPR's News Blog*, February 24, available at http://www.npr.org/blogs/thetwo-way/2012/02/24/147349639/occupy-wall-street-doesnt-endorse-philly-conference.

Percy, Walker. 2008. "The Loss of the Creature." In *Ways of Reading: An Anthology for Writers*. 8th ed., ed. David Bartholomae and Anthony Petrosky, 481–93. Boston, MA: Bedford/St. Martin's.

Perez, Celia C. 2009. "Zines by People of Color." *Library Journal*. Archive. November 5, available at http://www.libraryjournal.com/article/CA6703476.html.

Petrik, Paula. 1992. "The Youngest Fourth Estate: The Novelty Toy Printing Press and Adolescence, 1870–1886." In *Small Worlds: Children and Adolescents in America, 1850–1950*, ed. Elliot West and Paula Petrik, 125–42. Lawrence: University Press of Kansas.

Pielke, Roger. 2007. *The Honest Broker: Making Sense of Science in Policy and Politics*. New York: Cambridge University Press. http://dx.doi.org/10.1017/CBO9780511818110

Piepmeier, Alison. 2009. *Girl Zines: Making Media, Doing Feminism*. New York: NYU Press.

Pinar, William F. 2001. "The Researcher as Bricoleur: The Teacher as Public Intellectual." *Qualitative Inquiry* 7 (6): 696–700. http://dx.doi.org/10.1177/107780040100700603.

Porrovecchio, Mark. 2007. "Lost in the WTO Shuffle: Publics, Counterpublics, and the Individual." *Western Journal of Communication* 71 (3): 235–56. http://dx.doi.org/10.1080/10570310701515894.

Porter, James E. 1992. *Audience and Rhetoric: An Archaeological Composition of the Discourse Community*. Englewood Cliffs, NJ: Prentice-Hall.

Posner, Richard A. 2001. *Public Intellectuals: A Study of Decline*. Cambridge, MA: Harvard University Press.

Pratt, Nicola. 2004. "Bringing Politics Back In: Examining the Link between Globalisation and Democratization." *Review of International Political Economy* 11 (2): 311–36. http://dx.doi.org/10.1080/0969229042000249831.

Putnam, Robert. 2000. *Bowling Alone: The Collapse and Revival of American Community*. New York: Simon & Schuster.

Radway, Janice. 1991. *Reading the Romance: Women, Patriarchy, and Popular Literature*. Chapel Hill: University of North Carolina Press.

Radway, Janice. 2011. "Zines, Half-Lives, and Afterlives: Temporalities of Social and Political Change." *PMLA* 126 (1): 140–50. http://dx.doi.org/10.1632/pmla.2011.126.1.140.

Rau, Michelle. 1994. "From APA to Zines: Towards a History of Fanzine Publishing." *Alternative Press Review*. 10–13.

Raymond, Eric. 2001. *The Cathedral and the Bazaar*. Sebastopol, CA: O'Reilly Media.

Robbins, Bruce, ed. 1993. *The Phantom Public Sphere*. Minneapolis: University of Minnesota Press.

Roberts-Miller, Patricia. 2004. *Deliberative Conflict: Argument, Political Theory, and Composition Classes*. Carbondale: Southern Illinois University Press.

Rodriguez, Clemencia. 2001. *Fissures in the Mediascape: An International Study of Citizens' Media*. Cresskill, NJ: Hampton Press.

Rorty, Richard. 1982. "Pragmatism, Relativism, and Irrationalism." In *Consequences of Pragmatism (Essays 1972–1980)*, 160–75. Minneapolis: University of Minnesota Press.

Rosaldo, Renato. 1999. "Cultural Citizenship, Inequality, and Multiculturalism." In *Race, Identity, and Citizenship: A Reader*, ed. Rodolfo D. Torres, Louis F. Mirón, and Jonathan Xavier Inda, 253–61. Oxford, UK: Blackwell.

Rose, Shirley K., and Irwin Weiser, eds. 2010. *Going Public: What Writing Programs Learn from Engagement*. Logan: Utah State University Press.

Roseneil, Sasha. 2010. "Intimate Citizenship: A Pragmatic, Yet Radical, Proposal for a Politics of Personal Life." *European Journal of Women's Studies* 17 (1): 77–82. http://dx.doi.org/10.1177/13505068100170010603.

Sarewitz, Daniel. 2004. "How Science Makes Environmental Controversies Worse." *Environmental Science & Policy* 7 (5): 385–403. http://dx.doi.org/10.1016/j.envsci.2004.06.001.

Schilb, John. 2007. *Rhetorical Refusals: Defying Audiences' Expectations.* Carbondale: Southern Illinois University Press.

Sennett, Richard. 1974. *The Fall of Public Man.* New York: W. W. Norton.

Sheridan-Rabideau, Mary P. 2008. *Girls, Feminism, and Grassroots Literacies: Activism in the Girl Zone.* Albany: SUNY Press.

"A Shift in Revolutionary Tactics." 2011. *Adbusters.* #OCCUPYWALLSTREET, 13 July, available at http://www.adbusters.org/blogs/adbusters-blog/occupywallstreet.html.

Sirc, Geoffrey. 1977. "Never Mind the Tagmemics, Where's the Sex Pistols?" *College Composition and Communication* 48: 9–29.

Squires, Catherine. 2002. "Rethinking the Black Public Sphere: An Alternative Vocabulary for Multiple Public Spheres." *Communication Theory* 12 (4): 446–68. http://dx.doi.org/10.1111/j.1468-2885.2002.tb00278.x.

Trimbur, John. 1989. "Consensus and Difference in Collaborative Learning." *College English* 51 (6): 602–17. http://dx.doi.org/10.2307/377955.

Turner, Victor. 1967. *The Forest of Symbols: Aspects of Ndembu Ritual.* Ithaca, NY: Cornell University Press.

Vasagar, Jeevan. 2012. "Privately Owned Public Space: Where Are They and Who Owns Them?" *Guardian (Datablog).* June 11, available at http://www.guardian.co.uk/news/datablog/2012/jun/11/privately-owned-public-space-map.

Vygotsky, Lev. 1986. *Thought and Language.* 2nd ed., ed. Alex Kozulin. Cambridge, MA: MIT Press.

Wallace, David L. 2011. *Compelled to Write: Alternative Rhetoric in Theory and Practice.* Logan: Utah State University Press.

Wan, Amy J. 1999. "Not Just for Kids Anymore: Using Zines in the Classroom." *Radical Teacher* 55: 15–9.

Wan, Amy J. 2011. "In the Name of Citizenship: The Writing Classroom and the Promise of Citizenship." *College English* 74 (September): 28–49.

Warner, Michael. 2005. *Publics and Counterpublics.* New York: Zone Books.

Weisser, Christian R. 2002. *Moving beyond Academic Discourse: Composition Studies and the Public Sphere.* Carbondale: Southern Illinois University Press.

Weisser, Christian R. 2008. "Subaltern Counterpublics and the Discourse of Protest." *JAC* 28: 608–19.

Welch, Nancy. 2008. *Living Room: Teaching Public Writing in a Privatized World.* Portsmouth, NH: Boynton/Cook.

Wells, Susan. 1996. "Rogue Cops and Health Care: What Do We Want from Public Writing?" *College Composition and Communication* 47: 325–41.

Will, George. 1995. "Teach Johnny to Write." *Washington Post,* July 2, available at http://www.highbeam.com/doc/1P2-841900.html.

Williams, Bronwyn T. 2010. "Seeking New Worlds: The Study of Writing beyond Our Classrooms." *College Composition and Communication* 62: 127–46.

Wrekk, Alex. N.d. *Stolen Sharpie Revolution* [zine]. http://www.stolensharpierevolution.org/.

Wright, Frederick A. 2001. *From Zines to Ezines: Electronic Publishing and the Literary Underground.* PhD diss., Kent State University, Kent, OH; University Microfilms, Ann Arbor, MI.

Wu, Tim. 2011. *The Master Switch: The Rise and Fall of Information Empires.* New York: Alfred A. Knopf.

Wynne, Brian. 2006. "Public Engagement as a Means of Restoring Public Trust in Science—Hitting the Notes, but Missing the Music?" *Community Genetics* 9 (3): 211–20. http://dx.doi.org/10.1159/000092659. Medline:16741352.

Yancey, Kathleen. 2009. *Writing in the 21st Century.* Urbana, IL: NCTE. http://www.ncte.org/library/NCTEFiles/Press/Yancey_final.pdf.

Yorke, Chris. 2000. "Zines Are Dead: The Six Deadly Sins That Killed Zines." *Broken Pencil* 12: n.p., available at http://www.brokenpencilarchive.tuesdayafternoon.net/view. php?id=3191.

Zobl, Elke. 2009. "Cultural Production, Transnational Networking, and Critical Reflection in Feminist Zines." *Signs: Journal of Women in Culture and Society* 35 (1): 1–12. http:// dx.doi.org/10.1086/599256.

INDEX

ABOUT THE AUTHOR

Frank Farmer is associate professor of English at the University of Kansas. He is the author of *Saying and Silence: Listening to Composition with Bakhtin* (Utah State University Press, 2001) and editor of *Landmark Essays on Bakhtin, Rhetoric, and Writing* (Routledge, 1998). He received his PhD in rhetoric and composition from the University of Louisville and has published in several of the leading journals in the field, including *College Composition and Communication, College English, JAC, Rhetoric Review, Written Communication,* and *Rhetoric Society Quarterly.* He has received a number of awards for his teaching and most recently has served as chair of the Modern Language Association's Division Executive Committee on Language and Society. He resides with his wife, Linda, in Lawrence, Kansas.

Made in the USA
Columbia, SC
21 August 2017